PHOTOSHOP® CS4
QuickSteps

About the Authors

Gary Bouton has been illustrating and producing videos for over 30 years; the co-author came from a background in advertising and has been teaching his crafts through books for the past 18 years. To his credit, the titles include guides to Adobe Photoshop, CorelDraw, modeling and animation software, and *Xara Xtreme: The Official Guide*, for McGraw-Hill. With his wife Barbara, the Boutons support Gary's books through www.theboutons.com, where readers can also find a lively discussion forum dedicated to digital graphics, free content downloads, and several non-free commercial goods. Currently, Gary is working on post-production editing and CG effects for music videos for Australia-based *Monkey Pants Media*.

Carole Boggs Matthews has been around computers as a programmer, systems analyst, technical consultant, and founder, co-owner, and vice president of a software company. She has been on all sides of computer software products, from designer and builder to an accomplished user of software in her business. Together with Marty Matthews, her husband, she has authored or co-authored over 50 books, including *Adobe Photoshop CS QuickSteps*, *Adobe Photoshop Elements QuickSteps*, *Microsoft Office PowerPoint 2010*, and *Microsoft Word 2010 QuickSteps*.

PHOTOSHOP® CS4
QuickSteps

GARY DAVID BOUTON
CAROLE MATTHEWS

New York Chicago San Francisco
Lisbon London Madrid Mexico City
Milan New Delhi San Juan
Seoul Singapore Sydney Toronto

The McGraw-Hill Companies

Library of Congress Cataloging-in-Publication Data

Bouton, Gary David, 1953-
  Photoshop CS4 quicksteps/Gary David Bouton, Carole Matthews.
    p. cm.
  Includes index.
  ISBN-13: 978-0-07-162537-1 (alk. paper)
  ISBN-10: 0-07-162537-2 (alk. paper)
  1. Adobe Photoshop. 2. Photography—Digital techniques.
  I. Matthews, Carole Boggs. II. Title.
  TR267.5.A3B678 2009
  006.6'96—dc22
                                    2009023160

McGraw-Hill books are available at special quantity discounts to use as premiums and sales promotions, or for use in corporate training programs. To contact a representative, please e-mail us at bulksales@mcgraw-hill.com.

PHOTOSHOP® CS4 QUICKSTEPS

1234567890   CCI CCI   019

ISBN   978-0-07-162537-1
MHID   0-07-162537-2

SPONSORING EDITOR / Roger Stewart

EDITORIAL SUPERVISOR / Janet Walden

PROJECT MANAGER / Madhu Bhardwaj, International Typesetting and Composition

ACQUISITIONS COORDINATOR / Joya Anthony

TECHNICAL EDITORS / Lyra Ziegler, Carole Matthews, and Gary Bouton

COPY EDITOR / Bill McManus

PROOFREADER / Madhu Prasher

INDEXER / Claire Splan

PRODUCTION SUPERVISOR / Jim Kussow

COMPOSITION / International Typesetting and Composition

ILLUSTRATION / International Typesetting and Composition

ART DIRECTOR, COVER / Jeff Weeks

COVER DESIGNER / Pattie Lee

SERIES CREATORS / Marty and Carole Matthews

SERIES DESIGN / Bailey Cunningham

Contents at a Glance

1
2
3
4
5
6
7
8
9
10

Acknowledgments

A wonderful part of working with this QuickSteps series is the people who have worked on it. This book, as the others in the series, has been blessed with an exceptionally talented and hard-working team. Each person has been dedicated to making this book one to match their capabilities, which are substantial. One by-product of the book has been the supportive and cohesive team that has been developed. Although many members of the team may never personally meet, they have interacted in a professional and caring way. We offer a heart-felt thank-you to all on the team.

We would also like to thank Lyra Ziegler, who helped make this book better with her comments and technical corrections. Mark Clarkson, an author on the first edition of this book, kindly gave us permission to use some of his photos. We are very appreciative of his generosity. And a very special thanks to our friends and families for allowing the authors to use their pictures in this book. They worked hard and were compensated usually with pizza with all the toppings, except anchovies.

Introduction

QuickSteps books are recipe books for computer users. They answer the question "How do I...?" by providing quick sets of steps to accomplish the most common tasks in a particular program. The sets of steps are the central focus of the book. QuickSteps sidebars show you how to quickly do many small functions or tasks that support the primary functions. Notes, Tips, and Cautions augment the steps, yet they are presented in such a manner as to not interrupt the flow of the steps. The brief introductions are minimal rather than narrative, and numerous illustrations and figures, many with callouts, support the steps.

QuickSteps books are organized by function and the tasks needed to perform that function. Each function is a chapter. Each task, or "How To," contains the steps needed for accomplishing the function along with relevant Notes, Tips, Cautions, and screenshots. Tasks will be easy to find through:

- The Table of Contents, which lists the functional areas (chapters) and tasks in the order they are presented

- A How To list of tasks on the opening page of each chapter

- The index with its alphabetical list of terms used in describing the functions and tasks

- Color-coded tabs for each chapter or functional area, with an index to the tabs just before the Table of Contents

Conventions Used in This Book

Photoshop CS4 QuickSteps uses several conventions designed to make the book easier for you to follow. Among these are

- A 🔍 or a 🎨 in the Table of Contents or the How To list in each chapter references a QuickSteps or a QuickFacts sidebar in a chapter.

- **Bold type** is used for words on the screen that you are to do something with, such as click **Save As** or open **File**.

- *Italic type* is used for a word or phrase that is being defined or otherwise deserves special emphasis.

- <u>Underlined type</u> is used for text that you are to type from the keyboard.

- When you see the command, **CTRL/CMD**, you are to press the **CTRL** key in Windows or the **CMD** key on the Mac; **ALT/OPT**, press the **ALT** key in Windows or the **OPTIONS** key on the Mac.

- SMALL CAPITAL LETTERS are used for keys on the keyboard such as **ENTER** and **SHIFT**.

- When you are expected to enter a command, you are told to press the key(s). If you are to enter text or numbers, you are told to type them. Specific letters or numbers to be entered will be underlined.

- When you are to click the mouse button on a screen command or menu, you will be told to "Click **File | Open**," which means, "Click **File**, then click **Open**."

How to...

- **Start and Close Photoshop**
- **Learn About the Photoshop Workspace**
- **Open and Create Images**
- **Customize Photoshop**
- 🪐 **Understanding Interpolation Methods**
- **Work with Photoshop's Interface**
- 🔍 **Navigating Within a Document**
- **Work with Photoshop Controls**
- 🔍 **Using Photoshop's Online Help**
- 🪐 **Using Kulor**
- **Work with Panels**
- 🪐 **Using Scrubby Sliders**
- 🔍 **Selecting Screen Modes**
- **Display the Tools in Two Columns**
- **Work with Tool Options**
- **Switch Tools in a Menu**
- **Set Foreground and Background Colors**
- **Use the History Panel**
- 🔍 **Undoing and Redoing Actions**

Chapter 1

Stepping into Photoshop CS4

This chapter will introduce you to some of Photoshop's basic capabilities and its user interface. You will learn how to open and close Photoshop, how to navigate and use its screens and toolbars, and how to set up the program according to your personal needs. You will learn how to use Photoshop's Help and how to find additional help and tutorials online. You will also get a glimpse at the tools that Photoshop offers and an introduction to working with color and calibration.

Get Acquainted with Photoshop

Getting acquainted with Photoshop involves starting and closing it; setting preferences, such as how to display the mouse pointer; working with the Photoshop workspace and its menus, panels, and other components; opening and creating images; and using Photoshop's interface, including navigating, zooming, and working with panels.

This chapter assumes that you already know how to turn on the computer and load Windows and that Photoshop has been installed on your computer. Once Photoshop is installed, you start it as you would any other program.

Start and Close Photoshop

You can start Photoshop with a menu, shortcut, or keyboard combination. Figure 1-1 shows the Photoshop CS4 screen that awaits your creative efforts. Here are some common ways to start Photoshop:

- Double-click the Photoshop icon on your desktop.
- In Windows, click **Start | All Programs | Adobe Photoshop CS4**.
- In Mac OS X, either double-click the Photoshop icon in the Finder toolbar or on the Dock, or click **Go | Favorites** if you've made Photoshop a Favorite.

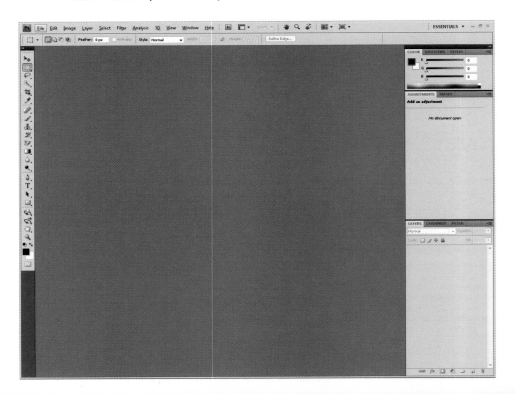

Figure 1-1: *Photoshop CS4 displays a window that is open and waiting for your creativity.*

Here are some common ways to close Photoshop:

- Click **File | Exit**. You will be prompted to save any unsaved work.
- In Windows, you can also click the **Close** icon ✕ in the upper-right corner of the Photoshop CS4 window.
- On the Mac, you can also click **Quit** from the menu bar.
- · In both operating systems, press **CTRL/CMD+Q**.

Learn About the Photoshop Workspace

Figure 1-2 shows an example of the Photoshop workspace. Yours may look slightly different, depending on what tools, documents, and windows you

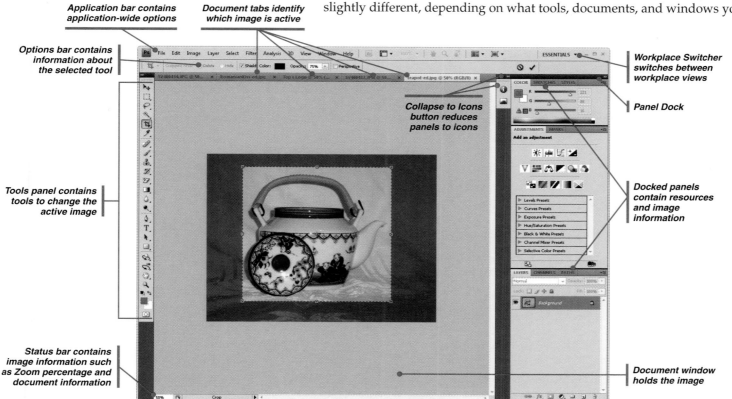

Application bar contains application-wide options

Document tabs identify which image is active

Options bar contains information about the selected tool

Tools panel contains tools to change the active image

Status bar contains image information such as Zoom percentage and document information

Workplace Switcher switches between workplace views

Panel Dock

Collapse to Icons button reduces panels to icons

Docked panels contain resources and image information

Document window holds the image

Figure 1-2: **The Photoshop workspace looks something like this.**

have open. Any of the items can be closed or moved about on the screen, as you'll see. In Windows, the empty workspace is gray.

The Status bar, shown in Figure 1-3, gives useful information about your currently selected document and tool. You can change the information displayed by opening the Options flyout menu on the Status bar and choosing the information to be displayed.

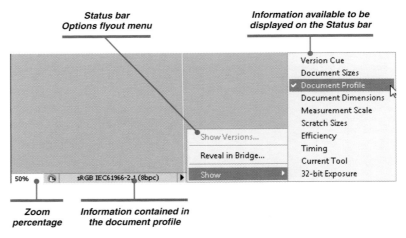

Figure 1-3: **The Status bar gives useful information about the current document and tool.**

Open and Create Images

You open a file in Photoshop in much the same way you open a file in almost any program.

OPEN AN IMAGE USING PHOTOSHOP OR BRIDGE

To open a file in Photoshop from the Application bar:

1. With Photoshop open, click **File** | **Open**.
2. Navigate the Open dialog box to find the folder containing your image.
3. Select the filename. Click **Open** or double-click the file's name to open the file in Photoshop.

TIP

To open multiple files in Photoshop, first select the files either by pressing **CTRL/CMD** while you click to select multiple files that are not contiguous or by pressing **SHIFT** while you click to select a range of files that are contiguous; then click **Open**.

Adobe's Bridge is a powerful way to browse, manage, and open your files. See Chapter 3 for in-depth information on how to use Bridge. To open a file with Bridge:

1. With Photoshop open, click **Launch Bridge** [Br] in the Application bar.

2. Use the Folders pane of the window, shown in Figure 1-4, to navigate to a folder containing images. Thumbnails of all images in the folder appear in the Thumbnails pane.

3. Click any thumbnail to select that file. A preview appears in the Preview pane on the right. Double-click a thumbnail to open the file in Photoshop.

*Figure 1-4: **Adobe Bridge is a powerful tool for finding, managing, and opening files.***

CREATE A NEW IMAGE CANVAS FROM A PRESET

Photoshop allows you to easily create an image canvas from a list of preset sizes and resolutions. To create a new, blank canvas for your image:

1. From the Application bar, click **File | New**. The New dialog box appears.

2. Type a name for the new image.

3. Click the **Preset** down arrow and choose a preset. Each selection gives you a different canvas size depending on its eventual use:

   ● Click **Default Photoshop Size** if you want the resulting canvas to measure 7×5 inches, have 72 pixels per inch (ppi) resolution, use a color mode of 8-bit RGB, and have a white background (see Figure 1-5).

   ● Click **Custom** to set your own size, resolution, color mode, and background color specifications.

   ● Click **Advanced** for advanced options relating to *color profiles* (a record of the color type of an image so that the image color is as accurate as it can be when read by various devices) and the pixel aspect ratios (for example, you can use this to display a square pixel image on a nonsquare device).

4. Click **Save Preset** to save the Preset settings.

5. Click **OK** to create a new image canvas.

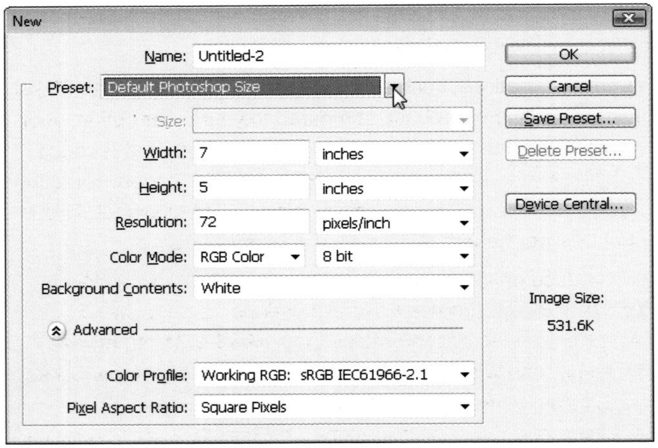

Figure 1-5: *You can choose a preset size for your new image.*

Customize Photoshop

Photoshop allows you to customize the way Photoshop works for you. You can set preferences that give you wide-ranging control over Photoshop. You can also customize the workspace and assign keyboard shortcuts, as you'll see.

SET PHOTOSHOP PREFERENCES

You can change the way Photoshop works by setting its *preferences*. You can change the look of the tool pointers, the color of guidelines, which units of measurement you prefer to work in (for example, inches, centimeters, or pixels), and more.

When you are first learning how to use Photoshop, it is best to leave the default preferences intact. After you understand the implications of the preferences, however, you can make changes to suit your needs.

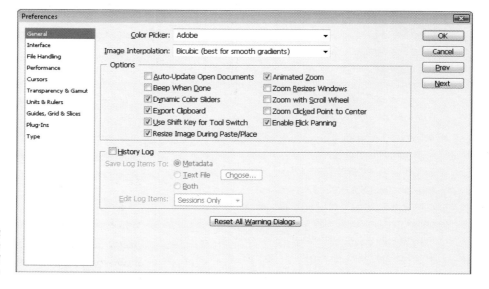

NOTE

Photoshop CS4 comes with several filters and software programs that work in conjunction with it to add features to Photoshop. When you install Photoshop CS4, these filters and programs are automatically installed in special subfolders of Photoshop's Plug-In folder. You may own other Photoshop-compatible filters or programs that are stored in different directories or that were installed prior to installing Photoshop CS4. To let Photoshop CS4 know where they are located so that you can still use them, click **Edit | Preferences | Plug-Ins**. In the Plug-Ins panel, click **Additional Plug-Ins Folder** and then browse for the folder in which the plug-ins are stored. Once Photoshop knows where the plug-ins can be found, it includes them as options in various menus, depending on what the plug-in does. For instance, they will be added to the list of filters in the Filter menu or to the list of file types in the Open, Save As, and Export dialog boxes. If there are too many plug-ins, the overflow options will be listed in the Other submenu (accessed by clicking the Filter menu).

TIP

A quick way to navigate to the Preferences dialog box is to press **CTRL/CMD+K**. This is a Photoshop keyboard shortcut—one of scores—that you'll want to commit to memory.

To set your preferences:

1. On the Application bar, click **Edit | Preferences | General**. The Photoshop Preferences dialog box appears, as shown in Figure 1-6.

2. Click the name of the panel, or click **Next** and **Previous** to cycle through Photoshop's ten pages of preferences. You see these choices:

   - **General** Set general-purpose options, such as those pertaining to the Color Picker (Adobe's Color Picker is generally more robust, compared to your other option, your operating system's Color Picker), the default image interpolation method (see the "Understanding Interpolation Methods" QuickSteps in this chapter), options for using SHIFT to switch between tools, and whether to zoom using the scroll wheel. This is also where you can specify where and how to save the History Log.

   - **Interface** Set screen interface options, such as the standard screen and menu color, and whether to show Tool Tips. You can also set options for panels and documents, such as whether to open documents as tabs, whether to remember where the panels are located, and whether to automatically collapse the panels into icons to save workspace. If you have an international edition of Photoshop, you can set the interface language here and the interface font size. The changes you make go into effect the next time you launch Photoshop.

*Figure 1-6: **Photoshop CS4 has many preferences you can change, beginning with the General preferences.***

QUICKFACTS

UNDERSTANDING INTERPOLATION METHODS

Interpolation is the technique used when you increase or decrease the number of pixels by *resampling* an image. When you *upsample* an image, you increase the number of pixels. Typically this leads to image harshness because no application can intelligently add pixels to an existing photograph. You should upsample images only when the need is absolute; reshooting an image usually provides you with better quality. When you *downsample*, you decrease the number of pixels. You set the default image interpolation method in the General preferences of the Preferences dialog box (see Figure 1-6):

Color Picker:	Adobe	▾
Image Interpolation:	Bicubic (best for smooth gradients)	▾
Options	Nearest Neighbor (preserve hard edges)	
	Bilinear	
☐ Auto-U	Bicubic (best for smooth gradients)	
☐ Beep W	Bicubic Smoother (best for enlargement)	
☑ Dynamic	Bicubic Sharper (best for reduction)	

- **Nearest Neighbor (Preserve Hard Edges)** Produces lower-quality images by simply duplicating pixels in an image. Use this option only for simple graphics such as screen captures and certain web graphics. You'll get the best interpolation by choosing a whole-number enlargement or reduction, such as 200%, 400%, and so on.

- **Bilinear** Produces a medium-quality image by calculating the average values of the pixels' color sampled horizontally and vertically.

- **Bicubic (Best For Smooth Gradients)** Uses more complex methods to change pixels by evaluating neighboring pixels in all directions and arriving at the resampled colors through weighted averaging. The results tend to be smoother color gradations.

Continued . . .

- **File Handling** Set options for saving files, determining file compatibility, and whether to use Version Cue workgroup file management, and the number of files retained for the list. Version Cue is used to track and manage projects that have several people working on versions of data.

- **Performance** Determine how much of the available RAM Photoshop can use and how many history states and cache levels you will have. These are used to improve responsiveness of screen refreshes and histogram speeds. Increase the Cache Levels for larger documents or those with many layers. Here you should also determine which scratch disks to use, and in which order they are to be used. A *scratch disk* is empty space on a hard drive where Photoshop stores Undo information and other data about images you're working on—it improves speed. You want your scratch disks to be fast and to have as much defragmented open space as you can afford.

- **Cursors** Choose from among standard options regarding how to display the painting cursors in a number of sizes and shapes. You can also set the standard shape for other cursors, and you can set the default Brush Preview Color.

  One preference that you might want to change is how tool cursors are displayed. By default, Photoshop shows each tool cursor as an icon, indicating which tool is active. Instead, you might want to use a cursor that shows the size and shape of the active tool. Click **Set Photoshop Preferences | Cursors** to select your preference.

- **Transparency & Gamut** Choose default settings for transparency, such as grid size and grid colors, and gamut warning color and opacity.

- **Units & Rulers** Choose default units for ruler measurements and type, column width, and gutter size, new document default print and screen resolutions, and whether the point/pica size default is in PostScript or traditional typefaces.

- **Guides, Grid & Slices** Choose color and style defaults for guides; color defaults for Smart Guides; color, style, and grid structure defaults for grids; color defaults for slices; and whether to show slice numbers.

- **Plug-Ins** Provides an Additional Plug-Ins Folder, and specifies whether Extension Panels can connect to the Internet and whether the Extension Panels should be loaded.

- **Type** Determine whether to use smart quotes and whether to show Asian text options or English font names. You can set the size for previewing fonts, and whether the font names are displayed in English.

Unless you have a sound, compelling reason to make changes, leave all preferences at their default settings. Click **Cancel** to close the dialog box.

QUICKFACTS

UNDERSTANDING INTERPOLATION METHODS (Continued)

- **Bicubic Smoother (Best For Enlargement)**
  Performs bicubic interpolation and then slightly softens the transitions between neighboring color pixels.

- **Bicubic Sharper (Best For Reduction)**
  Performs bicubic interpolation and then applies a subtle sharpening of the contrast between neighboring pixels. This is a good choice for retaining text legibility when you make a photo or a screen capture smaller.

TIP

To collapse the panels, click the **Collapse To Icons** button on top of the panel dock. To expand the panel, click the icon.

PREPARE AND SAVE THE WORKSPACE

Photoshop allows you to customize your workspace—decide which panels are open, what their positions are on the screen, and so forth—and then save that workspace. You can create one workspace suitable for browsing through large folders or images and another suitable for retouching scanned photos.

1. Close any panels you don't want open.

2. Open any additional panels and windows you require, and position them where you want them.

3. Click **Window | Workspace | Save Workspace**. The Save Workspace dialog box appears.

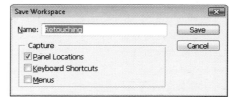

4. Type a name for the workspace, such as Retouching, and click **Save**.

To retrieve a custom workspace, click **Window | Workspace** and click the name of the workspace from the menu.

ASSIGN A KEYBOARD SHORTCUT

You can assign keyboard shortcuts for selecting tools, opening panels, and selecting menu commands. Some keyboard shortcuts are assigned by default: **B** selects the Brush or Pencil tool, for example, and **F5** opens and closes the Brushes panel. You can change these defaults and create new shortcuts to suit the way you work.

Here is how you assign a keyboard shortcut to a menu. The process is basically the same to create any shortcut.

1. Click **Edit | Keyboard Shortcuts**. The Keyboard Shortcuts And Menus dialog box appears.

2. Click the **Keyboard Shortcuts** tab, click the **Shortcuts For** drop-down menu arrow, and click **Application Menus**, as shown in Figure 1-7.

3. Under Application Menu Command, click the specific menu group arrow, such as the **Window** arrow, to expand the list of menu items.

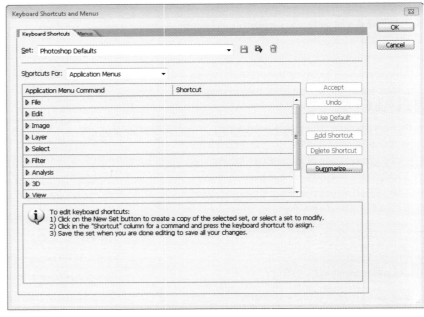

Figure 1-7: *Use the Keyboard Shortcuts And Menus dialog box to assign new keyboard shortcuts.*

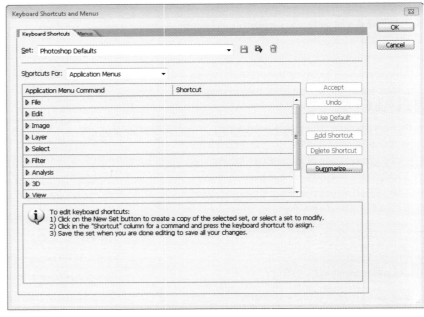

NOTE

To hide menu items, click **Edit | Keyboard Shortcuts**. In the Keyboard Shortcuts And Menus dialog box, click the **Menus** tab. In the Menu For area, click **Panel Menus** or **Application Menus**. Double-click a command to expand the list. Click the eye icon to hide the menu. When you have hidden menu items, an additional menu option, Show All Menu Items, is attached to the bottom of the menu; when clicked, it shows all menu items, including the hidden ones.

Step Backward	👁	None
Fade...	👁	None
Cut	👁	None

4. Scroll down and click the specific menu for which you want to create a shortcut, such as **Navigator**. A text box appears to the right of the command name.

5. Press the key combination you want to assign to the menu, such as **ALT+F6**. Shortcuts must include the **ALT/OPT** or **CTRL/CMD** key, a function key, or both. Click **OK** to accept the change.

Pressing this key combination now opens and closes the menu you want. In the preceding example, pressing **ALT+F6** opens the Navigator panel, a shortcut to clicking **Window | Navigator**.

If you try to enter a shortcut key that is already in use, you will be warned. You can choose to proceed and assign another shortcut to the conflicting command, or to undo your change. If you want to restore the original factory settings, click **Use Default**.

NOTE

Zooming in and out does not in any way alter the actual image.

TIP

By default, at extreme resolutions, Photoshop displays a grid around pixels, which can be visually distracting. You can turn off the grid by choosing **View | Show** and then disabling **Pixel Grid**.

Work with Photoshop's Interface

For the most part, Photoshop uses standard interface conventions for opening and closing dialog boxes and windows, entering and changing values, and so forth, but it also offers some unique controls.

ZOOM IN AND OUT

When you edit images, being able to zoom in on small details within the image is a big advantage When working with images in Photoshop, you can zoom in until the image is displayed at, for example, 16 times its actual size (that is, 1600 percent larger). At 1600 percent, each pixel in the image is 16×16 pixels on the screen. Similarly, you can zoom out until an entire image is only a few pixels wide.

ZOOM WITH THE ZOOM TOOL

With an image open and selected in Photoshop, click the **Zoom** tool in the Tools panel, or press **Z**, to select the Zoom tool. The Zoom tool, which includes Zoom In and Zoom Out, is displayed in the Options bar:

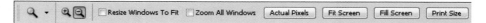

- Click repeatedly within the image to zoom in.
- To zoom out, press and hold the **ALT/OPT** key. The Zoom tool changes from a plus sign (+) to a minus sign (–). Press **ALT/OPT** and click repeatedly within the image to zoom out. Release the **ALT/OPT** key to zoom in again. You can also click the **Zoom Out** tool in the Options bar.
- In the Options bar, click **Fit Screen**, **Fill Screen**, or **Actual Pixels**.

ZOOM USING OTHER TECHNIQUES

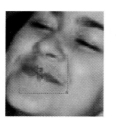

- **Marquee selection**   Click and drag the part of the image you want to zoom in on. A marquee is created that specifies the area on which to zoom. The image will then either zoom in or out, depending on the Zoom tool selected.

Use the Hand tool to drag the selection box

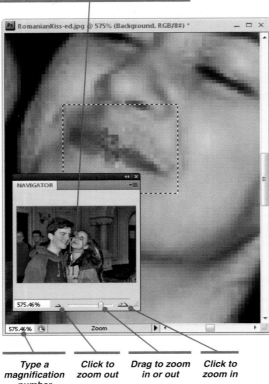

Ps RomanianKiss-ed.jpg @ 575% (Background, RGB/8#) *

NAVIGATOR

575.46%

575.46%　　Zoom

| Type a magnification number | Click to zoom out | Drag to zoom in or out | Click to zoom in |

Figure 1-8: Use the Navigator panel to control the Zoom tool.

TIP

To change the color of the selection box in the Navigator panel, click the **Options** menu in the upper-right corner of the tab bar and click **Panel Options**. The Panel Options dialog box will open. Click the Swatch to change colors and click **OK**.

- **Status bar**　Type a zoom amount in the text box at the far left of the Status bar.
- **Hand tool**　Double-click the **Hand** tool in the Tools panel to zoom the current image to fit on the screen.

ZOOM WITH THE KEYBOARD

- With an image open and selected in Photoshop, press and hold **CTRL/CMD** and repeatedly press the **plus** (+) key to zoom in.
- Press and hold **CTRL/CMD** and repeatedly press the **minus** (–) key to zoom out.
- Press **CTRL/CMD+0** to zoom the current image to fit on the screen. Press **ALT/ OPT+CTRL+0** to zoom the current image to 100 percent.

ZOOM WITH THE NAVIGATOR PANEL

1. Open and select an image in Photoshop. If the Navigator panel is not displayed, as shown in Figure 1-8, click **Window | Navigator**.

2. Drag the slider to the right to zoom in; drag it to the left to zoom out.

   –Or–

   Click the larger mountain icon at the right of the slider to zoom in, and click the smaller mountain icon at the left of the slider to zoom out.

   –Or–

   Type a zoom amount in the Navigator text box and press **ENTER**. For example, to display your image at twice its actual size, type 200; for half the image's actual size, type 50.

ARRANGE YOUR IMAGES IN THE WINDOW

To arrange your images within the workspace:

- Click **Window | Arrange** and then choose an option:
  - **Cascade** to display the images in a cascading stack
  - **Tile** to display each image in its own smaller window sized so that all can be displayed
  - **Float In Window** to display the active image floating in its own window

- **Float All In Windows** to display all images floating
- **Consolidate All To Tabs** to dock all images and display names in individual tabs
- **Match Zoom, Match Location, Match Rotation, Match All** to display images with similar zoom properties, similar location or matched as to which part of the image is displayed, similar degree of rotation, or similar zoom plus location properties.

    –Or–

- Click the **Arrange Document** icon on the Application bar and select the view you'd like based on the visual thumbnail. You can also find choices described in the preceding bullets.

Work with Photoshop Controls

Use sliders, drop-down lists and controls, flyout menus, and swatches when working with Photoshop.

USE SLIDERS

Many Photoshop controls use sliders to change values. To use a slider control in Photoshop, click the down arrow to open the slider, and drag the slider to the left to decrease the value or drag it to the right to increase the value.

USE DROP-DOWN LISTS

Drop-down lists in Photoshop are indicated by a little down arrow. To access a drop-down list:

1. Click the down arrow.
2. Click your selection in the list.

–Or–

1. Click within the displayed text of the drop-down list.
2. Use the **UP ARROW** and **DOWN ARROW** keys to scroll through the list.

QUICKSTEPS

USING PHOTOSHOP'S ONLINE HELP

Photoshop has a comprehensive online Help system available. To access Help:

- Press **F1**.

–Or–

- On the Application bar, click **Help | Photoshop Help**.

The Photoshop Help and Support page opens in your default web browser. On the right sidebar, click **Photoshop Help (web).** Navigate through Help by searching for keywords in the left sidebar or by using the Search feature.

For those times when you can't always rely on a web connection, seriously consider downloading the Help file in PDF format from Adobe's online Help site, for reference when you don't have a web connection. It's a 40MB Acrobat document.

USE FLYOUT MENUS

Flyout menus are indicated in Photoshop by a small arrow in a dialog box or by a small arrow at the corner of a tool in the Tools panel.

To use a flyout menu:

1. Click the flyout arrow.
2. Click your selection in the menu.

Click the arrow to display a flyout menu

USE SHORTCUT MENUS

You access shortcut menus (also called context menus), which display additional options, by right-clicking within the canvas—that is, right-clicking the image. You can also access shortcut menus for various panels by right-clicking inside them. To close a shortcut menu, either select an option and begin using the tool, or click anywhere outside of the current canvas or image.

CHOOSE COLORS

Photoshop has several panels and dialog boxes for picking colors with which you can then paint using the Tools panel's painting tools. These include the Swatches panel and the Color panel, as well as the foreground and background swatches, which, when clicked, open the Color Picker. From a swatch, simply click a color to select it.

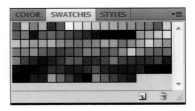

ARRANGE DOCUMENT WINDOWS

As you can see in Figure 1-9, document windows contain tabs when more than one document is open. You can dock, undock, stack, and unstack your documents.

- To select a window, click its tab.
- To move a document window to a different location on the workspace, simply drag it by its title bar or tab.

QUICKFACTS

USING KULOR

Because Photoshop can display user-created panels, and because Photoshop usually wants an active connection to the Web, a new color "system" in CS4 is the Kulor panel, accessed by clicking **Window | Extensions**. Users and Adobe Systems post small palettes of harmonious and exciting color schemes, ideal for web page design. To use a Kulor color, click the **Add Selected Theme To Swatches** icon, and the color set is available on the Swatches palette.

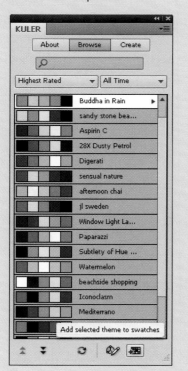

Figure 1-9: *You can arrange a document on your workspace by dragging its window from one location to another.*

- To undock a document from its default position on the document title bar, drag it free. To dock it, drag it back to the document title bar.

- To create a stack of documents, for easier viewing or to make batch adjustments to the group, drag one document over another until the titles are stacked.

Work with Panels

Photoshop's workspace contains a number of small windows, called *panels*, that you can use to choose colors, set paragraph formatting options, sample the RGB (Red, Green, Blue) values of pixels in an image, manage paths and layers, and so forth.

Panels are grouped together with other related panels. Each panel has its name displayed on a tab on the top. When the panels are grouped to the right of the document window, they are called *docked*. When the panels are dragged free of the dock, they are called *floating*.

QUICK**FACTS**

USING SCRUBBY SLIDERS

Text boxes containing values that also have labels, such as you find in most of the panels or on the Options bar (such as Font Size and Opacity), can be operated like a slider.

Just drag the cursor left or right on the label; left decreases the corresponding value in the box, while dragging right reverses the operation.

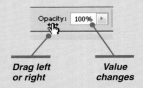

Drag left
or right

Value
changes

OPEN OR CLOSE PANELS

- To open a panel, click **Window** and click the name of the panel you want to work with—for example, **Brushes** or **Layers**.

- To switch between panels in a group, click the name tab, as shown here.

- If you delete a panel by clicking its Close icon in the upper-right corner, you can restore it by clicking **Window** and then clicking the name of the panel.

MOVE, DOCK, OR UNDOCK PANELS

- To move a single panel or a group of panels docked together, drag the title bar.

- To separate a panel from a group of panels, click its tab and drag it. A panel may be part of the docked group, part of a stacked group not in the panel dock, or floating in its own panel window.

RESIZE OR HIDE PANELS

- You can resize a panel in the Panel dock by dragging its lower-right corner. Some panels cannot be resized.

- Press the **TAB** key to hide all panels and toolbars and have an uncluttered workspace. Press **TAB** again to restore them to their original positions. While still displaying any toolbars currently open, press **SHIFT+TAB** to hide or show only the panels.

MAKE PANELS INTO ICONS

- To collapse a panel into an icon, click the Collapse To Icon button.

- To expand a panel from an icon to a full-sized panel, click the Expand button.

QUICKSTEPS

SELECTING SCREEN MODES

Photoshop offers three different screen modes. You can display them one at a time by pressing **F** repeatedly to cycle through the screen modes. You can also click **View | Screen Mode**, and then click the screen view you want from the submenu.

- **Standard Screen mode** Your image is placed within a window. You can view multiple images at once in Standard Screen mode, as shown earlier in Figure 1-9.

- **Full Screen mode** Only your currently selected document is visible. All frames, scroll bars, title bars, menus, and so forth are hidden, as shown in Figure 1-10. To temporarily reveal the Tools panel or the panels, place your cursor over that area. In Full Screen mode, the main menu is moved to the top of the Tools panel. In Full Screen mode, you can move your image around the screen by holding down the **SPACEBAR** to temporarily select the Hand tool and then dragging the image. To preview only your current document in Full Screen mode, like a screen slideshow, pressing **TAB** hides all panels and tools. Pressing **TAB** a second time returns the panels to view and enables you to more easily continue to switch tools and viewing modes.

- **Full Screen Mode With Menu Bar mode** The same as Full Screen mode, but the menu remains at the top of the workspace.

*Figure 1-10: **Full Screen mode hides all documents but the one currently selected.***

Explore Photoshop's Tools

Photoshop's primary tools are kept in a panel called the Tools panel. The Tools panel, shown in Figure 1-11, is open by default. If it is not visible, click **Window | Tools**. Figure 1-11 shows the Tools panel for Photoshop Extended and contains a couple more tools (the Rotate tools) than Photoshop Standard.

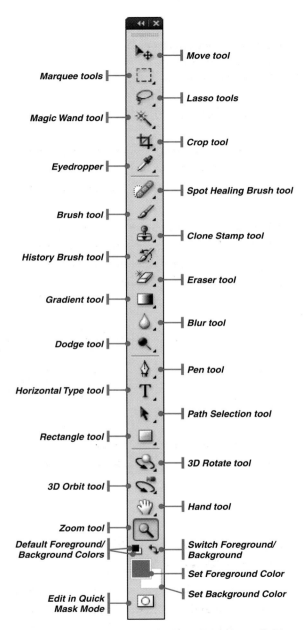

- Move tool
- Marquee tools
- Lasso tools
- Magic Wand tool
- Crop tool
- Eyedropper
- Spot Healing Brush tool
- Brush tool
- Clone Stamp tool
- History Brush tool
- Eraser tool
- Gradient tool
- Blur tool
- Dodge tool
- Pen tool
- Horizontal Type tool
- Path Selection tool
- Rectangle tool
- 3D Rotate tool
- 3D Orbit tool
- Hand tool
- Zoom tool
- Default Foreground/Background Colors
- Switch Foreground/Background
- Set Foreground Color
- Set Background Color
- Edit in Quick Mask Mode

*Figure 1-11: **The Tools panel displays the tools available for your use.***

While up to 25 buttons and controls are shown in the Tools panel at any given time, more tools are available for you to use. Many of Photoshop's tools are grouped in sets in the Tools panel. Whenever a tool icon has a small black triangle at the bottom, that indicates you can access a flyout menu containing additional tools.

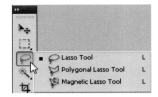

Display the Tools in Two Columns

To display the Tools panel shortened into two columns, click the **Collapse** button on the top of the Tools panel. To return it to the one-column default display, click the button again.

Work with Tool Options

All tools in Photoshop have options you can control: size, shape, color, and so forth. Let's take a close look at setting the options for a common tool, the Brush tool.

CHANGE THE BRUSH TOOL OPTIONS

The Brush tool serves as a good introduction to setting tool options in Photoshop; the same controls are available for many other tools, including the Smudge, Blur, Burn, Dodge, and Eraser tools. Some guidelines to keep in mind are

- Access basic options for most tools, including the Brush tool, by right-clicking the image and changing settings, an example of which is shown here in the Brush Preset Picker dialog box for the Brush tool.

- From the dialog box, you can change the size of the brush, as well as its hardness, by dragging the **Master Diameter** and **Hardness** sliders to the right or left. The harder the brush (drag right),

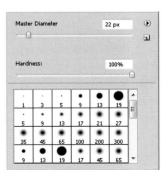

the more distinct the brush strokes created, as shown here, where the top brush stroke is set to 0 percent hardness (soft, almost fuzzy) and the bottom is set to 100 percent (very distinct and abrupt).

- Scroll down and choose a brush tip from the gallery of presets at the bottom of the dialog box.

- To load new sets of brushes from the Brush Preset Picker, click the Options menu button in the upper-right area and choose a new set of brushes from the menu.

- Close the dialog box, either by starting to paint or by clicking somewhere outside the dialog box.

More options for tools are available on the Options bar, located beneath the main menu, as shown in Figure 1-12. The one you'll probably use most is the Opacity setting, which controls the amount of opacity for all tools that use paint, including the Gradient tool and the Type tool groups.

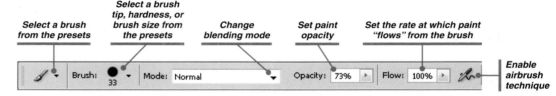

Figure 1-12: *The Options bar offers different properties for most Tools panel tools.*

To really get the most out of the paintbrush, press **F5** or click **Window | Brushes** to open the Brushes panel. You'll learn more about advanced brush options in Chapter 8.

Switch Tools in a Menu

You can use the tool shortcuts to toggle between tools within the same Tools panel flyout menu. On the flyout menu is the shortcut key.

For example, press and hold **B** to select the Brush tool. Press **B** again to switch to the Pencil tool. Press **B** once more to switch to the Color Replacement tool, before finally pressing **B** to return to the Brush tool again.

TIP

Press **X** to swap foreground and background colors.

NOTE

Click the foreground or background color swatch on the Tools panel to display the Color Picker, which enables you to choose a color that might not be available to choose as a sample in the current document.

NOTE

By default, Photoshop allows you to undo the last 20 changes to a document. To increase or decrease this number, click **Edit | Preferences**, click **Performance**, and type the number in the **History States** text box.

Set Foreground and Background Colors

Painting, drawing, fills, type, and many Photoshop filters depend on the current foreground and background colors. You can set these manually by taking a sample of a color, thereby changing the foreground or background color. Then you can select the paint, drawing, fill, type, or other tool to use with the sampled color.

SAMPLE FOREGROUND AND BACKGROUND COLORS

With an image file open in Photoshop:

- To set the foreground color, select the **Eyedropper** tool from the Tools panel and click in the image a color that you want to use.

- To set the background color, select the **Eyedropper** tool from the Tools panel and press **ALT** and click a color in the image.

RESTORE DEFAULT FOREGROUND AND BACKGROUND COLORS (BLACK AND WHITE)

To restore Photoshop to its default black and white foreground and background colors:

- Press **D**.

–Or–

- Click the **Default Foreground And Background Color** button on the Tools panel.

Use the History Panel

The History panel contains a snapshot of the 20 most recent changes in your document. Every time you make a change to the image, Photoshop adds a new image state to the History panel. When the number of changes exceeds 20, the older states are discarded from the History panel and replaced by the newer ones. Each state is named for the tool, filter, or other operation that created it—Brush tool, Pencil tool, Invert, and so forth. The Open layer is at the top, unless you have made more than 20 changes, in which case that initial layer is overlaid with a more recent one. Click the **Open** layer to view the state of the image when it was first opened. Click any of the other layers to view the state of the image created by performing the change named on the layer.

2

3

4

5

6

7

8

9

10

TIP

If you're not sure if a change is an improvement or not, press **CTRL/CMD+Z** repeatedly to switch between the original image and the changed image to compare them.

To revert to a previous state, click that layer in the History panel, and save the file or begin working on it again. Any changes that existed in the panel after this state will be discarded from the History panel as soon as you save the work or make new changes.

The following procedure explains how Photoshop's History panel keeps track of recent changes and allows you to easily compare earlier states and revert to an earlier state:

1. Open an image in Photoshop and make your changes to it.
2. Click **Window | History** to open the History panel. An example is displayed in Figure 1-13.

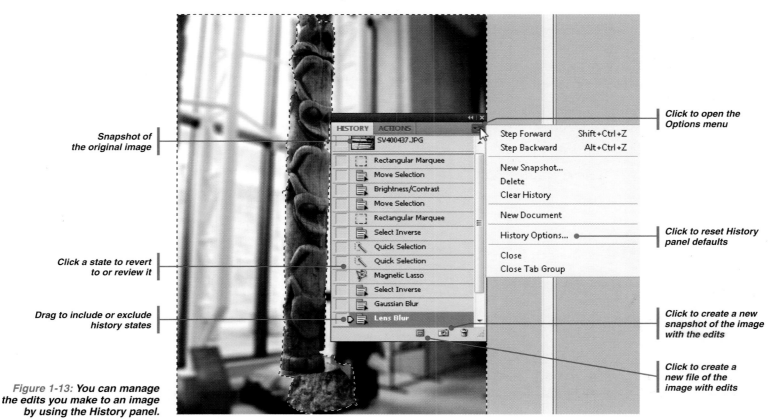

Snapshot of the original image

Click a state to revert to or review it

Drag to include or exclude history states

Figure 1-13: **You can manage the edits you make to an image by using the History panel.**

Click to open the Options menu

Click to reset History panel defaults

Click to create a new snapshot of the image with the edits

Click to create a new file of the image with edits

QUICKSTEPS

UNDOING AND REDOING ACTIONS

In addition to the History panel, you can also use the Undo and Redo commands to undo your most recent actions.

- To undo the most recent action, press **CTRL/ CMD+Z** or click **Edit | Undo**.

- To redo the most recent change, press **CTRL/ CMD+Z** or click **Edit | Redo** *operation*.

The Undo command only undoes the most recent operation. If you want to undo more than one operation, use the Step Backward command:

- To move backward through recent changes, press **ALT+CTRL+Z** or click **Edit | Step Backward**.

- To move forward again through recent changes, press **SHIFT+CTRL+Z** or click **Edit | Step Forward**.

- To step backward or step forward through the History states, you can also click the **Options** menu and click the option Step Backward or Step Forward.

TIP

You can double-click a default snapshot name to rename it with a more meaningful name.

3. Click a layer to select it. The image will revert to that state.

- All states after the selected state will be dimmed, but they are still available if you click them.

- If you begin to work with the image at this point, all succeeding states are deleted.

- You can drag the slider along the edge of each history state up or down to exclude or reinstate history states.

MAKE A HISTORY PANEL SNAPSHOT

Twenty undo actions may seem like a lot, but you can use them up before you know it. Twenty quick strokes with the Brush tool, for example, will do it. The History panel can take a snapshot of an image at a particular point in time. This snapshot will remain available until you delete it or close the document.

To take a snapshot of an image:

1. If the History panel is not open, click **Window | History**.

2. If you want to take a snapshot of an earlier state, click that layer in the History panel. The image reverts to that state.

3. Click the **Create New Snapshot** button at the bottom of the panel, as shown in Figure 1-13.

REVERT TO A SNAPSHOT

1. If the History panel is not open, open it by clicking **Window | History**.

2. In the History panel, click the snapshot. The image reverts to that state.

How to...

- *Understand Bitmaps*
- *Understand Vector Shapes*
- *Understanding Compression*
- *Understand Dimensions vs. Resolution*
- *Understand Image Size, Resampling, and Resolution*
- *Choose a Color Mode*
- *Using Indexed Color Mode*
- *Scan an Image in Photoshop*
- *Import Digital Photos*
- *Download Your "Negatives" to Bridge*
- *Saving as DNG*
- *Save Your Files*

Chapter 2
Creating, Importing, and Saving Images

With Photoshop, you can organize, sort, search for, preview, and open files on your hard drive or network, as well as import images from scanners and digital cameras. First you will learn about the differences between vector-based and bitmap-based images.

Work with Image Types

Computer graphics files—images, photos, drawings—can come in different file formats, color models, and compression schemes. Fortunately, Photoshop allows you to work with almost any image file in use today, as well as some legacy file formats.

Understand Bitmaps

Bitmap images (sometimes called *raster images*) are composed of rectangular color cells called *pixels*. Think of a pixel as a placeholder for color within a grid that makes up an image—a pixel doesn't have a fixed size; you can change the size of pixels relative to the overall image in Photoshop, as discussed later in this chapter. If you open a color photograph in Photoshop and zoom all the way in by holding down the **CTRL/CMD** key and pressing the plus (+) key ten times, you can clearly see the pixels that make up the photograph. The number of pixels is proportional to image *resolution*: the more pixels per inch, the higher the resolution. Most of the different image-file formats you'll encounter—including PSD, BMP, PICT, GIF, JPG, TIF, and PNG—are bitmap formats. (See Table 2-1 for more information about the individual file types.)

Table 2-1: *Short Description of Common File Types*

PSD	Photoshop native file format. Saves all Photoshop-specific features such as layers, effects, Smart Filters. Retains image resolution and accepts color management profiles. Compatible between Windows and Mac OS.
(TIFF) TIF	Tagged Image File Format. Saves *almost* all Photoshop-specific features such as layers, but not dynamic effects, layer masks, and so on. Can retain image resolution info and color management profiles. Compatible between Windows and Mac OS.
PDF	Adobe Acrobat Portable Document File. Saves compressed page with full-color images. Compositions can be saved and reopened in Photoshop with text embedded with subset of font used. Ideal file format for sharing searchable text and graphics as Web documents.
PNG	Portable Network Graphic. Supports 8- and 24-bit color depths, can be saved as a single layer file containing transparency. Compatible with many other graphics software, can be placed in Word documents, email inline graphics, and most Web browsers will display PNGs correctly (if you do not use transparency).
(JPEG) JPG	Joint Photographic Experts Group; supports 24-bit color, can retain image resolution and color management profiles. Uses lossy compression, occasionally visible in image, the *de facto* image format for Web pages.
GIF	Graphics Interchange Format. Limited to an index of 256 maximum colors, usually displays dithering in photographs. Does not use RGB color composite channels, useful for logos on the Web, and GIF animations can be created and exported in PS.
DNG	Digital Negative. File format you can use in Camera Raw (editor) to save digital camera photos from nearly all camera manufacturers, retaining all exposure settings and metadata. Photoshop can open a DNG file and you can perform editing work outside of Camera Raw. DNG standardizes the wide variations in file formats used by different camera manufacturers. TIFF and JPEG images can also be saved as DNGs via Camera Raw.
AI	Adobe Illustrator file, not a bitmap, but instead a vector graphic. You can place an AI file in a PS composition as a Smart Object, and paste AI data from the clipboard directly into a document in PS as vector paths.
EPS	Encapsulated PostScript. PS can write this type of file, and usually can open one. Typically an EPS file contains bitmap information although it can contain vector paths as well. Used mostly for placing in desktop publishing documents, EPS files are actually printer data that must be interpreted by Photoshop to be viewable and editable. EPS files are much larger than an equivalent PSD image.
BMP	Older Windows bitmap file format. Can save 24-bit color information, BMP files cannot retain image resolution data or color management profiles.
PICT	Macintosh native image file format. Can save 24-bit color information and an alpha channel for masking. Photoshop is one of the few programs that can read and write a PICT file that can be opened and edited by both Windows and Mac users.

NOTE

Photoshop supports a black-*or*-white color mode called Bitmap mode. It is *not* the same thing as a bitmap image. Since Bitmap mode is black *or* white, pixels can be either black or white, with no in-between grayscale shades that you see in black and white photography.

NOTE

When working with a composition in Photoshop that contains layers or effects, you can make a clipboard copy of the composition that can be pasted into almost any program. Press **CTRL/CMD+A** to select all, then click **Edit | Copy Merged**. Photoshop makes a flattened copy of all the special elements in the composition that cannot be opened in, for example, Word, and copies the image data to the clipboard as standard bitmap data, without changing the composition in PS.

NOTE

Your computer's monitor is a raster device, displaying one or more dots of color that correspond to a pixel in an image. At a resolution of 800×600, your monitor displays 480,000 pixels at a time. Because your monitor is raster based, lines in vector-based images might not be perfectly smooth onscreen unless the application uses an anti-aliasing filter to display the artwork.

Bitmaps:

- Contain comprehensive information about an image, subtle color differentiation, shading, and complexity.

- Are resolution-dependent; photo quality varies proportionately to image dimensions, so high-quality photos that contain megapixels of visual data can be quite large in saved file size.

- Can be recognized using most programs, making them nearly universally accessible.

- Can be decreased in image size or dimension with little degradation in quality, but increasing size can result in the loss of quality—usually focus, with the introduction of blotchy, unwanted artifacts.

Magnified area showing pixels

Understand Vector Shapes

Whereas bitmaps are made up of pixels, vector-based images are made up of points, lines, and curves, which combine to form the paths that visually describe the vector shape. A vector-based image file doesn't record the position and color of every pixel; rather, it records the position and color of every curve (called *paths* when you use Photoshop's Pen tool). Whereas a bitmap-based image file is like a photo or painting, a vector-based file is more like a coloring book, containing only outlines and fills. Adobe Illustrator and CorelDraw are vector-drawing programs that can import bitmaps, whereas Photoshop is a bitmap-editing program that contains a few tools for creating and editing vectors.

Because they are composed of shapes rather than individual pixels, vectors can be scaled up or down as far as you like without losing the original design quality. When vectors are resized, the positions of the points, lines, curves, and paths are

QUICKFACTS

UNDERSTANDING COMPRESSION

To mitigate the size of bitmap images, you can *compress* them. Consider a red circle on a white background.

Imagine recording every pixel in that image, starting with the upper-left corner and reading from left to right and top to bottom, just as you read a page of text. You would write, "pixel 1: white; pixel 2: white; pixel 3: white…" and so forth, until you finally reached a red pixel—pixel 199. Suppose, instead, that you wrote, "pixel 1 is white and so are the next 197 pixels in this row." That's an example of *lossless* compression; no visual or file data has been discarded in the compression process. Instead of 198 numbers—the color of each of the first 198 pixels—you have two numbers: the number of pixels of the same color and the color itself. Typically, programs that apply lossless compression to bitmap images use a variation on LZW compression (a lossless data compression

Continued . . .

mathematically calculated and scaled. For example, these two images look identical at normal size, but when they are enlarged, you can see the difference.

Bitmap image   Vector artwork

Here are two characteristics of vectors:

- Vector artwork is usually smaller in saved file size than a bitmap equivalent piece of art.
- Vector files are not as commonly accepted by other programs as bitmaps.

Vector-based image files are generally much smaller than raster image files. If a vector-based image file of a red circle on a white background weighs in at 2000 bytes (2KB) in vector format, it will be about the same file size *regardless of the image size*. A ten-inch circle will be the same file size as a one-inch circle. In contrast, a bitmap of the same circle grows larger as you increase the dimensions, because file size for bitmaps is resolution dependent. This isn't to say that vector files are always small—if you had the patience to draw a vector piece of art with 3000 vector paths, it's likely that the file size would be larger than a bitmap equivalent of the same art.

Vector-based files are best suited to such things as clip art, logos, and bold graphics with large, smooth areas filled with relatively simple colors. Common vector file formats include Adobe Illustrator (AI), SVG (the Web's Scalable Vector Graphic), WMF (Windows metafile), and proprietary formats such as CorelDraw's CDR and Xara's XAR formats. Of these pure vector file formats, Photoshop can only import Illustrator paths, either from the Clipboard into a document or by placing the design as a Smart Object.

Photoshop files can include both vector and raster components. A given Photoshop PSD file can have all vector components, all raster components, or some combination of the two. Photoshop files can include several forms of vector objects: text, shapes, and paths.

QUICK**FACTS**

UNDERSTANDING COMPRESSION

(Continued)

algorithm created by Abraham Lempel, Jacob Ziv, and Terry Welch in 1984). Photoshop has the capability to compress losslessly to its own file format (PSD) and also to TIFF and PNG. Think of lossless compression the same way you consider Zip and StuffIt file compression; the compressing process simply removes redundant data, substituting more efficient code, similar to the example of the red circle. But unlike file compression formats, image files do not need to be decompressed—Photoshop does this on-the-fly whenever you open a file.

Compression is a good thing, but there's a catch. There is also a *lossy* compression type—JPEG and GIF, for example, use lossy compression—in which visual data is averaged, and some original data that the compression scheme believes is unimportant data is discarded. Although the file size will be smaller, often an advantage, once image information is gone, you cannot get it back. JPG (or JPEG) compression is the worst offender. Figure 2-1 shows an example of a TIF file next to a JPG file. JPG uses a lossy algorithm that actually throws away information in order to squeeze the image down to a smaller size, and at higher compression settings, the degradation becomes quite apparent. For instance, JPG compression discards pixels with similar hues. Keep in mind that a pixel is a mixture of colors. For example, in the RGB (Red, Green, Blue) format, the pixel is a mixture of a shade of red, green, and blue, so some adjacent pixels with similar mixtures of red, green, and blue hues might be lost.

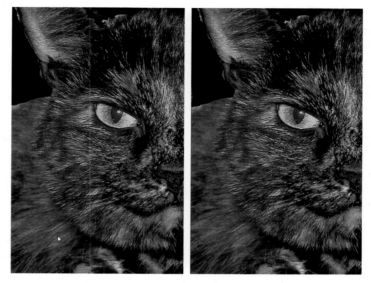

Figure 2-1: On the left you see the original image vs. the heavily compressed JPG image on the right. You can see the loss of detail in the image to the right.

Understand Dimensions vs. Resolution

Because bitmap images are *resolution dependent*, the dimensions of your photo are inversely proportional to its resolution. Resolution is the frequency of pixels per unit of physical, traditional measurement; 300 pixels/inch, 240 pixels/cm, and 120 pixels/pica are all examples of resolution, expressed as a fraction, or more commonly in the United States as "ppi"—pixels per inch. Consider an image of 300×300 pixels. At a resolution of 72 dpi, the *document* dimensions will print out a bit larger than four inches square. At a resolution of 150 dpi, it will print out at two inches square. At a resolution of 300 dpi, document dimensions will print out at an inch square. However, the image's *pixel* dimensions remain unchanged at 300×300 pixels. You can examine and change an image's dimensions, resolution, and printed size by clicking **Image | Image Size**.

Understand Image Size, Resampling, and Resolution

In Photoshop you have the option in the Image Size dialog box to resize an image, or to *resample* it. Resampling alters original photo visual information. This might not be what you desire, so read this section carefully.

- Resizing leaves the original pixels in your photo unchanged. When you increase dimensions, you decrease resolution, and vice versa.

- Resampling an image changes the number of pixels in the file, making the dimensions, resolution, and saved file size smaller or larger. Resampling might be necessary in your work, but usually the result is some loss of photo focus, because Photoshop either discards original pixels or creates new ones; in neither case is 100 percent of the finished image made up of only the pixels your camera took. See the "Understanding Interpolation Methods" QuickFacts in Chapter 1 for additional information on setting standards for sampling and resampling.

CHANGE IMAGE RESOLUTION

To change an image's resolution *without* changing its pixel dimensions at the same time:

1. Click **Image | Image Size**. The Image Size dialog box appears.
2. Deselect **Resample Image**.
3. Type a new **Resolution** value and click **OK**.

To change an image's resolution *and* its pixel dimensions:

1. Click **Image | Image Size**.
2. Click the **Resample Image** check box.
3. Type a new **Resolution** value. Under Pixel Dimensions, the Width and Height fields automatically update to reflect the new resolution.
4. Click **OK**.

RESAMPLE AN IMAGE

When you decrease the size of a bitmap image and leave the option Resample Image checked in the Image Size dialog box, you throw away some of the pixels. Normally this is not a problem because the smaller image diminishes the viewer's ability to discern details that are missing. When you *increase* the size of that same original image, Photoshop needs to add pixels to it. In a nutshell, Photoshop wasn't around at your shoot to see what details need to be added, so it has to guess via a process called "interpolation" and the result is always some sort of degradation to your original image: detailed images suffer the most, whereas simple landscape scenes tend to hide the artificially enlarged file. To minimize the obviousness of upsampling a photo, try to increase the size no more than 10 percent at a time. See the "Understanding Interpolation Methods" QuickSteps in Chapter 1.

To change the pixel dimensions of an image:

1. Click **Image | Image Size**. The Image Size dialog box appears.
2. Check the **Resample Image** checkbox.
3. Under Pixel Dimensions, type a new **Width** or **Height** for the image. The other dimension automatically updates.

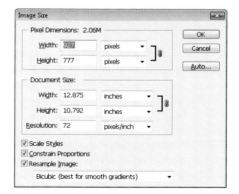

–Or–

Under Document Size, type a new **Width** or **Height** for the image. Photoshop automatically updates the other dimensions.

Choose a Color Mode

Taking the time to think about color when you are creating an image can be a wise decision. Four common color modes are grayscale, RGB, CMYK, and LAB color. The mode you choose depends on whether you will be printing your images from

USING INDEXED COLOR MODE

Indexed Color mode structures an image quite differently from the way in which RGB Color mode structures images. RGB Color mode images are built out of additive channels of red, green, and blue; the color capability, for example, of an 8-bit/pixel RGB image is 16.7 million possible colors. In contrast, Indexed Color mode images use a color table header within the saved file structure that has a maximum color capability of 256 possible colors. This Indexed Color mode table in the header of the file is commonly called its *palette*. Indexed color mode images typically are smaller than their RGB Color mode equivalent. How successfully an Indexed Color image can represent an RGB photo depends largely on the photographic content of the original photo. Photoshop *dithers*—alternates available colors in the palette to make a checkerboard sort of image—to simulate missing colors, which, depending on the visual complexity of the original image, can make the file size larger than a full-color JPEG equivalent image. In most cases, you should use Indexed Color mode only for the Web and on images with large areas of solid color, such as logos. GIF is the most common file type that uses Indexed Color mode.

You cannot create a new Indexed Color-mode file in Photoshop, but you can convert an existing image to Indexed Color mode, or you can save a file in any color-mode file as an Indexed Color-mode GIF file via Photoshop's **File | Save For Web & Devices** command.

NOTE

Your Working CMYK View mode is completely dependent on the choice you make under **Edit | Color Settings**. Usually (for the United States), US Web-Coated SWOP is a good working CMYK Working Space option to choose from the drop-down list.

your own paper, using a printing press, or using your images on the computer, such as in a web page.

1. Click **File | New**. The New dialog box appears.

2. Select a file size from the **Preset** drop-down list, or manually enter image dimensions and resolution.

3. Click the **Color Mode** drop-down arrow and choose one of the following options:

   - **Bitmap** mode images use black or white color values. They have a depth of 1 bit. This mode will probably be of interest only if you need to convert a monochrome (Grayscale mode) photo or other image so that it prints crisply at large sizes. In the Bitmap mode dialog box, you have options for Diffusion Dithering and Pattern Dithering a grayscale photo down to black or white. Bitmap mode can produce visually interesting, stylized results such as a view through a ground-glass window. However, a document in this mode cannot be edited using most of Photoshop's sophisticated selection and painting tools—the Brush tool, for example, will not produce soft edges, and regardless of any color you choose with which to paint, you'll only be able to paint with the nearest match to black, or white.

   - **Grayscale** images have no color; rather, a grayscale image is 256 shades of black, from pure black (0) to pure white (255). In photography, grayscale is known as "black and white."

   - **RGB Color** (Red, Green, Blue) is the standard color mode for images displayed on your monitor. RGB mode images are assigned a value from 0 (black) to 255 (white) for each of the red, green, or blue values of a pixel. Images for web pages and other computer applications should almost always be RGB. Although the inks used in personal inkjet printers are based around CMY and K pigments, most of today's printers have internal circuitry that performs the conversion between RGB images and the CMYK equivalent inks. For all intents and purposes, CMYK (and the newer hex ink) printers are based on RGB imagery.

   - **CMYK Color** (Cyan, Magenta, Yellow, Black) is the standard color mode for commercial offset printing. Very seldom will you find a personal printer that prints a CMYK mode photo correctly (see RGB mode above). Pixels are assigned a percentage value representing color—so the lightest colors have the smallest percentages in each of the four color channels. Images destined to be published on a commercial printer ultimately might need to be changed to CMYK mode, but generally this is not the responsibility of the photographer. To see an image in a screen simulation of CMYK mode, click **View | Proof Setup | Working CMYK**. *Don't forget* to switch this back to RGB, or your future editing work will be in print and not monitor mode.

- **LAB Color** is considered a device-independent color mode; its values apply to inkjet printing, reflexography (printing on plastic or film), and other devices that apply a pigment, dye, even pure light, to a surface. It's a good mode to work in if your assignment is, for example, a photo or logo that needs to color match the printed version of the logo on a T-shirt or bumper sticker. LAB color mode is based on the human vision spectrum, rather than empirical values in RGB additive and CMYK subtractive color modes. Briefly, LAB mode provides you with, "What you see onscreen is more or less what you'll get when you print this to paper, film, or other surface." Unfortunately, LAB mode images cannot be saved to common file formats, but the good news is that LAB and RGB color spaces almost completely overlap: essentially, they're the same except for their structure. The color values are made up of light (L), green-red values (A), and blue-yellow values (B) from +128 to −127 for each.

4. Click **OK** to create the file.

CONVERT AN IMAGE TO A DIFFERENT COLOR MODE

Even though an image exists in a certain color mode, you can change it. You would want to do this if you have an image destined for a web site or online gallery, for example.

From the Application bar, click **Image | Mode** and choose an option: **RGB Color** or **Grayscale**.

CONVERT A COLOR IMAGE TO GRAYSCALE

Click **Image | Adjustments | Desaturate**. This removes the color but leaves the image in its color mode. You can, for example, paint on color with the Brush tool.

–Or–

1. Click **Image | Mode | Grayscale**. Photoshop prompts you to confirm either that you want to flatten the image (assuming you have more than one layer) or that you want to discard color information.

2. Click **Flatten** to reduce the image to one layer, or click **OK** to discard the color information. You can now only paint on the image in shades of gray.

USE GRAYSCALE ALTERNATIVE

You can use the Black and White adjustment feature as an alternative to creating a grayscale image. Click **Image | Adjustments | Black & White**.

NOTE

To move from a higher bit-per-pixel mode to a lower one, you must travel progressively (in several steps) down the ladder, so to speak. For example, an RGB image must become Grayscale mode before you can access Bitmap from the menu.

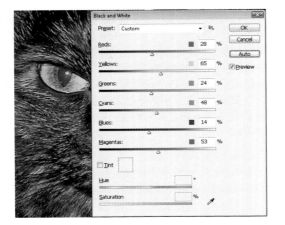

In the Black And White dialog box, click the **Preset** drop-down arrow and choose a filter, and then mix the channels so that they give you the effect you want. You get a much better looking image than you do when traveling directly from RGB Color mode to Grayscale mode. The added benefit is that the image is still in RGB Color mode, which means not only that you'll save on the black cartridge when you print to inkjet (your inkjet printer will use all the cartridges and not just the black one), but you can also add RGB color images to this apparently grayscale photo, to create stunning visual effects using Photoshop layers.

CONVERT AN RGB IMAGE TO INDEXED COLOR MODE

1. From the Application bar, click **Image | Mode | Indexed Color**. The Indexed Color dialog box appears.

2. In the Colors text box, type a number between 2 and 256 to set the number of colors to be used. Photoshop shows you a preview of the image as it appears when converted to that number of colors.

3. Choose the type of dithering you want Photoshop to use. Generally, for photos, Diffusion type produces the most eye-pleasing color reduction.

4. Click **OK** to accept the conversion.

Use Scanners and Digital Cameras

Photoshop allows you to import images directly from scanners and digital cameras connected to your computer.

Scan an Image in Photoshop

To scan an image from within Photoshop:

1. Make certain the drivers are installed for your scanning hardware; the disc that came with your scanner will serve you well, but it's usually better to download the latest drivers from the manufacturer's web site. The scanner could have been in a warehouse for several months, and reputable scanner manufacturers offer easy installation files from their web sites. Then, make sure the scanner is connected to your computer using either a USB or FireWire cable, and that it's powered on. Many of the newer power-efficient scanners go into sleep mode after a period of inactivity.

TIP

Scan the photograph using at least the resolution at which it will be displayed. The standard for displaying on a computer monitor is 72 dpi. If the photo will be printed, scan at the same resolution as will be used when it is printed (for example, 300 dpi). Scanning at a higher resolution is acceptable; scanning at a lower resolution is not. Even so, more than 300 ppi is usually unnecessary unless you're planning to print an enlarged version of the original material.

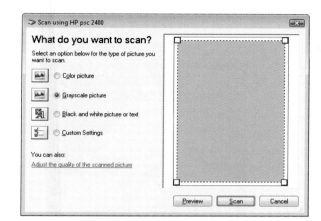

Figure 2-2: *The scanning interface will lead you through scanning your images.*

If you're scanning an heirloom black and white photograph, you'll get better editing results (see Chapter 9) if you scan in color, RGB mode. You'll be surprised how much visual content is disguised or hidden under years of photographic emulsion aging.

TIP

If you scan to a file on your hard drive or network, open the file normally in Photoshop.

2. From the Application bar, click **File | Import**. A submenu appears, listing the devices from which Photoshop can import.

3. The choices on the menu will vary, depending on your operating system and the devices physically attached to your computer. The Mac OS typically uses TWAIN drivers for scanners, while Windows systems can use TWAIN or WIA support to get the data from the scanner into Photoshop. Click the menu choice that applies to your scanning device from the **Import** list, and then click **OK**. WIA support for a Canon combo scanner/inkjet is shown here.

4. The combination interface and device driver displays options for your scan, as shown in Figure 2-2:

- Click the type of image you want to scan: **Color Picture**, **Grayscale Picture**, or **Black And White Picture Or Text**, for instance.
- Click **Custom Settings** to enter unique specifications.
- Click **Adjust The Quality Of The Scanned Picture** for advanced properties that allow you to adjust the brightness or contrast, resolution of the picture type, and the picture type.

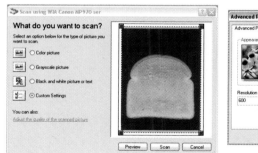

- Click **Preview** to see onscreen an image of what will be scanned.

5. Click **Scan** to perform the scan. The scanned image opens in Photoshop.

SCAN LINE ART

Although most scanning software has a setting for scanning line art, you will get better results by scanning the image as a grayscale photograph:

1. Scan the photo into Photoshop as a grayscale (black and white) photograph.

2. Press **ALT+CTRL+0** or double-click the **Zoom** tool to zoom to 100 percent.

3. Click **Image | Adjustments | Threshold**. The Threshold dialog box appears.

4. Using the Threshold command will render your image in black or white, with the same apparent results as Bitmap mode, except the image retains its original color mode. Drag the **Threshold Level** slider to the left to make lines lighter; drag it to the right to make lines heavier (see Figure 2-3).

5. Click **OK** to accept the threshold adjustment.

6. Use the Eraser and Brush tools to clean up any extra spots and specks.

You'll learn more about converting and retouching images in Chapter 6.

Figure 2-3: **You can scan a line drawing and change the line weight using Photoshop.**

Import Digital Photos

To import digital photos into Photoshop:

1. From the Application bar, click **File | Import**. In the submenu that appears, choose your camera from the list of devices.

2. Click **OK**; the connection is made and the camera is ready to download the pictures.

   –Or–

Figure 2-4: The Adobe Photo Downloader will automatically retrieve your photos from your digital camera, store them in the folder you want, and number and rename the files.

The Adobe Photo Downloader will automatically retrieve your photos if the card reader is connected to the computer (see Figure 2-4).

3. Select one or more photos, complete any settings, and click the appropriate button (**OK**, **Get Photos**, and so on) to import the photos into Photoshop. The exact appearance and operation will depend on your camera.

Download Your "Negatives" to Bridge

Adobe Bridge can act as a host for downloading raw image files from your camera or memory card reader. Bridge also offers more options for downloading—such as auto-naming your files and selecting only the ones you want—than the software that came with your camera. Once you've powered up your camera and connected its cable to your computer, and your computer acknowledges the connection:

1. Click the **Get Photos From Camera** icon.

   This displays the Adobe Bridge Photo Downloader dialog box. Click the **Get Photos From** drop-down list to choose the right connection to your camera or card reader. Bridge acknowledges device drivers, what you're actually seeing on the list, regardless of whether the device is connected at the moment or not!

2. Click **Browse** to locate a destination for your images. You can also create subfolders in case your camera's images were taken on several dates: click the **Create Subfolders** drop-down list to specify the format for the date the subfolder(s) are labeled with.

NOTE

If Windows users don't have Bridge open when the connection is made between the computer and camera, a dialog box might open—one triggered by the camera device—and you'll be prompted with choices for what to do with the newly discovered data. You can then choose **Download Images Using Adobe Bridge CS4** from the list.

3. You might want to rename the files with a custom name or a particular sequence for the date taken. Choose these options from the **Rename Files** drop-down list.

4. Click **Advanced Dialog** to preview your images and access more features, such as applying a template to all the images you download.

5. Type in basic user-defined metadata such as credit and copyright information, or choose a saved template for your downloaded images. In future Bridge sessions, you can load the saved metadata, making cataloguing and copyrighting scores of photos a simple task. This is covered more thoroughly in Chapter 3.

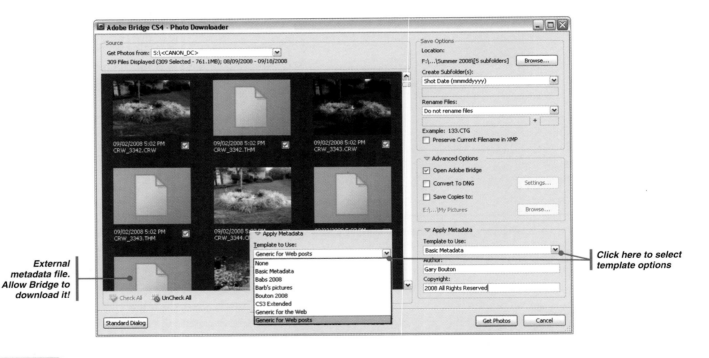

External metadata file. Allow Bridge to download it!

Click here to select template options

SAVING AS DNG

The Save As DNG option lets you save an image from your camera to Adobe's file format for Digital Negative (DNG) files. The advantage to saving a camera raw file as a DNG is that as an Adobe standard, the file will be able to be opened with all the camera data at any time in the future. In contrast, because there are so many different formats for camera raw files from different hardware manufacturers, you're not assured in the future that a proprietary camera raw file can be opened. The disadvantage to saving as DNG is that Photoshop and only a few other applications can read a DNG file.

TIP

If you click Cancel while Bridge is downloading your images, you'll get an information box that tells you that the images it has downloaded prior to the cancellation have been successfully written to hard disk.

6. Click **Get Photos**. Depending on the number of photos you have stored on the camera, this might take a while.

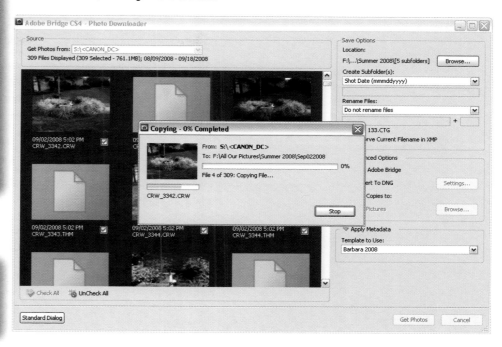

When the images you've chosen have completely downloaded, they appear in the Content panel, and you can confirm the hard disk location of the new images on the Folder panel.

Save Your Files

Photoshop offers you the option to save a photo in its original format, or as any other file type that is valid for the file's color mode, bit depth, and anything "special" about your editing work, such as transparency, alpha channels, and Photoshop effects.

SAVE AN EXISTING FILE

To save changes to an existing file, click **File | Save** or press **CTRL/CMD+S**. However, if you've added Photoshop-specific data to the file—text as editable text, layers, shapes—that sort of stuff you're best off choosing **File | Save As**. Otherwise, Photoshop saves the file using the Photoshop PSD file format.

SAVE A NEW, RENAMED, OR REFORMATTED FILE

To save a new file or to save a previous file with a new name or file format (for example, to save a JPG as a TIFF):

1. Click **File | Save As**. The Save As dialog box appears.
2. Type a file name in the **File Name** field.
3. Choose a file format from the **Format** drop-down list.
4. Click **Save**.

How to...

- *Use the Bridge Workspace*
- *View and Write Metadata*
- *Working with Metadata and Sidecar Information*
- *Create Labels*
- *Batch Rename Files*
- *Use Image Stacks*
- *Open the Camera Raw Editor*
- *Defining the Properties of a Processed Raw File*
- *Work with Camera Raw Editor's Tools*
- *Refine Images with Other Adjustments*

Chapter 3

Using Adobe Bridge and the Camera Raw Editor

If you're using a digital camera that saves to the Raw file format, this chapter gets you up and running on how to process Raw photos before performing any edits in Photoshop. As you'll see, you can adjust exposure, color temperature, and a host of other parameters, much in the same way you might push-process traditional, physical film, modify its exposure during printing, and so on. This chapter also shows you how to use Adobe Bridge to tag your images with identifying information, organize your images, and preview a collection of images.

Work with Bridge

It's easy to take hundreds of photos in a single session with digital cameras. Suppose you're looking for a *specific* photo you want to color correct and print today. Adobe Bridge is the best start to sorting through a collection of photographs, which you can do without launching Photoshop. Bridge can

CAUTION

Executable files (program files) will indeed launch if you double-click their icon in Bridge's Content panel, so exercise caution.

display every type of media that Adobe programs support. It displays all sorts of bitmap image formats, can play movie files and audio files, and enables you to browse PDF documents in its Preview panel. Files that aren't supported show up with an icon instead of a thumbnail preview. Bridge connects user content to the appropriate Adobe application.

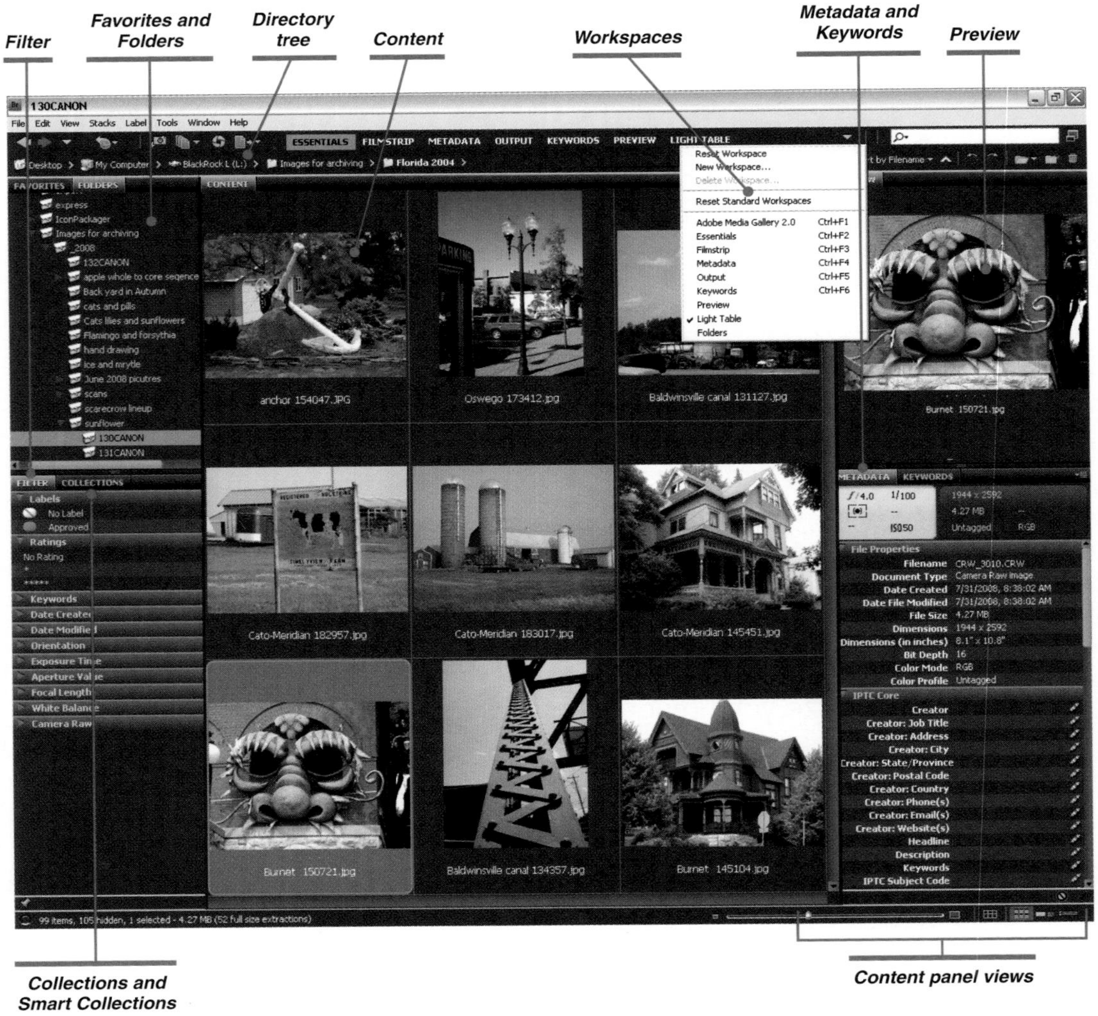

Figure 3-1: The user interface to Adobe Bridge has areas for viewing images and information, and offers common tasks via the menu, context menus, and tools.

Use the Bridge Workspace

You can perform scores of useful tasks in Bridge's workspace, an interface that's not visually intimidating. Figure 3-1 shows the interface after a folder has been loaded: the callouts describe the default workspace areas, discussed shortly.

USE FOLDERS AND FAVORITES

The Folders panel looks and acts exactly like a folder window you navigate using your operating system, except files within folders are displayed in the Content panel, not in the Folders panel. The current folder you're viewing is also at the end of a hierarchical directory tree at the top of the interface, enabling you to navigate up and down the directory tree without using the Folders panel.

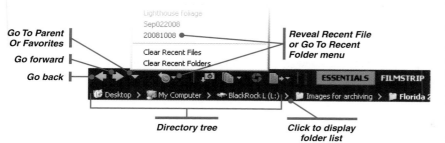

Go To Parent Or Favorites

Go forward

Go back

Reveal Recent File or Go To Recent Folder menu

Directory tree

Click to display folder list

When you first open Bridge, you have a Favorites list, and by default it's populated with system folders such as My Pictures and My Documents. Conveniently, you have a directory tree above the Favorites and Folders grouped panels, plus folder navigation icons. Regardless of whether the Folders panel is hidden by the Favorites panel, it's always easy to navigate to a desired folder.

- To switch back and forth between the displays you've used, click the back arrow and forward arrow buttons above the directory tree.
- To select a folder and display its contents, click a folder icon on the tree.
- To see a list of subfolders within a folder, click the "greater than" icon that separates the folders on the directory tree.
- To go to a recently accessed folder, click the **Go To Parent Or Favorites** icon.

Once you have the contents of a folder displayed in the Content panel, it's easy to add images to the Favorites panel and to open them:

- To add one or more images to the Favorites list, click the thumbnails in the Content panel, and then drag them onto the Favorites list.
- To add noncontiguous images to your Favorites, press **CTRL/CMD** and click the filenames in turn; to select contiguous thumbnails, press **SHIFT** while you click the first and last filenames in the list.
- To open a Favorites image in Photoshop CS4, double-click its filename or icon.

USE COLLECTIONS AND SMART COLLECTIONS

Collections and *Smart* Collections are Bridge methods for organizing your photos, but they differ in the way they work and the way you set them up. A Smart Collection is created by conducting a search based on criteria you define (explained in the steps to follow) and Smart Collections dynamically update whenever you've added photos to a folder that matches your search criteria. In contrast, you create a regular Collection by manually dragging image files into a folder you create.

NOTE

When you drag a file using Bridge, you aren't moving the physical location of files. You're simply making a favorite image of yours easier to retrieve in future Bridge

The Collections panel lets you organize files located all over your hard drive, and organize them in indexed collections that can be easily accessed and loaded into Photoshop. Similar to Favorites, a collection doesn't move files on your hard drives; your collections are shortcuts to different places where your images are located.

A Smart Collection can be used to organize only the Camera Raw images you've taken. To create a Smart Collection:

1. Right-click over the list area of the Collections panel and then click **New Smart Collection**, as shown next—or click the icon on the bottom right of the panel. The Smart Collection dialog box appears, where you define the criteria for your collection that will update as you add new files to a folder or a folder's subfolders.

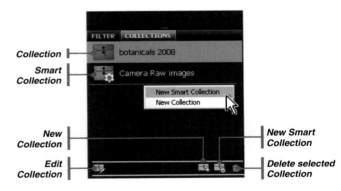

Figure 3-2: Choose almost any sort of criteria for your search to have Bridge build a Collection for you.

2. Under Source, click the **Look In** down arrow and choose **Browse**.

3. Use the directory window to browse to a folder that contains images for which you want a collection, choose it, and then click **OK**.

4. Click the leftmost **Criteria** down arrow and then choose **Document Type**. As you can see in Figure 3-2, you have a very wide range of selections when creating a Smart Collection criteria.

5. Set the middle drop-down list selection to **equals**. Which selections are available to you in the middle and right drop-down lists depends on your first criteria choice.

6. Click **Camera Raw Image** from the far right drop-down list. You can type the first letter of your file type to make Bridge automatically scoot to this area on the list.

TIP

Using the Criteria selections, it's easy to create an "anything but" collection: choose "does not equal" from the drop-down list.

3

7. The Results field offers a drop-down list where you choose if "any" or "all" criteria are met (then the files are added to your new Collection). Check the **Include All Subfolders** box and, because this is your first time using the Collection feature and you are yet to index any images, Bridge-style, check the **Include Non-indexed Files** box.

8. Click **Save**. When Bridge indicates it's finished, you see a new entry on the Collections list and its title is highlighted with the default name entered. Type the name you want for the collection, and then click outside the text field to make your entry complete and deselect the text.

USE THE FILTER PANEL

Essentially, when you open a collection or any folder, you can hide images that aren't tagged to specific criteria. The Filter panel works in combination with Keywords, Labels, or other data you've tagged to specific images—see "Create and Find Keywords," later in this section. In Figure 3-3, a filter has been defined to show only images labeled with the Approved tag; out of dozens of photos in the selected folder, only two appear in the Content panel, because the rest of the images don't fit the "Approved" criterion.

Figure 3-3: Use a filter to hide in a folder images that don't meet your search criteria.

To filter your display of images:

1. Tag your images using the criteria you want, such as Keywords or Labels.

2. Click the **Filter** tab, such as shown in Figure 3-3.

3. Click the option you want to use to filter your selection of images. The files corresponding to the criteria will be displayed in the Content panel.

EXPLORE THE CONTENT PANEL

The Content panel is where, by default, you can view thumbnails of photos and other bitmap-type files, as well as videos. You can change your view in the Content panel, however, to display View content as details and View content

View content as thumbnail **View content as details**

IPTC Subject Code

Zoom   Lock Grid   View content as list

Figure 3-4: Views of the Content panel can provide different visual and text data.

as list format that shows very small thumbnails but well-organized image-related data.

- To increase or decrease the size of the thumbnails in the Content panel, drag the slider left or right.

- To prevent accidental resizing of the grid that the thumbnails make up while you work in the Content panel, click the **Lock Grid** icon.

- To put image properties to the right of thumbnails (decreasing the thumbnail size), click the **View Content As Detail** icon.

- To view a folder's content as a list, click the **View Content As List** icon.

In Figure 3-4 you can see the icons; by default, View Content As Thumbnail is your viewing option.

WORK WITH IMAGE VIEWS

As discussed in "Process Camera Raw Images" later in this chapter, Bridge can display previews of varying quality, and without reading embedded processing information. Click the **Options For Thumbnail Quality And Preview Generation** button down arrow on the address bar to see the options for displaying images.

- **Prefer Embedded**   Choose this option when you want to preview images that contain camera data and any other additional image processing data (such as exposure and color temperature). With this option chosen, the Content panel loads and displays images in a collection or a selected folder noticeably faster.

- **High Quality On Demand**   This option does not automatically generate high-quality (high-resolution) images, which in turn saves hard disk space. To enable a high-quality screen version of an image, right-click the image and choose Generate High Quality Thumbnail from the context menu.

- **Always High Quality**   This option creates high-quality thumbnails whenever you load a folder.

- **Generate 100% Previews**   If you choose this option, you'll get an attention box that extols the virtues of a 100% preview, but also cautions you that this option will require an unspecified amount of hard disk space.

A 100% Preview is not the actual size of the image you've selected—the 100% Preview is screen resolution, typically 72 pixels per inch. The 100% Preview option lets you display a selected file in Full Screen mode (press **ENTER**; press

ENTER a second time to return to Bridge). While in Full Screen mode, you can use the mouse wheel to zoom in and out of the image: scrolling away from you zooms in, scrolling toward yourself scrolls out.

BUILD WORKSPACES

The tabs above the directory tree are used to configure Bridge. In Figure 3-5, you can see four of the more popular workspaces for Bridge.

Figure 3-5: Choose the workspace layout that best suits your task within Bridge.

If you're a photographer, you probably want to stick to the default Essentials or the Light Table configuration. The following list describes your options for viewing files:

- To show your images in a Filmstrip layout, choose Filmstrip from the drop-down list (or press **CTRL/CMD+F3**).

- To show images in a Light Table layout—which maximizes the Content panel so you can view and arrange images just like a physical light table—choose Light Table from the drop-down list.

- To only show an image's Keywords, choose Keywords from the drop-down list (or press **CTRL/CMD+F6**).

● To return to the default workspace layout, click Reset Standard Workspaces from the drop-down list.

View and Write Metadata

Metadata is literally "data *about* data"; photographers can access data about when a photo was taken, f-stop, film speed, and image size, all of which was recorded by the camera. Users can write additional metadata, too: Bridge can display and save many different "pages" (fields) of metadata with notes you might want to tag to images.

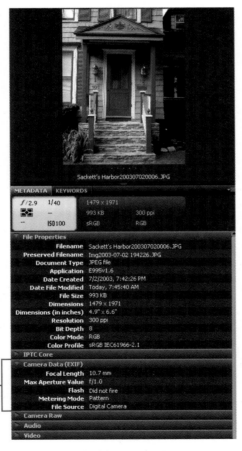

EXIF data ⊢

LOOK AT AN IMAGE'S CAMERA DATA (EXIF METADATA)

When you click the Metadata tab, you'll see several fields of data, which you can expand and collapse by clicking the triangle to the left of the field category. The two most pertinent interface areas for judging what might need to be corrected in a photo are the File Properties and Camera Data (EXIF—**Ex**changeable **I**mage **F**ile format), metadata that is not editable. In the following example, the JPEG file was taken at a narrow f-stop and the flash did not fire; this is valuable information to remember and use in the Camera Raw editor to correct, in this case, sharpness and color-casting (images tend to cast warm when a flash fails to fire).

WRITE IPTC METADATA

There are several ways to add user data to an image, but perhaps the simplest is to use the IPTC (International Press Telecommunications Council) Core tab to add notes, credits, and other information. And, no, you don't have to be a card-carrying press member to use the feature!

1. Expand the IPTC Core tab by clicking the triangle to the left of its title on the Metadata panel.

2. Click a field to highlight it and open it for an entry.

3. Enter the desired information.

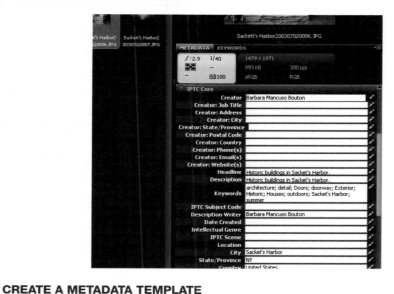

CREATE A METADATA TEMPLATE

To create XMP metadata (Adobe's **E**xtensible **M**etadata **P**latform) for an image in a more comprehensive fashion than using the Metadata IPTC Core feature, you use File Info feature, but it's usually a smarter workflow approach to create a template first, with reoccurring fields filled in. To make an XMP template:

1. From the main menu, click **Tools | Create Metadata Template**.

2. Type a name in the **Template Name** field. For example, "Generic for Web posts" is easy to remember; you add your name, contact information, and a copyright status, and this is written into all the images that use this template.

3. Click to the left of the items to check those items that you want automatically filled in the template whenever you attach this template to images. Description, Keywords, and Copyright Notice are good ones that quite often contain the same text content.

WORKING WITH METADATA AND SIDECAR INFORMATION

Metadata is written to files as header information—brief text information (not visible in image viewers) within certain file types that support metadata; JPEG, TIF, DNG, and PSD are usually good choices. However, other file formats such as PNG, cannot internally hold metadata, but can still be written *about* the file *externally* as *sidecar* information. Sidecar data comprises small files marked with the .xmp file extension.

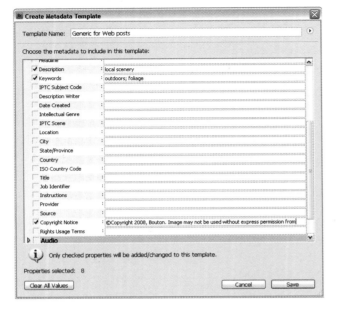

4. Fill in the fields you've chosen.

5. When you're done filling the fields—and you're certain your spelling is correct—click **OK** and Bridge saves the template.

USE YOUR XMP METADATA TEMPLATE

To use a template you've created:

1. Click to select one or more images in the Content panel.

2. Right-click and then choose **File Info** from the context menu.

3. Click the **Import** button. You'll get an attention box asking whether you want to overwrite existing metadata as one of the options—no, you probably don't. Click the bottom button (keep original metadata, but append matching properties from template), and then click **OK**.

4. Choose the template you want to use from the Metadata Templates folder in the dialog box; click **Open**.

5. Enter custom data that relates to individual images. You can also add Favorites stars and Keywords (covered next as panel features).

CREATE AND FIND KEYWORDS

Using Keywords is a fast and nonambiguous way to tag a file or several files with a word the user can remember, and later images in a folder or collection can be filtered to display only the photos that are tagged with a specific Keyword.

Follow these steps to create a new Keyword and tag an image with a Keyword:

1. Load a folder of images in Bridge so you can see the images in the Content panel.

2. Decide on a keyword to which you can refer later. In Figure 3-6, there are hundreds of photos of a carnival in a folder, but the photographer wants later to only locate the photos of the Ferris wheel.

NOTE

By default, the Keywords panel has categories such as People, Places, and Other Keywords. Click an entry in a category to create a new entry within that category. Click the + symbol to add a new Keyword, or right-click and then choose **New Keyword** from the context menu.

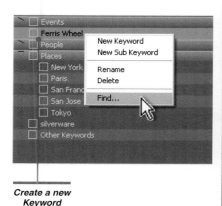

Create a new Keyword

Figure 3-6: Narrow searches by tagging images with Keywords.

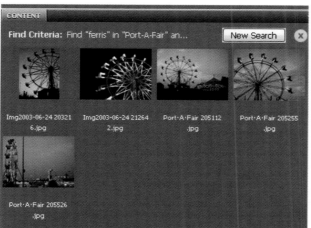

3. Type the name of your new category in the open text field; press **ENTER** to finalize your new entry and close the text editing box.

4. Click an image thumbnail (or click several images if they can use the same Keyword) and then check your category check box.

That's it; the image is now tagged with the keyword. If you'd like to verify that you have tagged the photo(s), click an image that isn't tagged (to clear the Keyword panel), and then click an image you tagged—you'll see a check appear to the left of the Keyword you created in Step 3.

Displaying images in the Content panel that are tagged with a Keyword requires that you perform a search on a Collection, or a folder you've loaded. To find, for example, only the photos that in the previous steps were tagged with "Ferris wheel":

1. Right-click this Keyword in the Keywords list and choose **Find** from the context menu.

2. In the Find dialog box, if the criteria looks correct, either click **Find** or press **ENTER**.

TIP

To increase the size of the Preview panel, click and drag its edge away from its center. This action doesn't change the size of the thumbnails in the Content panel.

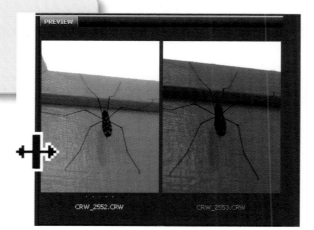

USE THE PREVIEW PANEL

The Preview panel shows you one or more of the currently selected images in the Content panel. To select two or more photos that are not displayed in sequence, hold **CTRL/CMD** while you click the thumbnails.

One of the handy features of the Preview panel is that it has a *loupe*; you can check an image for focus and other properties before sending, for example, a Camera Raw image off for processing in Adobe's Camera Raw editor. To open the loupe to your view of a Preview image:

1. Hover your cursor over the area of the Preview panel image: you should see a Zoom tool.

2. Click the image area you want to examine. Your cursor turns into a Hand tool; drag the Preview image to examine the smallest details in different areas.

3. Click to return to the Zoom tool.

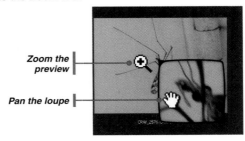

Zoom the preview

Pan the loupe

Create Labels

If you don't have thousands of digital photographs, but only a few dozen, there are features in Bridge that are ideally suited to address modest, "local" imaging needs.

APPLY AND SORT LABELS

An Adobe Label on a photograph is written as metadata; in Bridge you have five levels of importance with which you can tag an image (or several at once through multiple selections).

To label photos:

1. Right-click the image thumbnail in the Content panel.

2. Choose **Label** from the context menu and then click a label type.

The image now has a brightly colored horizontal bar, a different color for each label type, below the thumbnail.

BlackRock L (L:) > Images for archiving > Jewelery silverware etc

CONTENT

DSCN7355.JPG

DSCN7367.JPG

~~ar Filter~~	Ctrl+Alt+A
Show Rejected Items Only	
Show Unrated Items Only	
Show 1 or More Stars	Ctrl+Alt+1
Show 2 or More Stars	Ctrl+Alt+2
Show 3 or More Stars	Ctrl+Alt+3
Show 4 or More Stars	Ctrl+Alt+4
Show 5 Stars	Ctrl+Alt+5
Show Labeled Items Only	
Show Unlabeled Items Only	

To review those images you've labeled with a label:

1. Click the down arrow to the right of the star icon, the **Filter Items By Rating** drop-down arrow.

2. Choose an option that suits your specific browsing need; the Content panel then only displays items that have a label you've previously applied.

TAG FAVORITES

Tagging an image as a Favorite is similar to labeling it, but there's no "To Do" or any other action associated with a Favorite. Favorites are ranked as no stars and one through five stars. You can quickly search a collection or a folder to show only your Favorites in the Content panel. To give a thumbnail a star or two:

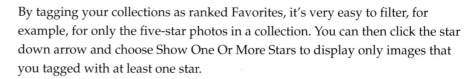

1. Click an image thumbnail, and then click your cursor over the tiny dots just above the name of the file in the Content panel; increase the size of the image to see the dots if needed. The second through last dots represent stars in increasing order.

2. To remove a Favorites ranking, click the first, leftmost dot.

By tagging your collections as ranked Favorites, it's very easy to filter, for example, for only the five-star photos in a collection. You can then click the star down arrow and choose Show One Or More Stars to display only images that you tagged with at least one star.

Batch Rename Files

As part of organizing, you might want to rename some or all files in a specific folder. To do this in Bridge:

1. Select the images you want to rename.

2. Right-click and then click **Batch Rename** from the context menu.

3. In the Batch Rename dialog box, you can leave the Destination Folder option set to Rename In Same Folder if you then check the **Preserve Current Filename In XMP Metadata** check box. Doing this keeps the original filename and it doesn't matter now what the new filename will be—you can later look up the original photo name by viewing the metadata.

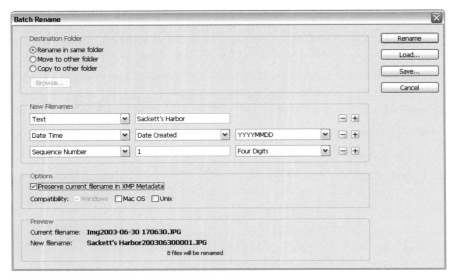

4. In the New Filenames area, it's best to rename the files using text, and not numerically (the other option in the first drop-down list). Type the new name prefix for your selected photos in the entry field to the right of Text.

5. The Date Time is probably best left at its default, unless you want to sort by month or other criteria in the future.

6. You can remove other fields if you have no use for them by clicking the minus (–) button at the right of a row.

7. The Sequence Number is usually the best option for file renaming; in Figure 3-7 you can see that the text for a group of images is labeled with the location, Sackett's Harbor, and by starting at 1, and allowing four digits as the suffix for the "Sackett's Harbor" prefix, 9999 images can have the same prefix in the name.

8. Click the **Rename** button. The files are renamed, and you're returned to the folder in Bridge's Content panel, with your newly renamed—and much easier to review—photos.

Figure 3-7: Batch rename photos to make your time sorting images much easier.

Use Image Stacks

Creating stacks of images not only enables you to see more of a collection, but is also terrific for thumbing through to see, for example, which photo out of a series has the best exposure or camera angle. To make a stack:

1. **CTRL/CMD**+click several image thumbnails in the Content panel.

2. Right-click and choose **Stack | Group As Stack** from the context menu.

To unstack a stack, Choose **Ungroup from Stack** from the right-click context menu or choose **Stack | Ungroup From Stack**.

An image stack is readily identified by the unique number tag at the top left of an image thumbnail.

You'll note that in this section, the main menu in Bridge has not been thoroughly documented; this is for a good reason. Almost all the commands you use and features at your disposal in Bridge can be accessed from the right-click context menu, or can be performed by dragging on an interface element or a thumbnail.

You've just learned the smart way to work in Adobe Bridge and will be hard-pressed to find a significant item on the menu (except for Help) that cannot be accessed through the methods you've just learned in this chapter.

Travel from Bridge to Photoshop

It's easy to open an image—or a number of selected images—in Photoshop from Bridge: right-click over the image(s) and choose **Open With | Adobe Photoshop CS4 (Default)**. In seconds you have your selected images in a tabbed window in PS CS4. As you can see next, the Open With submenu includes other applications you can launch; which programs are listed depends on the programs you own, and the operating system's associations with the file type, such as JPEG, TIF, and others.

You can also use the Open command on the context menu to launch Photoshop with your selected image(s), but only if CS4 is the default application; an application you've installed after you install CS4 might have made the association, for example, for PNG file types, so to be sure you're launching Photoshop, use **Open With** instead of Open.

Raw file types have many different extensions because no two camera manufacturers can agree on a common file format. A Raw image is an *unprocessed* image and therefore needs to pass through Adobe Camera Raw Editor *before* it can be edited in Photoshop. There are two ways to spot a camera Raw image in the Content panel:

- The Metadata File Properties area states that the selected image is a Raw file in the Document Type field.

- For Windows users and others who use file extensions, a camera Raw file has an unusual file extension such as CRW (Canon), NEF, NRW (Nikon), MRW (Minolta), or any of more than 15 other popular ones. Additionally, Adobe has an omnibus file exchange format for Raw files with the extension DNG.

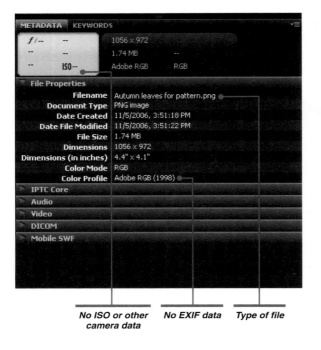

No ISO or other camera data **No EXIF data** **Type of file**

As a rule, when you right-click a thumbnail in Bridge and choose Open, JPEG, TIFF, and Camera Raw file types are sent to the Camera Raw Editor before you can open them in Photoshop; Adobe specifies these files types as ones that can retain camera metadata internally.

Process Camera Raw Images

Chances are good that any digital camera model from 2002 and later will take camera raw images (in addition to JPEGs and TIFFs). Camera raw images produce the highest-quality images to date, but unlike JPEG and other file formats, you can define a raw image's exposure, color temperature, and other properties, very much like the traditional darkroom enhancing you can perform on a film negative when printing a photo.

Open the Camera Raw Editor

A camera raw image isn't developed: you need to *create* a processed image based on the raw "negative" file—which also makes it less likely you'll accidentally alter your negatives. To open one or more raw images for processing:

- In Bridge, select the images, right-click, and click **Open In Camera Raw** from the context menu. Camera raw files as well as file formats saved to your camera's memory card, such as JPEG and TIFF, will open in the Camera Raw Editor.

  –Or–

- In Photoshop, click **File | Open**, select the image (alternatively, Marquee-select several images or press **CTRL/CMD** and click nonsequential images), and then click **Open**. Note that Camera Raw will only open if you choose one or more raw files—JPEGs and TIFFs will not trigger the Camera Raw Editor.

The "darkroom" for raw film processing is the Camera Raw Editor, shown in Figure 3-8.

The elements in the interface are as follows:

- **Tools panel** Here you can find the tools for removing Red Eye, adding a graduated tint, and many other features you can also use directly in Photoshop. The tools are a convenience if you're in a hurry and don't have time to launch Photoshop for a minor correction or enhancement.

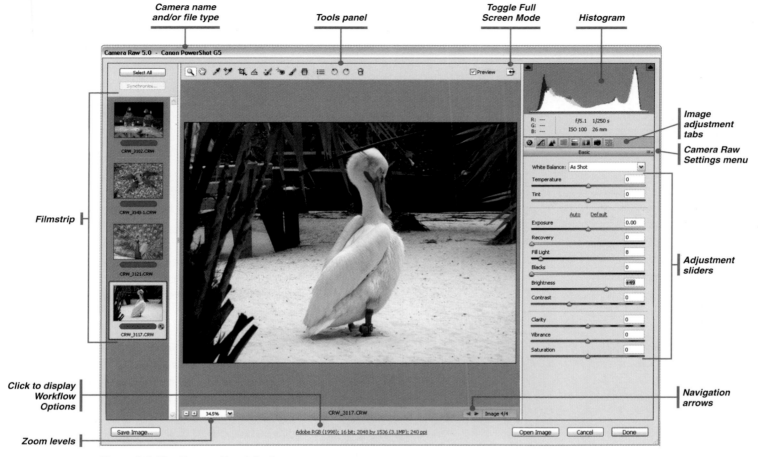

Figure 3-8: The Camera Raw interface

- **Filmstrip**   To the left of the interface you'll find one or more images you've chosen for processing. Click one to edit it and preview it in the main window.

- **Toggle Full Screen Mode**   This button offers alternative views between a normal and a maximized interface onscreen.

- **Camera name and/or file format**   On the title bar (hidden when in Full Screen mode) you'll see the name of the camera when a camera raw file is loaded. When a JPEG or other image file format is loaded, you'll see the file format here.

- **Image adjustment tabs** By default, you can process images using the Basic adjustment tab sliders and settings. There are additional adjustment settings on the other tabs, described in the following section.

- **Histogram** Here you can see how many pixels are at various brightness levels in the selected image: the red, green, and blue channels are overlaid with a white composite channel. You can adjust the distribution of pixels at different brightness levels using the Tone Curve tab in the adjustment tabs section. See Chapter 4 for details on working with Levels, Curves, and other Photoshop adjustments for correcting and enhancing the shadows, midtones, and highlights in your photos.

SAVE OR RESET YOUR PROCESSING WORK

Before you get too far into Camera Raw image processing, it's good to understand what the buttons along the bottom of the interface do and mean:

- **Save Image** Click to save an image—with or without any adjustments. The Save Options dialog box opens. If you want to save a copy of a camera raw image, choose Digital Negative (DNG) from the Format drop-down list. You can also save to TIFF, JPEG, and Photoshop's native file format. To save with the most future editing options, choose Digital Negative Or PSD—saving a JPEG as a JPEG only allows further degradation of the file because JPEG is a lossy file format.

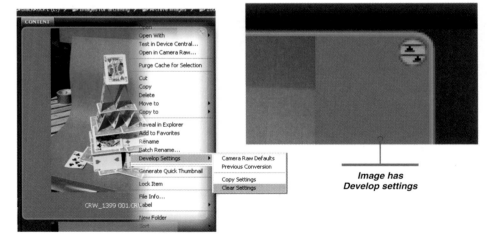

Image has Develop settings

- **Open Image** Click to open the file as a Smart Object in Photoshop. The image will need to be saved in Photoshop using **File | Save** or **File | Save As**; Smart Objects do not have a file format and they are not saved to hard disk.

- **Cancel** Click to return to Bridge. Alternatively, press **ALT/OPT** and the Cancel button becomes the Reset button, which, when clicked, discards all your editing of the image in the Camera Raw Editor.

- **Done** Click to apply the edits. You're returned to Bridge. Note that a small icon appears to the upper right of an edited image. Because edits are nondestructive in the Camera Raw Editor, you can elect to remove all edits at any time within Bridge. Here you can see an image that has been cropped. To remove the crop, right-click the thumbnail in Bridge's Content panel and then choose **Develop Settings | Clear Settings** from the context menu.

DEFINING THE PROPERTIES OF A PROCESSED RAW FILE

To get the most out of your Photoshop editing work, it's important to save a copy of your Raw image in a color space and color depth that allows high-fidelity corrections with the least loss of original camera data. Here are the steps to ensure that every pixel of your photo arrives in Photoshop with as much editing potential as you need:

1. Click the **Workflow Options** text label below the current image.

2. Choose **Adobe (1998) RGB** for the color space. This is the largest color space available; the larger the color space, the more freedom you have to create dramatic changes to image areas in Photoshop—such as burning and dodging—without creating flat, super-saturated areas that look unnatural.

3. Choose **16 Bits/Channel** as the depth. A 16-bit image contains a broader range of tones than standard 8-bit-per-pixel photos, enabling you to play with exposure without introducing banding or other artifacts. The trick is to create smooth areas when you edit in Photoshop; 16-bit-per-pixel images provide the capability.

4. It's best to leave the Size setting of your image at the size at which it was taken; when an image is resized, pixel color values are reassigned and this sometimes leads to blurring the photo.

5. It's also best to leave the Resolution setting at its current value. Changing resolution can create the same image softening as changing the image's size. Size and resolution are both best changed using Photoshop's advanced features.

UNDERSTAND THE CAMERA RAW SETTINGS MENU

Say you've taken several raw images at about the same time, and they're all consistently running colder than you'd like. The Camera Raw Settings menu is invaluable for saving processing settings you perform on one image, and then applying the setting to several photos:

1. Make your corrections using the adjustment sliders and/or other controls on the image adjustment tabs.

2. Choose **Save Settings** from the menu, check the boxes that you want to apply to other images, and then click **Save**.

3. Load an image to which you want to apply the saved settings.

4. Choose **Load Settings** from the menu and choose the file you saved in Step 3.

Other options on the menu can be used to reset the defaults to a raw image (thus removing any custom processing settings), load the conversion you used previously, and write an external XMP file for an image you've processed that cannot store metadata internally, such as PNG images.

USE ZOOM LEVELS

Choose from the drop-down list to increase and/or decrease your view in the main image window. Also, to the left are + and – buttons; if you want to zoom in or out by predefined multiples, you click either of these buttons.

WORKFLOW OPTIONS

Eventually you'll want to perform a little advanced editing in Photoshop, even with the best of photos. When you click the blue underscored label beneath the current image, the Workflow Options dialog box appears, in which you can define the color space, color depth, size, and resolution of the image as it will open in Photoshop.

Checking the Open In Photoshop As Smart Objects check box sends your processed image to Photoshop as a Smart Object. Smart Object layers display a unique identifier in the corner of their thumbnail on the Layers panel. You can also click Open Object to open the raw image in Photoshop as a Smart Object.

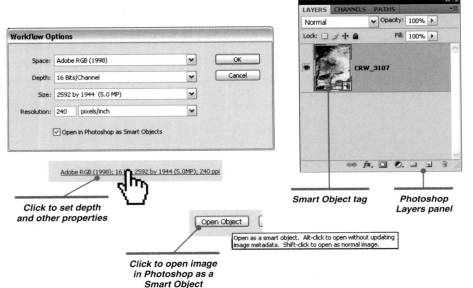

Smart Objects are in a special "wrapper"; some but not all edits can be performed on Smart Objects. The purpose of a Smart Object is to retain all the original properties of the file, to make edits nondestructive. Figure 3-9 shows an example of the Workflow Options dialog box and the identifier for a Smart Object as displayed on Photoshop's Layers panel.

Click to set depth and other properties

Click to open image in Photoshop as a Smart Object

Smart Object tag

Photoshop Layers panel

Figure 3-9: Use the Workflow Options dialog box to save the raw image for editing at custom resolutions and depth.

NAVIGATION ARROWS

These arrows take you from the current image to the previous and next ones only if you've loaded several images in the Camera Raw editor for editing—a single loaded image doesn't call these arrows and, in this case, they're hidden. You can manually navigate through your images by clicking their thumbnails in the Filmstrip panel.

ADJUSTMENT SLIDERS

This is the area where the most significant global changes are made while you process your images in the Camera Raw editor. It's often best to make adjustments starting at the top of the panel, working down.

- Use the White Balance drop-down list to make a baseline correction to the image. Then use the sliders to refine the color and tone corrections.

- Use the Temperature slider to change the color casting of the photo. Drag left to cool the image, and drag right to warm up a cold image.

- Use the Tint slider to compensate for Temperature corrections. Add a green tint by dragging the slider left, and add magenta by dragging to the right.

- Click the Auto button to allow the Editor to estimate the parameters for the sliders below; click the Default button to reset the sliders.

- Drag the Exposure slider to the right to increase the global brightness of the image (most noticeably in the lighter areas). Drag to the left to darken the image. Use the number box to enter precise values: every whole value you type in is equivalent to a camera's f-stop.

- Drag the Recovery slider to the right if your Exposure setting is making white areas too brilliant (called "clipping to white" or "whiter than white"). Drag the slider to the left to diminish the effect of Recovery.

- Drag the Fill Light slider to the right to add detail to shadow areas of your photo without brightening the absolute blacks in the image. Drag left to lessen the effect.

- Drag the Blacks slider to the right to add overall contrast and punch to the photograph; doing this expands the areas in the photo that are mapped to absolute black. Drag to the left to contract the areas in the photo that are mapped to absolute black (0,0,0).

- Drag the Brightness slider to the right to compress the highlight range and expand the shadow range in the photo.

- Drag the Contrast slider to the right to narrow the range of midtones in the image. Drag left to lessen the effect, broadening the midtones primarily, with secondary, less impact on the shadow and highlight tone regions.

- Drag the Clarity slider to the right to apply sharpening to the midtone region of objects in the scene. You might see an improved sense of depth in photos where fine details are bunched together, for example foliage or a plate of pasta. If objects visibly begin to display a halo effect while you're viewing the main preview at 100% viewing resolution, back the slider to the left a little.

- Drag the Vibrance slider to the right to add saturation to dull image areas without oversaturating areas that already are quite "juicy."

- Drag the Saturation slider to the right to add saturation; drag the slider to the left to eventually create a black and white photo at −100.

Work with Camera Raw Editor's Tools

Many of the tools you'll find in the Camera Raw Editor are also available within Photoshop, and in several cases you have more options for performing tasks with precision within Photoshop. However, the Editor's tools, shown

TIP

If after adjusting Brightness the image still isn't exactly the way you envision it, readjust Exposure and Blacks. Tonal controls in the Camera Raw editor are interrelated.

in Figure 3-10, are an excellent starting point for photographers; learn these tools and you'll feel more at home in Photoshop.

The tools offered in Camera Raw are quite similar to those in Photoshop. Here is what they perform:

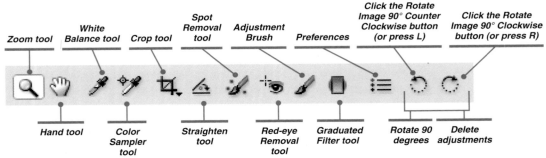

Figure 3-10: *The adjustment tools available in the Camera Raw Editor*

- Zoom into the current image by clicking it with the Zoom tool. Press **ALT/OPT** and click to zoom your view out; you can also Marquee-drag to zoom into a specific area of the image.

- Shift your view of a magnified image by dragging in the image window with the Hand tool. Hold the spacebar to temporarily toggle to the Hand tool from other tools such as the Zoom tool.

- Change the color temperature and tint of an image by clicking with the White Balance tool an image area you think should be a completely neutral color.

- Mark specific image areas for future reference using the Color Sampler tool. This is a terrific feature to see the true value of a color pixel so you can better evaluate the white balance of an image. Click the Clear Samples button to get rid of the markers. You can drag a marker anywhere in the image by click-dragging. To remove only one marker, hold **ALT/OPT** and click over it.

- Crop an image using the Crop tool:

  - By default, the aspect ratio of the Crop tool is unconstrained; click-drag to create a crop.

  - To choose a preset crop aspect ratio, drag on the **Crop Tool** button to reveal a menu.

  - To create a custom aspect ratio, choose **Custom** from the drop-down list, and then type the ratio numbers you want.

  - To rotate the crop area you've defined, hover the cursor around a corner until it turns into a bent double-arrow, and then click-drag any of the four handles bounding the crop area.

Color value   Color Sampler tool

Take new sample

Move color sample

Move crop   Crop area   Scale crop   Rotate crop

Figure 3-11: *Adjust the angle, size, and position of your crop after you've defined it by click-dragging with the Crop tool.*

- To scale the area you propose to crop, hover the cursor around a corner until it turns into a straight diagonal double-arrow, and then click-drag any of the four handles bounding the crop area.

- To move the crop area, drag inside of the crop area.

As shown in Figure 3-11, you can perform significant editing through cropping, but the beauty of Camera Raw is that these are nondestructive edits; you can undo a crop or a rotation at any time in the future.

The following list offers practical uses for the other tools:

- Straighten the horizon of a photo by click-dragging with the Straighten tool. After performing the correction, the tool changes to the Crop tool—the image needs to be cropped after straightening; see the previous section.

- To repair noise, unwanted spots, or other visual debris in a photo, use the Spot Removal tool. Beginning at the unwanted area, click-drag to create a circle, which appears as a dashed red outline (see Figure 3-12). A dashed green outline of the same size appears—this is the sample area for replacing the damaged area.

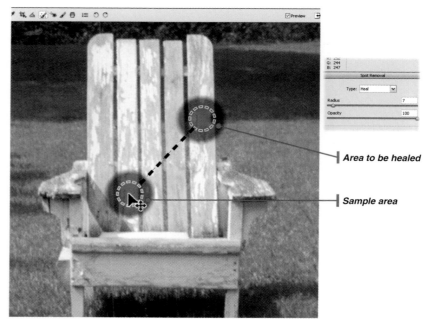

Area to be healed

Sample area

Figure 3-12: *Use the Spot Removal tool to repair image areas.*

1 2 3 4 5 6 7 8 9 10

To move the sample area, drag inside of it to reposition it. Use the Radius slider under the Histogram to adjust the size of the damaged area as well as the sample area. Use the Opacity slider to make the repairs more subtle. By default Heal mode is used, but if you need a more significant replacement, use the Clone mode available on the drop-down list above the Radius slider.

- Remove the red-eye effect from portrait photography by first zooming to 100% viewing resolution. Drag a selection area around the red eye, and then adjust the size of the area to be corrected by dragging on the edges of the selection. Use the Pupil Size slider below the Histogram to increase or decrease the pupil area in the photo. Drag the Darken slider (to the right) to darken the pupil inside your selection and the iris outside your selection.

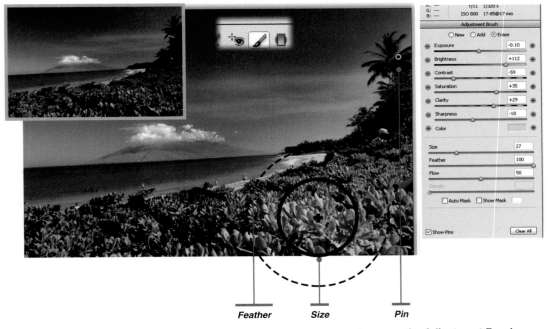

Feather   Size   Pin

Figure 3-13: *After performing coarse adjustments to exposure and colors, use the Adjustment Brush to tweak minor areas.*

- Use the Adjustment Brush to make small, local exposure corrections to a photo, after you're happy with your color temperature and tint work. Stroke over an area that needs minor correction, and then set the Exposure, Brightness, Contrast, and other sliders to adjust only the areas you've stroked over. To see the affected areas as a color overlay in the image, check the Auto Mask check box and then hover your cursor over the pin in the image that indicates where you began stroking the adjustment. The dashed outline around the brush indicates the falloff—the Feather amount—to create a degree of transition between adjusted and original photo areas. In Figure 3-13, you can see that the original image is good, but the right side is slightly in the shade. Using increased Brightness and a little Color tinting, the Adjustment Brush used over the shaded areas makes this photo exceptional.

- Use the Graduated Filter tool to create effects that your camera didn't originally use through custom filters. Additionally, you can perform the same correction options as those you use with the Adjustment Brush using the Graduated Filter tool, to visually ease an effect as a transition between it and the original photo. After choosing this tool, click the New radio button, and then drag the cursor from where you'd like the effect to begin to where you feel it should end. Then make your adjustments using the sliders at the right of the interface. At any time you can change the direction of the gradient and its position by dragging on either the start or end point for the gradient, the green and red markers, respectively.

- Click the Preferences button to specify defaults when loading images (or press **CTRL/ CMD+K**). Some of the options are better performed manually in Photoshop, such as sharpening and tone adjustments. Clicking this icon opens a dialog box where you:

  - Choose from the Save Image Settings drop-down list if you prefer to save XMP metadata in a sidecar file or have the metadata written directly into the image file.

  - If you trust Camera Raw's Auto settings, you can elect to apply the Auto settings by default to all future images you open by checking **Apply Auto Tone Adjustments** in the Default Image Settings field.

  - If you want to speed up color-corrected previews of camera raw files, choose how much hard disk space you feel you can afford and then set the location for the cache data in the Camera Raw Cache field. This option is a trade-off: if you have thousands of images, conceivably you can take up a lot of hard drive space with caching. Conversely, it's a pain to delete image caches and have to slog through thousands of camera raw files, waiting every time for Bridge to build a cache for the custom metadata in the file.

  - If you took JPEG and/or TIFF file format images with your digital camera, you can choose to open these files with any custom metadata editing you've performed (such as Adjustment Brush and Healing Brush edits). You choose this option in the JPEG and TIFF Handling field in Preferences.

  - Rotate the image 90 degrees counterclockwise or clockwise by clicking the **Rotate** buttons.

Refine Images with Other Adjustments

The other adjustment tabs have features that can help you move your images closer to what you envision, through both correction and enhancement options, and with some special effects opportunities:

- **Tone Curve tab**   Use to correct and emphasize those brightness regions that might be lacking in the current image. The Tone Curve tab operates in two modes: Parametric and Point. Drag the sliders in Parametric mode to emphasize or reduce

NOTE

If rotating a photo is the only adjustment you need to make, you can do this directly in Bridge, using the buttons directly to the right of the Sort Manually legend.

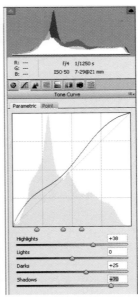

specific brightness ranges such as Highlights and Darks. The graph displays adjustments as a line that takes on several curves, depending on what you do with the sliders: the curve bends upward in the regions to which you increase the emphasis. Below the curve is a histogram that shows how many pixels in the image lie at what brightness level. If an image looks muddy, for example, a good approach to manually correcting this defect is to brighten and/or lessen the contrast in the brightness range where the most pixels are located on the histogram. More pixels usually equals more discernable image information. To use a click-and-drag technique instead of the sliders to work with the Tone Curve tab, switch to Point mode. You have presets in Point mode you can apply, or manually drag points on the curve on the graph to adjust the brightness—the tone quality—of your image.

- **Detail tab** Use to sharpen image detail and to lessen image noise. As you grow more experienced with Photoshop, you'll probably use the Camera Raw Sharpening sliders less often, because Photoshop's Sharpen filters are more complete, sophisticated, and robust than Camera Raw's. However, the Noise Reduction features on this tab are quite good and help reduce or eliminate entirely noise that is a product of JPEG lossy compression in images, particularly noticeable in clear blue sky image areas. You might often find dragging the Luminance slider to the right produces a better photo than dragging the Color slider.

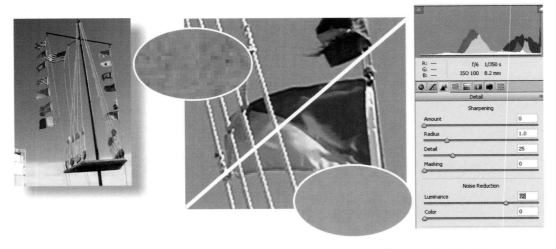

- **HSL/Grayscale tab** Use to reduce or change the hue, saturation, or luminance of any of the ROYGBIV spectrum that makes up a color image. Here, you can

make special-effects photos, emphasizing only one or two hues, or turn your color photo into a grayscale ("black and white") image. When colors have their saturation component lessened, there is an uneven balance between what becomes grayscale tones, so you have complete control, for example, over how bright the blues in an image become when you want to make a black and white photo from a color image. Note that Photoshop's Image | Adjustments Black And White and Hue/ Saturation features offer better control over color-to-grayscale conversions, but this feature in the Camera Raw Editor is good for a "quick fix." Also, adjustments you make to photos in Camera Raw aren't permanent: they can be reset at any time using the Develop Settings | Clear Settings command.

- **Split Toning tab** Use to create images that look like you used infrared film, or just to add a funky effect to a photo. Here, you set the hue and saturation of the lighter image areas as a separate entity from the darker image areas. There is no right or wrong way to use this adjustment: it's just fun and you should simply experiment with it. Black and white images in particular, and compositions that don't have a lot of color, can benefit the most from Split Toning tab options.

- **Lens Corrections tab** Because even moderately expensive cameras may have charge-coupled devices (CCDs, the digital sensors) that have slightly different color sensitivities, photos might show chromatic aberration, usually most visible as purple fringing along the edges of objects in photos with high contrast. Use the Fix Red/ Cyan Fringe and the Fix Blue/Yellow Fringe sliders on this tab to reduce or remove chromatic aberration in the photo. Zooming into 100% and higher resolutions will help you locate and correct the defects. Drag the Lens Vignetting slider to the right to compensate for light falloff around the perimeter of the photo: usually, the longer the lens you use in photography, the more-visible vignetting that happens. Alternatively, you might want to deliberately add vignetting to a photo as an effect.

If this is the case, drag the slider to the left instead of to the right. If you've used the Crop tool before entering the Lens Corrections tab, you can use the Post Crop Vignetting sliders.

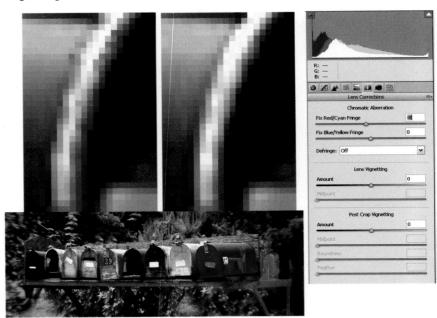

- **Camera Calibration tab** Use to compensate for the perceived difference between what you think you digitally captured and what the camera raw metadata is telling the Camera Raw Editor to show you. With moderately expensive cameras, the discrepancies should be minor, if any, but here's how to re-profile the metadata. See the following item for the step on how to save this profile and then apply it to future images you want to process.

- **Presets tab** Save any and all changes you've made in the Camera Raw Editor by choosing the Presets tab, and then click the drop-down menu. Choose **Save Settings**, and then leave checked all the settings you want saved to an XMP file. You can also simply export the XMP settings from the Presets menu. To apply the settings you've saved to new images, load the images in the Camera Raw Editor and then choose **Load Settings** from the Presets menu.

Chapter 4
Adjusting Tone and Color in Your Photographs

When we evaluate photos, we usually look at the overall color and brightness of different areas. However, digital photographs we see onscreen are arranged into red, green, and blue color channels, not exactly the arrangement artists would prefer when we want to make a pale violet in an image more saturated or darker. Fortunately, Photoshop has the features for isolating a brightness and hue region in a picture so that you can adjust it with different *color models*. This chapter shows you how to calibrate your monitor and build a profile so that your color-editing work is consistent from day to day. You can then perform sophisticated edits to photos that enhance them without detracting from your presentation.

Calibrate and Manage Color

Calibration is necessary at three stages of digital photography work:

- **When you take a photo,** the acquisition stage. See Chapter 3 on downloading camera files and working with camera metadata.
- **When you view,** the onscreen editing stage you perform in Photoshop, and when you've saved to file.
- **When you print** (covered in Chapter 12). When your input corresponds to what you see in Photoshop, and that work prints with corresponding colors, it's because your equipment is calibrated properly, which is the topic of this section.

But calibration is only half the equation to image editing with consistent results: color management through *color profiles* preserves the color space and other parameters of images you save; using color profiles is covered right after calibration in this chapter.

Use Adobe Gamma Control Panel

For color calibration, Mac users have the operating system's ColorSync, and should refer to the operating system manual for its use. Windows users need a helper application to calibrate monitors. Fortunately, a software calibrator called Adobe Gamma is included with Adobe products and is installed with Photoshop. Look under **Start | Control Panel** for Adobe Gamma.

Make sure your workspace lighting is subdued and consistent from day to day. Don't have any lights pointing at or reflecting in your monitor, and if possible, load as desktop wallpaper or in an image previewer an image whose colors and tones you are familiar with—the photo will make a good reference as you adjust your monitor's calibration. Follow these steps to calibrate your monitor:

1. Double-click the **Adobe Gamma** icon. Upon launch, Adobe Gamma asks you whether you want the Step By Step (Wizard) interface or the Control Panel—choose the **Step By Step (Wizard)** button, enter a Description (or load a profile), and then

NOTE

If you don't see Adobe Control Panel in Control Panel, go to C:\Program Files\Common Files\Adobe\Calibration. Consider dragging the control panel file to your Desktop as a shortcut; your monitor will age over time, and it's a good idea to recalibrate your system at least once every two months or so.

click **Next**. You'll see how to work with the Control Panel mode of calibration later in this section.

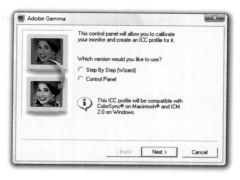 

2. To adjust the tones of your display for brightness and contrast, turn your monitor's controls so that the black square inside the black square is just a tad lighter than the outside square while keeping the white a bright white. Take your time; most of today's monitors have buttons and not dials and screen readouts. Click **Next** when you're done.

3. You can probably skip this wizard step on defining your screen's phosphors. The drop-down list has only a few choices of monitors, you'd be ill-advised to guess at the phosphor response, and today's flat-panel screens don't even use phosphors. Click **Next**.

4. You can adjust the gamma for all three color channels individually by unchecking the View Single Gamma Only check box, but unless your monitor is very old and burned in, leave the box checked and evaluate gamma as a composite. Drag the slider ever so slightly back and forth and squint a little at the target box; when the solid color visually fades into the stripes in back, you're all set. Click **Next**.

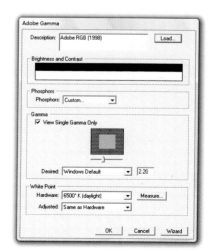

5. Unless you've looked up your hardware's white point in its manual, you're best off leaving the current Hardware White Point setting at its default. Click **Measure**; a dialog box advises you that Adobe Gamma is going

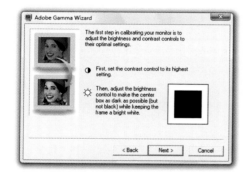

UNDERSTANDING GAMMA

Gamma is the amount of contrast in the midrange of a photograph. We usually divide an image's *tones*—the brightnesses, *not* the colors—into three ranges: the shadow regions, the midtones, and the highlights. Although there is no such thing as a "typical photo," most of the recognizable detail in images lie in the midtones; shadows and highlights *shade* the visual content of an image. This is why it's important to be able to read a Photoshop histogram, discussed later in this chapter.

to black the screen and have you choose from three squares to determine the most neutral square. Click **OK** and then click on either the left or right square to change the color cast of the center square. You might only need to do this once or twice to arrive at a perfectly neutral center square.

6. Click the center square to finalize your setting, and then click **Next**.

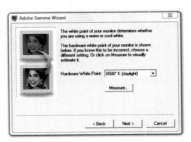 

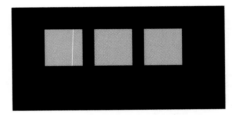

TIP

The color temperature derived at the whitest point onscreen is very hard to determine by eye alone; we recommend that you choose Same As Hardware.

7. Choose a white point from the Adjusted White Point drop-down list if you want to work with one onscreen that is different from the calibration done on the monitor hardware at the factory. Click **Next**.

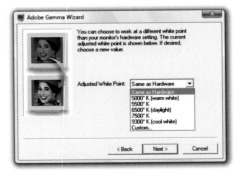

8. Click the **Before** and **After** buttons to compare what you see onscreen; this is why we recommended before you began to have an image onscreen as wallpaper. If you're happy with your new calibration, click **Finish**, and if not, click **Back** and adjust some of the settings in the previous steps.

9. After clicking Finish, you're prompted to save the ICC profile with a name. This file is then used by Photoshop and other well-engineered graphics applications to read the profile's instructions concerning how an image file should look both onscreen and when printed. It's a good idea to save the profile using today's date as its name for easy reference and as a reminder to reprofile your monitor every few months.

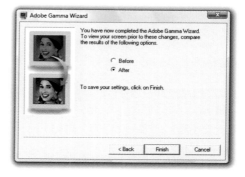

Now that you've stepped through Adobe Gamma wizard-style, there's really no need to use this mode the next time you want to calibrate. Choose Control Panel mode instead of Step By Step (Wizard) in the future (in step 1 of the preceding list). The Control Panel mode offers the same settings as the step-by-step mode; you can simply recalibrate your settings in one fell swoop in the future.

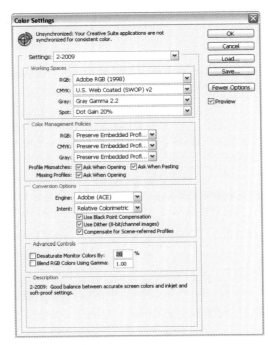

Figure 4-1: Use the Color Settings dialog box to allow color profiles a wide enough color space to properly display your images.

Get Photoshop to Use Color Settings

Now that you've calibrated your monitor, it's time to tell Photoshop how to use a *color space* for your imaging work. A fair analogy is that a color profile—which you just created for your system devices—is a set of instructions on how to build a house, whereas a color space determines *how much real estate* you have upon which to build your house. Choose **Edit|Color Settings**.

By setting up color consistency and warnings, as described in this section using the Color Settings dialog box shown in Figure 4-1, you ensure color consistency and high-fidelity output when editing images. The first thing you might notice is that if you own more than one Adobe product (such as InDesign and Illustrator), you'll see one of two icons at the top left of the dialog box.

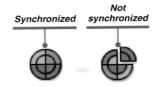

If this is your maiden voyage with color management, don't worry if you see the "not synchronized" icon, telling you that you're not using consistent color management between Adobe applications. If you've used color management in the past with other products, and you see the "not synchronized," the following section describes how to get everything in sync.

Once you've made and saved color settings, you can synchronize your color settings within the Adobe applications by setting and saving the color settings in one application and then choosing to use them in another. Applications made by companies other than Adobe sometimes can read and write color profiles, and many of today's inkjet printers understand ICC profiles.

Set Up Working Spaces

Photoshop will operate flawlessly if you tell it to use large color spaces in which to edit your images. When changing colors or brightness in images, you really need a large working space, because from moment to moment your edits are stepping outside of the default color space for an image file. It's a similar theory to mixing a drink in a glass: if you have plenty of room in the glass (color space), you're less likely to spill any liquids outside of the glass while mixing. The metaphor of "outside the glass" is *color gamut*, the available digital space for color expression in an image. The following steps show you how to set up a color space for Photoshop to recognize and use:

1. Choose **Edit | Color Settings** to open the Color Settings dialog box (see Figure 4-1).

2. In the Working Spaces area, choose **Adobe RGB (1998)** from the RGB drop-down list. Usually, it's best to work with an image—and save an embedded color profile—using the broadest possible color space. The sRGB color space is smaller than Adobe RGB and, as a consequence, some colors are clipped out of range if you work in this space, which is good for web posts but not for hi-fi imaging. If you own a wider color space setting than Adobe RGB (such as ProPhoto RGB or Bruce RGB), choose it instead.

3. Choose just about anything you please for the CMYK color space—the default is fine. The reason for the relative unimportance of the CMYK color setting is that most of the time you'll be editing RGB images. CMYK color settings are of the most importance when you're editing a CMYK mode photo for printing in a magazine. Soft-proofing of CMYK images is covered later in this chapter.

4. Choose the Gray setting that is specific to your operating system. For example, Windows uses a gamma of 2.2 while the Mac OS uses 1.8, deeper, which presents a more faithful representation of black and white photography. Again, you probably won't be editing Grayscale mode photography in Grayscale mode, so this is not a critical color setting unless you understand a specific commercial printing press's characteristics.

5. Unless you run an image setting device (commonly found at production houses, not common to most households), you're best off leaving the Spot setting at its default. Spot color is created by a printing plate in addition to the four C,M,Y, and K print production plates. Dot gain is the physical effect that occurs when an imaging plate renders ink or other pigment to a surface (usually paper). The dots of pigment tend to spread, and Dot Gain is a calculation specific to one print press to anticipate the ink spreading with this custom spot color.

TIP

If you're printing to a home inkjet printer, you do not need to, or want to, print a CMYK version of your RGB image. Most of today's even moderately priced inkjets take RGB information and perform a better conversion than can be achieved through manual conversion.. In fact, a CMYK mode image usually prints to inkjet with less color fidelity than an RGB image, even though the ink cartridges are CMY and K.

Receive Warnings on Missing and Mismatched Profiles

It's usually a good idea to save at least a copy of your work in PSD, JPEG, or TIFF file format, because these formats can *retain* color profiles. This means that a day or a year from now, your images open with correct color settings because metadata has been written into them about how bright an image should look, or how it will print.

In the Color Management Policies area of the Color Settings dialog box, it's a good idea to select **Preserve Embedded Profiles** for all three image modes. So if your current workspace (for example, Adobe RGB, as recommended earlier) is not the same as the space embedded as metadata in an image you open, you'll be warned about the mismatch and prompted for what you want Photoshop to do about this event.

To ask to be prompted for mismatches:

- Check the **Profile Mismatches Ask When Opening** box to receive an attention dialog box when you open an image that has a profile but the profile is not the same as the color space in which you're working in Photoshop.

- Check the **Profile Mismatches Ask When Pasting** box if you want an alert that you're pasting (or copying, or duplicating an image layer) into a document that does not share the same color settings as the image you're copying.

- Check the **Missing Profiles Ask When Opening** box if you want an alert that an image you're opening doesn't have a color profile. You might not want this option checked if you work with a lot of files that aren't JPEG, TIFF, or PSD file format (such as PNG files), because you don't want the interruption.

Here you can see a dialog box that's the result of opening a file—that has no color profile metadata information embedded—after defining Photoshop's working color space as Adobe RGB (1998).

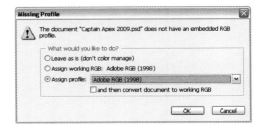

Your options are

- **Leave As Is (Don't Color Manage)**   Choose this option if you're only looking at a file, not editing it. If you don't color manage the file but *do* edit it, the chances are good you will inadvertently drive some colors out of gamut (expressible range within a digital color space).

- **Assign Working RGB**   This option assigns to the image you open a working (temporary, not saved or embedded) space you've specified in the Color Settings dialog box. This is a good, noncommittal road to take with most image editing; you work with the file in a wide color space, but do not save or convert the image to this working space's color parameters.

- **Assign Profile**   Use this option to actually convert the image's color space to one of the color spaces on the drop-down list. If you're confident the document you're opening has no tagged color space, or it's not the one you desire, click this option. Below it is a check box you'll want to check that makes the working color space the same as the profile you assign.

Use Conversion Options

In the Color Settings dialog box (see Figure 4-1), you can see in the Conversion Options area that Photoshop by default uses the Adobe Color Engine (ACE) as the color space in which it can convert an image's profile to the one you want. The ACE is based around CIELAB color, which is the largest color space commonly available to software applications, so there is little chance colors will be clipped out of the destination color space from their original color space. The second drop-down list in the Conversion Options area, Intent, enables you to specify a *rendering intent*, a "style," a set of specifications that can produce different results. Your options are as follows:

- **Relative Colorimetric**   This is the best choice for moving colors that cannot be faithfully reproduced in the destination color space from the original color space. Out-of-gamut colors are shifted to the closest reproducible color, and original colors are preserved, resulting in the most subtle, often unnoticeable color shifting. This is the default.

- **Perceptual**   This choice makes the overall photo look natural, as colors relate to one another. However, Perceptual does shift colors as out-of-gamut colors are fit into the destination color space.

- **Absolute Colorimetric**   This choice clips colors (discards them) when they fall outside the range of the destination color space. It's a useful conversion for proofing because it best represents how paper color influences image colors when printed. However, Absolute Colorimetric is not acceptable for converting an image you want to edit from its color space to a monitor color space such as Adobe RGB.

- **Saturation**   This is the best choice for moving an image's color space to a destination to be used for business graphics and logos, but not worthy of putting delicately shaded photographs into. This rendering intent accentuates brilliant hues, is good for overhead slide reproduction, and would be the last choice for serious photographic work.

Use Advanced Color Settings Options

Click the **More Options** button to extend the Color Settings dialog box to produce two more options for color settings, under Advanced Controls:

1. Check the **Desaturate Monitor Colors By** box (and leave the value at the default of 20%) to more accurately view 16 bit/pixel, 32 bit/pixel, HDR images, and other images that occupy a wider color range than your monitor can display. Colors will look duller, but the *relationship* between different colors is more accurate.

2. Check **Blend RGB Colors Using Gamma** (then type a value in the field) to view colors more accurately when you blend them on Photoshop Layers. In theory, a gamma of 1.00 is mathematically correct, but your monitor, depending on its age and the operating system you use, might display fringing on layers, or just look plain wrong. Leave it at the default of 1.00; if documents using layers are visually difficult to edit, try increasing the gamma; new settings take effect immediately in Photoshop.

Save Your Color Settings

Finally, you want to save your settings. A descriptive name is good to choose—such as the date. When you click **Save**, the dialog box for saving also provides the opportunity to make notes, which are then visible at the bottom of the Color Settings dialog box in the Description field.

Read a Histogram for Image "Evidence"

A histogram is displayed in the Histogram panel, the Curves and Levels dialogs in Photoshop. Being able to *read* a histogram will speed up your editing work, because an image histogram can tell you what is right, and specifically what is wrong, with the brightness in a photograph.

A histogram is a graph—Photoshop's histograms plot brightness along the X axis, from dark at left to light at right. Up and down along the Y axis of a histogram is the population, sometimes called the *pixel count*, for the current image. If the histogram looks "good," you have your work cut out for you trying to figure out how to enhance an image; if, on the other hand, there's something "wrong" about an image's histogram, it's easy to locate and then fix the problem using the features and tools in this section.

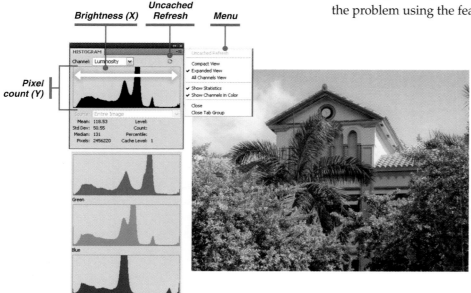

Brightness (X)   **Uncached Refresh**   **Menu**

Pixel count (Y)

Figure 4-2: The Histogram panel is your first stop to understanding the corrections a photo might need.

Work with the Histogram Panel's Features

Figure 4-2 shows the Histogram panel extended, with the menu displayed and the Channel drop-down list set to Luminosity. Access the Histogram panel via the docking strip or through the Window menu.

You'll probably get the best idea of how an image's colors map to a histogram graph by clicking the Channel down arrow and selecting the Luminosity setting. This setting works best because color influence is not figured into the histogram map, giving you a more stark or definitive understanding of the distribution of brightness in the image, although the Colors and RGB choices can also provide a graphical idea of how many pixels account for different brightness levels in the image.

Overall, if you have the room on your screen (many Photoshop users have two screens, which allow panels to be put on a separate monitor), choose a Channel setting and then, on the menu, choose **All Channels View** to extend the panel to include a color breakdown of the pixel count.

In addition to the information on the graph, when you choose Expanded View from the menu, you can see:

- **Mean**   Use the Mean value to assess an image's average brightness. For example, if your photo is of a sunny day and most of the visual content of the image is bright, yet the Mean value is below 128 on the histogram's scale of 0 to 255, the image is probably underexposed and could use a pass through the Curves or Levels command.

- **Std Dev**   Use the Standard Deviation information to evaluate how crisp or dull the image appears. For example, if the photo you took has a lot of bright and dark areas, and yet the Std Dev is below 40, chances are good that the image lacks contrast; again, turn to Curves or Levels to redistribute brightness values.

- **Median**   Use this value as a baseline for correcting the area that should be the midpoint between the lightest and darkest areas in the photo. For example, a hypothetically perfect photo would have a Median of 128, the middle of a range from 0–255 in brightness values. If an *average* photograph's Median is much below 128, this suggests the image requires lightening. There are, of course, exceptions to this rule—much of a histogram's reading depends on the visual content of the photo. The histogram shown in Figure 4-2 has a Median of 131, which is a little high but close to a "perfect" Median of 128. The variance is due to the visual content of the photo, explained in the following section.

- **Pixels**   Use this field to determine how many pixels are in an image, or a selected area. This is a useful readout when trying to calculate how many pixels (total) should make up highlight, shadow, and midtone regions in a properly exposed photo.

- **Level**   Hover your cursor over the histogram to see how bright a range of pixels is. A properly exposed photo most likely will read about 128 (on a scale from 0–255). If the Level is wildly off, and your own eye confirms this, you need to edit the area.

- **Count**   Hover your cursor over any point in the histogram to determine how many pixels have a specific brightness.

- **Percentile**   Hover your cursor over any point in the histogram to determine what percentage of the total image's pixels exist at or below this level. If, for example, 75 percent of all pixels fall below a brightness value of 35—and the photo is of a sunny day—clearly the photo is underexposed.

NOTE

You can use any Photoshop selection tool to select an image area, to then see the histogram of only that selected area.

CAUTION

If you see an exclamation mark inside a triangle, it means that the readout is being created from cached, not current, data. If you've been editing, zooming, or reading the histogram from a selection area, click the warning icon to refresh the data. Clicking the Uncached Refresh button will do the same thing; so does double-clicking anywhere inside the histogram graph.

UNDERSTAND AND WORK WITH CACHE

Caching is used by Photoshop to speed up operations: Photoshop predicts which data you will use in the immediate future and stores it in memory so that it doesn't have to refetch it from disk. You set Cache level in **Edit** | **Preferences** (or press **CTRL/CMD+K**) | **Performance**; typically, the default of 4 for Cache Levels is good, and higher settings not only take up more RAM but can also slow your work due to Photoshop prefetching data you don't want.

On the Histogram panel there is an Uncached Refresh button to recycle—refresh—uncached data, thus making the histogram more accurate as you zoom in and out or edit the image.

READ "GOOD" HISTOGRAMS

As a rule of thumb, if an image itself looks fine, then it *is* fine. Histograms displayed in Photoshop can be misleading and cause you to draw the wrong conclusions unless you can distinguish between a "good" and a "bad" (*balanced* and *unbalanced*) histogram for the brightness information it provides. In Figure 4-3, you can see three example images and their corresponding histograms. These are good images— they represent the visual data correctly, and yet there is a heavy population of image pixels at different levels of brightness:

Figure 4-3: Each image displays a different histogram, according to image content.

- The histogram for the picture of the flower shows that most of the pixels have very little brightness, and this is correct for the exposure and its visual content—the flower doesn't take up very much of the frame and is represented on the histogram as the upper brightness pixels, while the deep green background slopes off toward bright and dark, providing fair contrast for the overall picture.

- The photo of the wooden rooster contains a lot of visual detail in the midrange, and consequently there is a large pixel count in the middle area of the histogram, with a gradual decrease in brightness both toward the highlights and the shadow areas. However, the emphasis is on the lower (darker) midtones, and this is the sort of histogram that a good portrait photograph would have.

- The sky photo at right shows many more pixels in the highlight range, with few or none in the shadow regions. This is correct: there are no shadows in a brilliant but cloudy sky. Notice that there is a smooth slope toward darkness in the histogram, indicating that the light clouds make a smooth blend into the slightly deeper blue sky. Also, the falloff on the brighter side of the histogram is steep, indicating contrast—hence good visual detail—in the upper brightness regions, adding visual detail to the clouds themselves.

SPOT AN AWFUL HISTOGRAM

Figure 4-4 shows at left a before photo where a flash didn't go off in a dark museum. Its histogram before adjusting the photo shows two things:

- Almost all of the pixels are in the shadow area, with a steep ("contrasty") falloff before pixels are even represented in the upper midtones.

- These pixels are uniformly distributed; there's no contrast in the shadow area, but only a "lump" of dark, undifferentiated brightness values.

The photo has been corrected using the Levels command at right, a feature discussed later in this chapter in "Correct Tones with Levels." Not only have pixels been redistributed to occupy more of the midrange, but a "combing" effect is automatically performed in Photoshop, to stagger the brightness levels between adjacent tones. This effect in Levels produces differences in brightness by adding contrast between, for example, brightness levels 29 and 30 (on the scale from 0–255), and this results in clarity and more detail forced out of a photo that has a bad histogram. The result in Figure 4-4 is not world-class photography—such an image will never become a great photo—but if you're documenting an event and you have no light, adjusting the histogram levels can bring a picture back from illegible to legible.

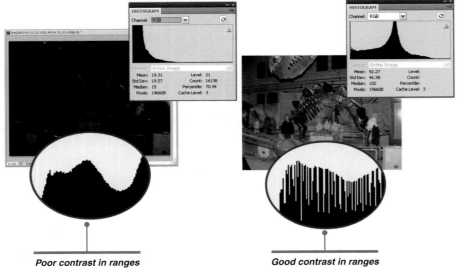

Poor contrast in ranges   **Good contrast in ranges**

Figure 4-4: Use your own eye first, and then the Histogram panel, to spot the brightness regions that are just plain wrong in a photograph.

Use the Curves Adjustment to Add Tonal Snap to a Photo

There are three Photoshop features dedicated to adjusting brightness levels—*tones*—in CS4: Curves (offers the most control and presents the most challenge), Levels (commonly used by the pros and is less complex than Curves), and Brightness/Contrast (good for a quick fix but also about as accurate as the knobs on a 1960s TV set). Brightness/Contrast, however, is so intuitive to use (as with a 1960s TV set) it is not covered in this chapter.

Now that you can read a histogram, it's time to get acquainted with the Curves tool's method for tuning the brightness regions in a photo using a path you can shape, laid on top of the image's histogram.

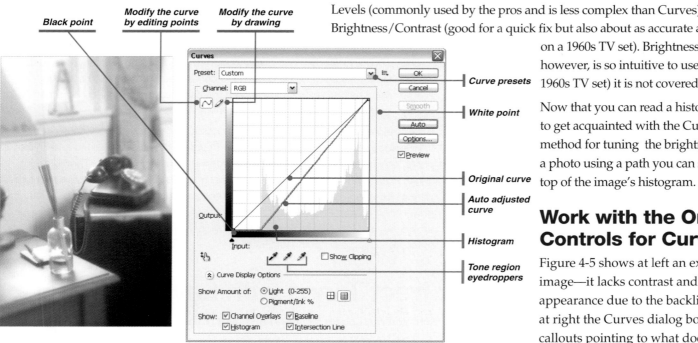

Callouts on figure (left to right / top to bottom):
Black point · **Modify the curve by editing points** · **Modify the curve by drawing** · **Curve presets** · **White point** · **Original curve** · **Auto adjusted curve** · **Histogram** · **Tone region eyedroppers**

Figure 4-5: Treat the grid above the histogram as your workspace for tone-correcting an image.

Work with the Onscreen Controls for Curves

Figure 4-5 shows at left an example image—it lacks contrast and is watery in appearance due to the backlighting—and at right the Curves dialog box with callouts pointing to what does what.

Adjust Tones, Region by Region

The following steps take you through working with the Curves command. First, load an image into the workspace (press **CTRL/CMD+O**, or double-click in the workspace), and then:

1. To automatically correct the levels of an image, click the **Auto** button. The result is that 10 percent of the darkest areas and 10 percent of the lightest areas are clipped—the values are removed from the tonal "map" of the image. The pixels' remaining brightness values are redistributed along a new, broader tonal range.

TIP

To set exactly how much of the bottom range and upper range are clipped, click **Options** and, in the Auto Color Correction Options dialog box, enter a percentage for Shadows or Highlights in the Clip text box.

2. To manually correct an image's brightness values, click the **Edit Points To Modify Curve** button , and then click points on the curve in "problem areas" along the line above the histogram. Then drag the points; the document window updates as you make changes:

   - To add contrast (and darken the image slightly), drag a point to the right. Dragging left decreases contrast and slightly lightens the tonal range where you originally clicked a point.

   - To lighten a tonal range, drag the point upward; dragging downward darkens the tonal range under the point you're dragging.

3. Click the **Draw To Modify The Curve** button (the pencil icon) only if you're feeling very skilled at this point, to draw the ideal curve tone mapping for the image. After drawing the curve, you can smooth the curve by repeatedly clicking the Smooth button.

4. If the photo only needs minor adjusting for tones, use the eyedropper tools beneath the Curves grid. Click the **Black Point** eyedropper tool and then click an area in the photo (not on the histogram) to define the darkest area in the image. Then click the **White Point** eyedropper tool and click in the image to set what you believe should be a pure white area in the photo. If your photo has an area that is a perfectly color-neutral gray, click the **Gray Point** eyedropper tool and then click the perfectly neutral gray in the image. It's okay if there is no perfect gray in the image, and you might be better off manually setting gray on the histogram.

Correct Tones with Levels

Often, you can use the Levels adjustment (**Image | Adjustments | Levels**, **CTRL/CMD+L**) more quickly than Curves for exposure correction; you don't have as many options, but the sliders in Levels get around the need to work with a tone curve. Like the Curves adjustment, you have eyedropper tools for selecting the Black, White, and (color-neutral) Gray points for choosing these points in a photo, and you also have the Auto button.

Use Basic Levels Adjustments

Figure 4-6 shows an example image that is a perfect target for correction using Levels: like the image corrected using Curves, the pumpkins photo is dull, but the tones aren't weak. Instead they are bunched together, hiding much tonal (and secondarily color) information.

1. With your image in the documents window, click **Image | Adjustments | Levels** to open the Levels dialog box.

2. To define the darkest area of a photo, drag the Input Black Point slider below the histogram to the right. You know now how to evaluate a histogram; this pumpkin image—looks fine in the shadow regions—there are lots of pixels in the low range so the slider isn't used in this example.

BEEFING UP A WIMPY PHOTO

Especially when working with a scene that is heavily backlit, the Curves feature is terrific for adding tonal "bottom" without ruining the delicate play of detail in the highlight regions. You use the traditional "S curve," demonstrated in the following steps. As you can see here, the histogram reports that true black on the tonal scale doesn't exist in the image, and that too much visual detail lies in the upper ranges instead of in midtones.

1. Move the Black Point slider below the histogram to the right, to the area on the histogram where pixels begin to populate the image.

2. If necessary drag the White Point slider to the left, to accentuate the brightest regions of the photo.

3. Click a point on the histogram toward the shadow region, where you see a lot of pixels on the graph. Then drag the point down (to deepen the tones) and to the right (to add contrast), using the visual feedback of what you see changing in the document window to evaluate when to stop dragging.

Continued . . .

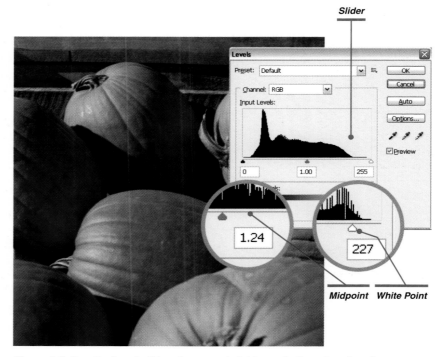

Figure 4-6: Use the Input sliders to remap brightness in three tonal regions.

BEEFING UP A WIMPY PHOTO

(Continued)

4. Click a point on the curve where there are a lot of pixels toward the upper midtones, below the highlights. Then drag the point a little upward (to lighten tonal range) and to the right (to add contrast). As you can see in Figure 4-7, the "S curve" is a gentle one; every image will need a different curve to correct overall exposure, and clearly the finished photo is better than the original to its left. Some color is gained in the process because brightness is inextricably linked to saturation; however, because you're working primarily with brightness in Curves, more tonal work has been accomplished than color work.

Figure 4-7: Use Curves to correct tonal ranges in a photograph.

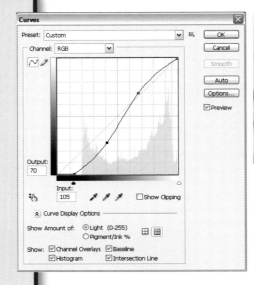

No black point

Not enough pixels in midtones

3. To increase the brightness in the highlights, drag the White Point slider to the left to about the point where pixels in the highlight range begin to become evident on the histogram.

4. To reveal detail in a muddy midtone range, drag the Midpoint slider to the left. Figure 4-6 shows the original image and close-ups of the White Point and Midpoint sliders at their new, desired location.

Work with the Midpoint Dropper and Color-Casting

The previous steps did not cover the eyedropper sampling for the tones in the pumpkin photo, and for good reason. Most of the time, you can achieve good midtone contrast and exposure by manually dragging the Midpoint slider. However, when you can clearly see an element in a photo that should be a neutral midtone, such as the wood toward the back of the pumpkins photo, you can define the midtone range using the Midpoint Dropper tool to not only achieve tonal balance but also remove color-casting at the same time. If your photo, after it was corrected in the previous steps, looks good but areas are casting the wrong hue, before you click OK, you have the opportunity to play a little more with the new midpoint in the photo. Then tune the color-casting by choosing only a single color channel for final refinements:

1. Click the middle eyedropper icon, and then look carefully for an image area that should be a neutral gray.

2. Click on this area in the document window.

3. If in addition to correcting the color-cast, clicking the (color neutral) midpoint in the image makes the midtones too dense, drag the Midpoint slider slightly to the left. The Midpoint slider and the Midpoint Dropper tool operate independently of each other. As shown in Figure 4-8, the wood that is casted way too cold is warmed up to the appropriate hue for the image.

It's common when neutralizing the color at any brightness level to introduce unwanted color-casting in other areas. For this reason, this chapter covers color correction that's mostly independent of tone correction, but there's also a quick fix in Levels—you correct tones in one selected color channel of the image. This a terrific feature, but you need to take a crash course in digital *color opposites* to make the most of Levels corrections in channels. Digital images are typically broken down into red, green, and blue color channels. When you edit levels in, for example, the image's blue channel, you move the tonal range in the photo toward this color when you drag the White Point or the Midtone slider to the left.

Figure 4-8: Use the Midpoint Dropper tool in combination with the Midpoint slider to correct and neutralize midtone image areas.

When you drag sliders to the right, you move the color-casting to that color channel's color opposite—yellow, in this case. Here is a traditional artist's color wheel that represents the hue spectrum; you'll want to refer to this wheel in later sections of this chapter, as well as in other chapters.

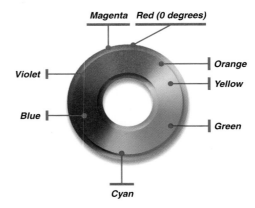

Magenta   Red (0 degrees)

Violet

Orange

Yellow

Blue

Green

Cyan

Clearly, the color opposite across the wheel from blue is yellow. Because the wood in the pumpkins photo was color neutralized, the orange of the pumpkins might have been moved a little too far into the blue hues. To correct colors in Levels:

- If your warm colors are casting cold, choose Blue from the Channel drop-down list, and then drag the Black Point and/or Midpoint (Input) sliders to the right.

- If an image is casting too red, choose Red from the Channel drop-down list and then drag the Black Point or Midpoint Input sliders to the right.

- If an image has an unattractive greenish cast because it's a scan of an old photo or you used fluorescent lighting, choose Green from the Channel drop-down list and then drag the Black Point or Midpoint Input sliders to the right.

Use Exposure

Although the Exposure feature is primarily used in the creation of a High Dynamic Range (HDR) image—this adjustment can also be used on 8- and 16-bit photographs, primarily for tonal changes.

Figure 4-9: Use Exposure to correct an image after you've taken it, the same way you'd use exposure with your camera.

To use Exposure, click **Image | Adjustments | Exposure** to open the Exposure dialog box, shown in Figure 4-9. You have these options:

- **Exposure**   To increase the brightness of lighter areas with much less impact on the shadow areas, drag this slider to the right.

    - **Offset**   To decrease the shadows and midtones with much less effect on the highlights, drag this slider to the left. Dragging right reverses the effect.

    - **Gamma Correction**   To add contrast to the midtones, drag this slider to the right. Dragging left broadens the midtone range and can often help restore image detail.

The thumbnails in Figure 4-9 were driven to extremes with Exposure to serve as a better visual example.

The Exposure dialog box shown at right displays a realistic group of settings for a typical photo.

Restore an Image with Shadows/Highlights

The Shadows/Highlights tone correction feature is invaluable for restoring photos taken with strong backlighting. It lightens the shadow areas with very little effect on midtones or highlights. To adjust the shadows and highlights:

1. Click **Image | Adjustments | Shadows/Highlights**.

2. Click **Show More Options** to access the complete set of controls.

3. Under Shadows:

- Drag the Amount slider to the right to lighten shadow areas in the photo.

- Drag the Tonal Width slider to the right to increase the range of pixels lightened in the shadow region; think of this as an "intensity" slider.

- Drag the Radius slider to the right to lighten more pixels that neighbor one another. The result is similar to adding contrast to the lightened shadow areas.

4. Under Highlights:

- Drag the Amount slider to the right to "recover" areas that might become blown out from too excessive of an Amount value under Shadows.

- Drag the Tonal Width slider to the right to affect more highlight areas.

- Drag the Radius slider to the right to increase contrast in the highlight areas.

5. Under Adjustments:

- Drag the Color Correction slider left to decrease saturation; drag right to add saturation.

- Increase midtone contrast by dragging the Midtone Contrast slider to the right; dragging left decreases contrast in the midtones.

6. To save a file with these settings—useful if you have lots of photographs that need the same correction, click **Save**, name your file, and click **Save** again. To apply the saved file, with a new image loaded, click **Load** and then locate the file you saved.

NOTE

Dragging left on any of the sliders (that can be dragged left) produces the opposite effect as from what is stated here.

Concentrate on Color, Not Tones

Getting a poorly exposed image to a polished state involves working with color as well as tone. The excursions in the sections that follow show how the other **Image | Adjustments** commands address working with color, correcting it, and occasionally distorting it for trick photography effects.

Use Color Balance

Color Balance (**CTRL/CMD+B**) works in three tonal ranges (just like Curves and Levels), moving these ranges' colors independently (shown earlier) to color opposites. Additionally, the Color Balance dialog box has a Preserve Luminosity check box that you'll want to leave checked most of the time. Unchecked, when you make color balance changes, tonal changes will occur, because color and brightness are linked digital image properties.

- To cool down the midtones in a photo, click the Midtones button and then drag the Yellow–Blue slider more toward Blue. Dragging toward Yellow warms the color temperature for the midtones, adding a flattering effect to many portrait photos.

- To tint an image's midtones, drag the Magenta–Green slider either way.

- To further enhance skin tones and to color-correct for fluorescent photography, drag the Cyan–Red slider to the right.

Figure 4-10 shows the original image at left, and at right you can see how the fellow's pale, ruddy forearm is easily enhanced by finding the tonal area (midtones commonly contain human skin information) and then warming the color temperature up with the Yellow–Blue slider. Use the Highlights button and the Shadows button and then correct as discussed above for these tonal regions if necessary.

Figure 4-10: Use Color Balance to cast the three tonal regions to warm, to cold, or to tint a photo.

Correct Hue and Saturation

Choosing **Image | Adjustments | Hue/Saturation** (CTRL/CMD+U) provides a convenient way to adjust color properties in an RGB image without resorting to the fairly unintuitive color opposites convention. The Hue/Saturation dialog box offers Hue, Saturation (the purity, the distinctiveness of a Hue), and Lightness sliders, for adjusting all the characteristics of an RGB image without the inconvenience of dealing with the red, green, and blue color channels.

You'd be ill advised to correct all the hues in a photo with Hue/Saturation—Color Balance and other Photoshop features address color balance more precisely and intuitively—but if you need to desaturate or change the hue of only part of the color spectrum, Hue/Saturation is your ticket.

Change a Specific Hue in a Photo

Adjacent is an attractive street scene of pre-War buildings. However, the choice of green accent paint distracts the viewer from the overall loveliness of the photo. Because "reality" is distorted every day in magazine ads and newspapers using Photoshop, toning down the bright green paint is not so much an artistic lie as it is an editorial image enhancement: *what if* the owner used better taste in paint color?

1. Press **CTRL/CMD+U**, or click **Image | Adjustments | Hue/Saturation** to open the Hue/Saturation dialog box, shown in Figure 4-11.

2. Choose the color you want to modify from the drop-down list, which by default is loaded with the Master spectrum (all hues in the image). You have to choose a color to make the Eyedropper tool used in the next steps available.

3. Click the Eyedropper tool and then click over the area in the document window where some of the color that you want to change is located.

4. If you want a narrower range of the hue you clicked in the photo to change, drag the vertical sliders on the spectrum bar at bottom inward; dragging them outward increases the breadth of the hue you change.

Figure 4-11: Use one or more hues from the drop-down list to correct only part of a photo.

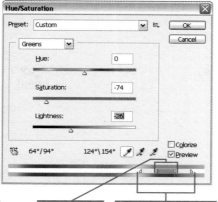

Vertical sliders   Fall-off triangle sliders

![NOTE]

The Lightness slider affects the overall luminosity of a hue. You cannot, therefore, accomplish the same dense, rich changes as you would on tones using Curves or Levels. You might want to go back to Curves or Levels to make tonal changes after using Hue/Saturation.

5. Fall-off is "fuzzy" area outside of the hue you've targeted; some bounding hues will be partially changed, while others won't. To increase the fall-off to include some neighboring hues, drag the fall-off triangle sliders outward. If you want a more precise and occasionally hard transition between edited hues and unaffected ones, drag the triangle sliders toward the vertical sliders.

6. To change the hue to the targeted hue, drag the Hue slider to the left or right.

7. To change the saturation of the targeted color—the most common and popular Hue/Saturation task—drag the Saturation slider left or right.

8. After changing hue and saturation, you may want or need to increase or decrease the targeted hue's brightness. Drag the Lightness slider left or right to accomplish this.

Figure 4-11 shows the correction in progress with a live update to changes in the document window. By keeping the vertical sliders to a fairly narrow range, the adjustment affected the green façade but not the green in the neighboring trees.

Create a Vintage Photo Using Hue/Saturation

There will be times when you want to diminish or completely remove the color from a photo, to let the audience concentrate on the composition of a picture, and not its colors. In Hue/Saturation, you have several presets that enable you to instantly convert your photo to a sepia version, convert it to a cyanotype (sometimes called a *steeltone*), or auto-reduce its color to produce an old-style photo. The following describes how to work with the Preset list and use some fancy manual moves to produce images whose colors are not intended to faithfully represent the originals.

With your photo in the document window, click **Image | Adjustments | Hue/ Saturation**. You have these options for working with sepia versions:

- To create a vintage sepiatone-style photo, click Sepia in the Preset drop-down list.

- To tint a photo to any other hue you like, click the Colorize check box and then drag the Hue slider to the desired color. Then adjust the Saturation slider and finally the Lightness slider to create an "orangetone," an "emeraldtone," or any other version of your photo.

- To create a black and white photo from your original, drag the Saturation slider all the way to the left.

There are other features in Photoshop, particularly **Image | Adjustments | Black & White**, described next, that offer more control in making a black and white image as well as a monochrome-tinted one.

Make Black and White Photographs

Because colors in digital images also have a brightness component, it's usually a bad idea to choose Image | Mode | Grayscale when you want a black and white version of your work. The grayscale version of, for example, red usually casts a deeper tone than you expect or want, while cooler colors result in fainter-than-desired grayscale equivalents. If you have a nice color photo that you want a grayscale ("black and white") copy of, or even a tinted image:

1. Click **Image | Adjustments | Black & White** to open the Black And White dialog box.

2. Take a spin through the Preset list. There is no such thing as a "typical" image, but the Neutral Density preset and the Red preset tend to work well with human portrait photography. Click the Auto button to get the widest range of grayscale detail from your color image—you might need to go back to the Levels adjustment afterward to open up some midtone brightness values.

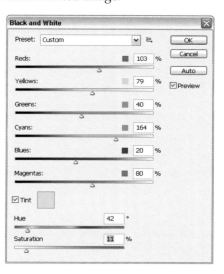

3. Manually, open up color ranges that seem to have too much contrast and are blocked in. On a color wheel, the secondary colors are neighbored by the primary hues displayed as sliders in this adjustment. For example, in Figure 4-12, the ginger tabby is orangish; orange is a secondary color derived from red and yellow, so by moving these sliders to the right—and watching the preview in the document window—the grayscale version of the cat becomes a little brighter with more detail.

4. If you'd like to tint your grayscale image, click the Tint check box, choose a hue (or click the swatch to choose using the Color Picker), and then drag the Saturation slider left or right to make the tint effect subtle or pronounced.

Figure 4-12: Use Black and White to correct the balance of colors as you remove hues from your photo.

Original

Straight to grayscale conversion

Black and White adjustment

Match Colors Between Photos

If you have a series of photos with similar visual content, but taken over time under different lighting conditions, the Match Color adjustment is indispensable for correcting one (or several) bum photos:

1. Open the good photo and then open the photo that requires color matching.
2. Click **Image | Adjustments | Match Color**.
3. Choose the good image from the Source drop-down list.
4. Drag the **Luminance** slider (if necessary) to brighten or darken the image. The document window displays an instant preview, so it's a good idea to move the Match Color box out of the way for a good working view.
5. Drag the **Color Intensity** slider to saturate or desaturate the finished image as needed.
6. Click the **Neutralize** check box to remove color-casting if needed.
7. Drag the **Fade** slider (this is an artistic judgment call) to blend the Color Match result with the original photo. In essence, it diminishes the effect as you drag the slider to the right.

Figure 4-13: Reconcile the color and exposure differences between photos using Match Color.

Match Color result photo

Original photo

Match Color source photo

8. If you have several poorly exposed photos, click **Save Statistics**, save the file, and then click **Load Statistics In Future Sessions** to load your saved settings and apply them to the other photos.

You also have the option to use a selection tool to select only a portion of a photo for the Color Match adjustment. Take care, however, if an image area or the entire photo bears no color or tone resemblance to your source image, because you'll get unacceptable, or at very least surreal, results (if this is your intention, go for it). Figure 4-13 shows a very hard assignment: matching a brilliant beach scene and one that was taken during a summer storm.

Flatten the file before converting it; right-click over any layer title on the Layers Panel (press F7 to display it) and then click **Flatten Image on the context menu**. The interaction of colors between layer blending modes changes when the mode changes.

Use a Photo Filter

You've seen very strong color alterations with Hue/Saturation, but if you need a hint instead of a shove, the Photo Filter adjustment is very good at imitating the traditional tinted lenses that photographers screw onto the shooting lens:

1. Choose an image that is casting too cold as an example, and then click **Image | Adjustments | Photo Filter**.

2. Click **Warming Filter (85)** in the Filter drop-down list.

3. This might not be the right hue for your image, so click the **Color** button, and then click the swatch to go to the Color Picker (the Select Color Filter box).

4. Choose a color that's warmer (more toward red), and then click **OK**.

5. Drag the **Density** slider left or right to increase or decrease the amount of the filter.

6. If you uncheck Preserve Luminosity, the brightness of the color you selected will be taken into account and you might get a denser image than you like. As a rule, leave Preserve Luminosity checked.

If you have a warm image, on the other hand, that needs a little cooling, choose one of the Cooling Filters from the drop-down list. Also, you can perform a little color correction in Photo Filter using cyan, red, or any of the other choices.

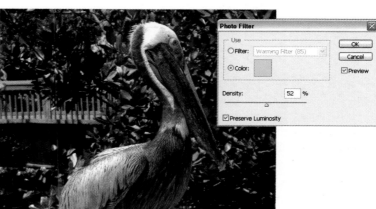

Change Saturation and Color Cast in Variations

A nice "one-stop shop" on the Adjustments menu is Variations. This command opens a large interface in which you can choose thumbnails that represent variations on colors, arranged like the color wheel shown earlier in the chapter. It's very simple to click your way through the thumbnails, choosing the color opposites to neutralize shadow, midtone, and highlight areas in your image. Additionally, you have Saturation and Lightness controls—Variations is a very good feature for prepping an image for personal inkjet printing; what it lacks in controls compared to Color Balance and Hue/Saturation it makes up for in immediate visual feedback and the ability to control Hue, Saturation, and Lightness all in one fell swoop. Click **Image | Adjustments | Variations** to open the Variations dialog box, shown in Figure 4-14, and then:

1. Begin by clicking **Midtones**, the tonal region where much visual detail lies.

2. If you want to make gross color adjustments, leave the Fine–Coarse slider at its default. But if you want to make subtle changes, drag the slider two notches or so toward Fine.

3. Look at the Original thumbnail at upper left. If it's too blue, click the **More Yellow** thumbnail, the color opposite of blue. Similarly, work your way around the other color primaries and secondary colors—click the color's opposite to neutralize any unwanted color cast.

4. If you want the midtones to be darker, click the **Darker** thumbnail on the row of thumbnails at right. Or choose **Lighter** if you want to open the midtones.

5. Click the **Shadows** button and then perform the same operations as you did in Steps 3 and 4.

6. Click the **Highlights** button and repeat Steps 3 and 4.

7. After analyzing the Current Pick thumbnail, if the colors look good but are too faint, click the **Show Clipping** check box. This feature puts a green-tinted overlay on areas that are super-saturated and will look and print as a flat (really ugly) color with no variation in tone.

TIP

You can click the same thumbnail to apply a "double dose" of the same color correction. This is a particularly welcome technique when you're previewing fine, not coarse, variations.

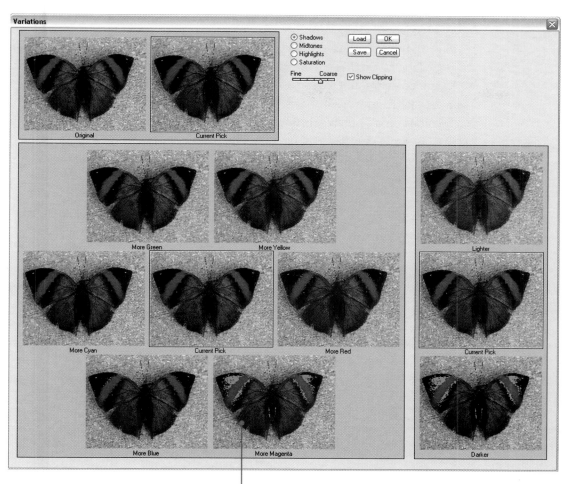

Variations

○ Shadows
○ Midtones
○ Highlights
○ Saturation

Load   OK
Save   Cancel

Fine   Coarse

☑ Show Clipping

Original

Current Pick

More Green

More Yellow

Lighter

More Cyan

Current Pick

More Red

Current Pick

More Blue

More Magenta

Darker

Color clipping

Figure 4-14: Use Variations to make tone and color changes and preview them all in the same interface.

8. Click the **Saturation** button, and then click **Less Saturation** if the Current Pick thumbnail has any of this clipping overlay on it. If the image needs more saturation, play with the Fine–Coarse slider, and then click the **More Saturation** thumbnail until you can detect clipping, then back off the saturation by clicking the **Less Saturation** thumbnail.

9. If you have several images that need the same type of correction, click **Save** and save the settings; you then can load them in the future. Click **OK** to return to the document with your changes applied.

Figure 4-14 shows a use of the Variations adjustment to make the background a little warmer and the wings of the butterfly cast a little colder, but keep the red about the same.

Replace Certain Colors

One of the most dramatic editing effects you can apply to an image is to change a color in an area without changing others: you can make one orange grape in a bunch, change a tacky necktie's color in a group portrait, and make "reality" whatever you envision it to be. There are two ways to change a color: use the Replace Color adjustment, or use the Color Replacement tool on the Tools panel.

Use Replace Color

With all the examples in this chapter, it really helps if you know how to create a selection so that you're not affecting areas you don't want to change—see Chapter 5 and you'll get more out of this chapter. However, you don't need to be a selection wizard to use Replace Color. Follow these steps to see how to replace a color that is distinctly different from other image colors:

1. The Quick Selection tool is perfect for stroking a selection in an area where there's one, pronounced, clearly defined color, such as a stripe on a candy cane, beach ball, or garment. Drag the **Magic Wand** tool on the Tools panel to access the Quick Selection tool—it's part of this nested tool group.

2. Using the Quick Selection tool, stroke just a little over the area you want to define for color replacement. This is a "safety" step for precise editing, but not absolutely necessary to use Replace Color. If the entire area is not selected, click the **Add To Selection** button on the Options bar and then complete the selection.

3. Click **Image | Adjustments | Replace Color**.

4. Choose Localized Color Clusters only if you want to choose several different colors to replace with one new color.

5. Click the **eyedropper** tool at the far left of the Replace Color dialog box, and then click inside the color area you selected in Step 2. If you elect not to use a selection to speed up your work, you might need now to click the **Add To Sample** eyedropper tool to select a broader range of sampled color to replace.

Select area

Figure 4-15: The Replace Color adjustment can produce surreal imagery, or repair work that will go undetected.

6. Drag the **Saturation** slider to the right temporarily so that you can see the replacement color swatch. Then drag the Hue slider until you see the replacement color swatch more clearly. Then ease off on the Saturation until you have a photorealistic color; drag the Lightness slider left or right to fine-tune the replacement color. Alternatively, skip Step 6 and click on the replacement color swatch. Doing this displays the Color Picker.

7. To get a realistic replacement color, drag the **Hue** slider to get the hue you want; usually you can leave the brightness and saturation color field marker right where it is. Colors in the real world are less saturated than you might imagine—our eyes sometimes lie to us, and this is why paint stores let us take sample chips home.

8. Click **OK** in the Color Picker, and then click **OK** in the Replace Color dialog box.

Figure 4-15 shows the work in progress. If you wanted a red and green ball in this example image, you'd simply make a new selection using the Quick Selection tool and repeat these steps.

Work with the Color Replacement Tool

As you read Chapter 7 on blending modes, you'll see that the Color Replacement tool is a convenient, automated way to use color blend mode to replace a current color with one you define. For now, it's enough to understand that using the Color Replacement tool can be simpler for Photoshop beginners to create dramatic color changes in specific images areas. It's less intense than Replace Color, the results can sometimes look like you've hand-tinted a photo, and you have complete hands-on control over changes, rather than manipulating controls in a dialog box.

1. Click the **Color Replacement** tool on the Tools panel, in the Brush Tool group of tools.

1

2

3

4

5

6

7

8

9

10

2. Right-click in the document window to get the size and hardness parameters for the brush. Scale the size according to the area you want to recolor, and usually 80% Hardness will make definitive changes without a harsh, telltale edge around your editing work.

3. Choose a replacement color by either bringing up the Color Picker or, better still, scouting down a replacement color in your image to make it a "natural," subdued, medium-tone color—press **ALT/OPT**, click over an image area, and then release **ALT/OPT**.

4. Choose a sampling style from the Options bar; Continuous is usually the best choice. If you click the Once button, the tool will replace colors only in areas containing the color that you clicked to sample in Step 3. If you choose the Background color button, only areas in the image that have the current background color (on the Tools panel) will be changed.

5. In the Limits drop-down list, choose **Discontiguous**, which replaces color wherever you stroke. Contiguous replaces only those color pixels that directly neighbor one another, and this sometimes leads to splotchy retouching. If you need sharp, detailed edges in your retouching work, choose **Find Edges**.

6. Depending on the specific image, you might want to increase the Tolerance—this is how closely the colors you replace match the original colors. A lower Tolerance setting can lead to specks or splotches in your recoloring work.

7. Zoom into your image and then stroke over the areas you want to replace with the new color.

NOTE

If you choose the Once Sampling style, you can resample a replacement color at any time by pressing **ALT/OPT** and clicking a color in the document or by using the Color Picker.

Chapter 5
Making Selections

Selections are the key to using Photoshop to its fullest. Selections allow you to confine your edits to a limited area of an image. Any operations you perform on the image will affect only the selected pixels, as shown in Figure 5-1 where only the pixels within the elliptical selection are being replaced. You can perform almost any Photoshop operation—applying filters, adjusting colors, painting, erasing, cutting, copying, and so on—on the pixels within a selection; any unselected pixels are unaffected.

Figure 5-1: *Filters, adjustments, and other edits are only applied to the active selection, as shown in this elliptical selection.*

Create New Selections

Photoshop provides a number of ways to select areas of an image, such as by defining a geometric area using any of the Marquee tools, or by selecting specific pixel properties such as similar image colors. You can then modify selections once they are created. Photoshop gives you the power both to crop a photo, using either the Crop or other selection tools, and to manipulate your photos, using sophisticated techniques for defining areas to be changed and areas to be protected from change (called *masking*).

Use the Marquee Tool

You can use the Marquee tool to select a rectangular or elliptically shaped area. You also have options for a selection of only one single-pixel-wide row or column.

MAKE A RECTANGULAR OR ELLIPTICAL SELECTION

You can make a rectangular or elliptical selection using a special Marquee tool:

1. If the correct Marquee tool isn't selected, click the current **Marquee** tool icon in the Tools panel, and hold down the mouse button. The Marquee tool pop-up menu appears.

2. Click the **Rectangular Marquee** tool or the **Elliptical Marquee** tool.

3. Drag within the image to create the marquee selection.

   –Or–

   Hold down **SHIFT** while dragging to constrain the selection to a square or circle.

NOTE

Only the pixels *inside* of the marquee are selected.

TIP

You can select the Marquee tool and switch between the Rectangular and Elliptical Marquee tools by pressing **SHIFT+M.**

5

UICKSTEPS

CONSTRAINING YOUR SELECTIONS

You can make your selection conform to certain parameters to make it a specific height and width, or to make sure the selection retains the proportions of the image.

MAKE A SELECTION OF A FIXED SIZE

You can tell Photoshop exactly what size you want future rectangular or elliptical selections to be. With the Rectangular Marquee or Elliptical Marquee tool selected:

1. From the Options bar, click the **Style** down arrow and click **Fixed Size**.

2. Using the scrubby slider, drag the pointer over the **Width** or **Height** label to establish the width or height in pixels. Or you can type the number directly into the text box.

- Notice that if you type in the Width and Height text boxes, you also may have to type the units; the default units may be inches, not pixels, unless you have changed the default.

- To change the default size and units, press **CTRL/CMD+R** to display the ruler, right-click the ruler, and click the units you want, such as Pixels.

3. Click to establish the upper-left corner of the selection, and then drag inside the marquee selection to position it.

Continued . . .

Select by Color Using the Magic Wand Tool

Marquee selections are great for selecting circular and rectangular areas of an image, but sometimes you need to select all the pixels of the same *color*, regardless of the shape. Then it's time for the Magic Wand tool.

SELECT AN AREA WITH THE MAGIC WAND TOOL

1. Select the **Magic Wand** tool from the Tools panel.

- Set the **Tolerance** level on the Magic Wand Options bar. This tells Photoshop how similar in color pixels must be to be included in the selection. The larger the tolerance, the broader the range of similar colors that will be selected, based on the color pixel you initially click upon. A tolerance level of 32 (the default) is a good place to start.

- Click the **Anti-Alias** check box to soften the edges of the selection.

- From the Options bar, click **Contiguous** to select contiguous colors. *Contiguous* in this sense means "only pixels that touch one another."

2. Click within the area you want to select.

3. If too many pixels are selected, press **CTRL/CMD+D** to deselect the current selection, and then reduce the tolerance. If too few pixels are selected, increase the tolerance. Click within the selection to reselect the area using the new tolerance level.

The Magic Wand tool's Options bar, shown in Figure 5-2, gives you more control over the tool's selections. The "Refining Edges" QuickFacts gives you information about advanced edge control.

QUICKSTEPS

CONSTRAINING YOUR SELECTIONS

(Continued)

MAKE A SELECTION OF A FIXED-ASPECT RATIO

You can constrain the aspect ratio of a selection so that, for example, it is twice as tall as it is wide, regardless of the actual size of the area selected. With the Rectangular Marquee or Elliptical Marquee tool selected:

1. From the Options bar, click the **Style** down arrow and click **Fixed Ratio**.

2. Use the scrubby slider to set the ratio by dragging over the labels, or type directly into the **Width** and **Height** text boxes.

3. Drag in the document window to create the selection.

4. After making the selection, you can reposition it by dragging inside the marquee lines.

TIP

Both Fixed Size and Fixed Aspect Ratio settings for the Marquee selection tools offer value-swapping: you can reverse the orientation of your proposed selection with just a click on the Swaps Height and Width icon ⇄. So, for example, if you set up a 5×7-inch aspect ratio and then decide you want it to be 7×5, click the Swaps Height and Width icon and you're all set to select.

Contains tool presets · Add to the existing selection · Select the intersection of the existing selection and a new one · Click to smooth out the jagged edges of selections · Click to sample colors from the composite image

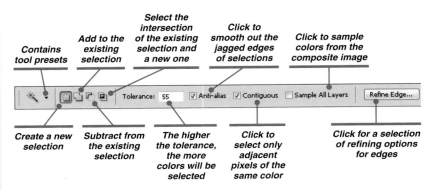

Create a new selection · Subtract from the existing selection · The higher the tolerance, the more colors will be selected · Click to select only adjacent pixels of the same color · Click for a selection of refining options for edges

Figure 5-2: For more control, use the Magic Wand Options bar.

MAKE CONTIGUOUS AND NONCONTIGUOUS SELECTIONS WITH THE MAGIC WAND TOOL

- If you click **Contiguous** on the Magic Wand Options bar, the tool will select only pixels of similar color that directly neighbor—actually touch—one another. Pixels of the same color elsewhere in the image will not be selected.

- If you deselect **Contiguous** on the Magic Wand Options bar, the tool will select all pixels of similar color, regardless of their location within the image.

Use the Quick Selection Tool

The Quick Selection tool (grouped with the Magic Wand tool) is used by stroking over an image area. The tool seeks similar color values, and then creates a marquee selection that stops when it detects dissimilar colors—it's indeed quick and invaluable when you need to select photo areas that are well defined by differing color values.

Like the Magic Wand, after you make an initial stroke in an image, the Options bar reveals Add To and Subtract From operation buttons, as well as the Refine Edge button (see the "Refining Edges" QuickFacts).

By adjusting the size and hardness of the Quick Selection Brush tool on the Options bar drop-down list, you can get into intricate edges of flower petals, machine parts, and similar photo areas. Figure 5-3 shows the ease and accuracy of the tool when an image clearly has well-defined color edges in its elements.

Figure 5-3: *Use the Quick Selection tool instead of the Magic Wand when electing both geometry and similar colors.*

TIP

When you have a complicated selection to make, you can sometimes use the Magic Wand tool to select the background based on color, and then use the Inverse feature to select what you really want. This only works if the background is of a similar color—it won't work on a scenic background when you're trying to select a person, for instance.

NOTE

The quality of "color," specific to the Magic Wand, the Quick Selection tool, and the Select | Color Range command, applies to both hue *and* tone. So if you have a monochrome image, such as a brick wall, don't be deterred from using these color selection tools. If a photo doesn't have pronounced colors but has a lot of variations in brightness (tone), you can indeed use these selection tools.

REFINING EDGES

The Refine Edge button appears whenever you've made a selection. When you click the button, the dialog box offers numerous controls for finessing the selection edge, but not the general shape of the selection itself. Your options are as follows, for adjusting the selection edge and previewing it:

- **Radius** Determines the extent from the existing selection edge at which the refining process occurs. Think of Radius as limiting or "choking" the refinement.

- **Contrast** Works in tandem with the Radius setting; if you use a high Radius, specify an accordingly high Contrast to remove noise from areas near the edge of the current selection.

- **Smooth** Takes the irregularities, the tiny slopes and sudden bends in the selection edge, and simplifies the selection outline.

- **Feather** Creates a transition along the border of the selection to go from fully selected, to partially selected, to not selected (masked). This effect is similar to traditional darkroom feathering, where photographers slightly blur image edges by waving a soft cloth or a physical feather along edges while the photographic paper is being exposed.

- **Contract/Expand** Makes the selection larger or smaller in size.

- **Previews of selection** You have a number of ways to preview your selection refinement work, which is handy if you have a visually complex background outside of the selection. Figure 5-4 shows an example of a selection enclosed in

Continued . . .

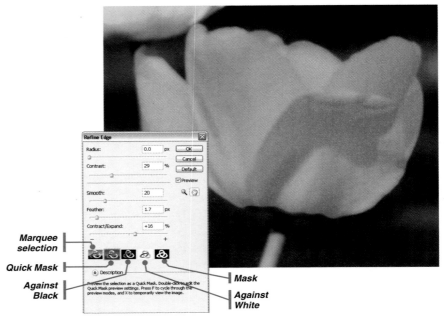

Figure 5-4: *The Refine Edge dialog box contains extended options for working with selections and edges.*

Use the Lasso Tools

Photoshop has three different Lasso tools: the Lasso tool, the Polygonal Lasso tool, and the Magnetic Lasso tool.

SKETCH A FREEHAND SELECTION

You can make a freehand sketch of the outline of your selection:

1. If the Lasso tool is not selected, click the current **Lasso** tool icon in the Tools panel, and hold down the mouse button. The Lasso tool pop-up menu appears. Click the **Lasso** tool.

2. Click within the image and drag to sketch a selection.

3. Release the mouse button to close the selection.

You can fine-tune the way the Lasso tool works by changing its options, shown in Figure 5-5.

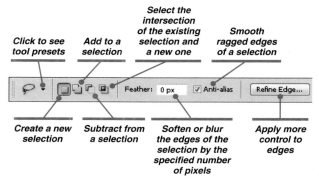

Figure 5-5: Change the Lasso tool and Polygonal Lasso tool options.

SELECT AN AREA WITH THE POLYGONAL LASSO TOOL

You can create a selection made up of a number of straight segments, by clicking to define points that surround an area:

1. If the Polygonal Lasso tool is not selected, click the current **Lasso** tool icon in the Tools panel, and hold down the mouse button. The Lasso tool pop-up menu is displayed. Click the **Polygonal Lasso** tool.

2. Click inside the image to define the starting point of your selection.

3. Move the mouse to a new position. A line segment follows the cursor.

> **TIP**
>
> While using the Polygon Lasso tool, you can also sketch an area, exactly like you would with the Lasso tool, by holding **ALT/OPT** and dragging. Release **ALT/OPT** and the tool's behavior reverts to the Polygon Lasso, single-click operation.

The edge detection width determines how wide an area Photoshop will search to detect the edge

The higher the value, the more often Photoshop anchors the selection in place

Width: 10 px   Contrast: 10%   Frequency: 57

The higher the value, the sharper the contrast must be to be selected

When selected edge detection width varies with pen pressure (requires a pen-sensitive tablet)

Figure 5-6: Change the Magnetic Lasso tool options to gain greater control.

> **TIP**
>
> You can press **ALT/OPT** and then drag the pointer to momentarily switch to the Lasso tool. When you release **ALT/OPT**, the Magnetic Lasso tool returns.

4. Click the image repeatedly to create your selection.

5. Double-click to finish the selection. Alternatively, single-click at your beginning point to close the marquee selection. When you're near your initial click point, the cursor changes to feature a tiny circle ✂, at which point you can close the polygon selection with a single click.

SELECT AN AREA WITH THE MAGNETIC LASSO TOOL

Use the Magnetic Lasso tool to select an image with sharp contrast in its edges. The Magnetic Lasso tool will attempt to automatically follow and "snap to" edges. You can fine-tune the way the Magnetic Lasso tool works by changing its options. The Magnetic Lasso tool shares many of the options shown in Figure 5-5 but contains a few additional options, shown in Figure 5-6.

1. If the Magnetic Lasso tool is not selected, click the current **Lasso** tool icon in the Tools panel, and hold down the mouse button. The Lasso tool pop-up menu is displayed. Click the **Magnetic Lasso** tool.

2. Click your image once near an edge of color or tonal contrast to begin creating a selection.

   - Move the cursor to a new position. A line segment follows the cursor. Photoshop places small, fastening points as it goes. These points are only for user reference and cannot be moved.

   - Press **BACKSPACE** at any time to delete the last anchor.

   - Click the image at any time to force the Magnetic Lasso tool to place a fastening point at the cursor location.

3. Double-click to finish the selection. Alternatively, when your cursor is close to the beginning point of the selection, a single-click will close the selection. Like the Polygon Lasso tool, a small circle at the lower right of the cursor indicates you're in position to single-click close the selection marquee.

NOTE

The Color Range command is unavailable for 32-bit images.

Select a Range of Colors

Using the Color Range command, you can select a range of similar colors or tones from an image. You can also select within an already defined selection area—create a rectangular selection, for example, and then use the Color Range command within that selection. You can either change an existing selection or replace it. The selections can be cumulative: make one selection, click **OK**, open the Color Range dialog box again to make another selection, and so on. To replace a selection, the previous selection must be deselected, most easily accomplished by pressing **CTRL/CMD+D** (**Select | Deselect**). To select pixels within a range of colors:

1. From the Application bar, click **Select** and then click **Color Range**. The Color Range dialog box appears, as shown in Figure 5-7.

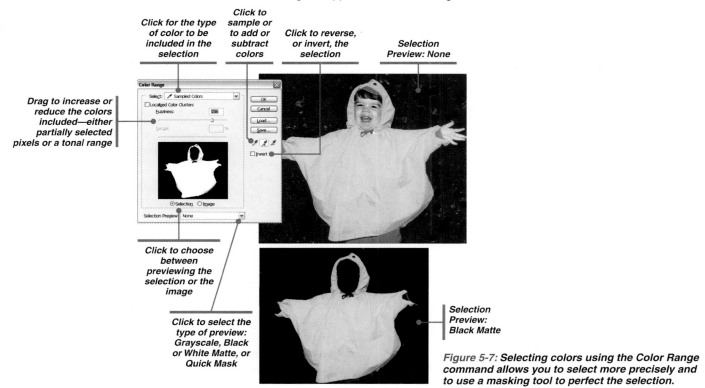

Click for the type of color to be included in the selection

Click to sample or to add or subtract colors

Click to reverse, or invert, the selection

Selection Preview: None

Drag to increase or reduce the colors included—either partially selected pixels or a tonal range

Click to choose between previewing the selection or the image

Click to select the type of preview: Grayscale, Black or White Matte, or Quick Mask

Selection Preview: Black Matte

Figure 5-7: *Selecting colors using the Color Range command allows you to select more precisely and to use a masking tool to perfect the selection.*

- Click the **Select** down arrow to select the color range that will be tested and selected. You will find most flexibility if you retain the default option of Sampled Colors—otherwise, your adjustment options are limited to presets covering primary colors and tonal ranges.

- Click the **Selection** button to then display selected areas you define (using the eyedropper in the document window) as white in the proxy window in the dialog box. Alternatively, click the **Image** button to make selections in the proxy window itself, while watching the results in the document window. Some users prefer this technique, but many stick with Selection.

- Click **Localized Color Clusters** to limit the search for selected colors to a proximity to where you click the eyedropper to make a sample. The Range slider becomes active after you check this box and click in the image.

- Drag the **Range** slider to determine the extent to the Localized Color Clusters option.

- Use the **Fuzziness** slider to adjust the range of color you selected with the eyedropper. The greater the value, the more partially selected colors will be included in the selection.

- Click the **Selection Preview** down arrow to select how the image selection will be displayed. Your choices are None (best used in combination with the Selection option below the proxy window), Grayscale, Black Matte, White Matte, and Quick Mask.

- With Selection chosen, click within the image to sample the color you want to select; click in the proxy window if you've chosen Image. White areas preview selected areas, black areas are masked (not selected), and gray areas will be partially selected. An example is shown in Figure 5-7.

- To select additional colors, click the **Add To Sample** (the eyedropper with the plus (+), or hold down the **SHIFT** key while clicking the image to activate it.

- To subtract colors from the selection, click the **Subtract From Sample** (the eyedropper with the minus (-), or hold down the **ALT/OPT** key while clicking the image to activate it.

- To make subtle refinements, click **Select** and click **Sampled Colors**, any of the **preset colors** on the list, **Highlights**, **Midtones**, **Shadows**, or **Out Of Gamut** colors.

2. When finished, click **OK**.

TIP

When using the Color Range command, press **ALT/OPT**, and the Cancel button changes to a Reset button. Click **Reset** to restore the original selection.

FEATHERING AND ANTI-ALIASING

Feathering and anti-aliasing smooth the edges of your selections. *Feathering* softens a selection by creating an intermediate transition between the inside selection and the exterior mask. The pixels bordering the selection are only *partially* selected. When they are copied, they will be partially transparent. If an effect or filter is applied to them, that filter or effect is rendered partially transparent.

Without feathering | | **With feathering of 20 percent**

Anti-aliasing is another Photoshop smoothing feature, not exactly the same as feathering, but related to smoothing in general. Because the components of digital images—pixels—are four-sided, it's difficult for many applications to reconcile a curved selection, such as one created with the Lasso tool, with the right-angled edges of the pixels in the underlying image. An element selected and copied without anti-aliasing and then pasted in front of a different-colored background will display an unsightly, ragged edge. Anti-aliasing smoothes round and other curved selections by adding edge pixels whose color is an average of pixel colors found inside and outside the very edge of the selection. The math is complex, but fortunately the feature is easy to use and provides high-fidelity editing results.

Without anti-aliasing | | **With anti-aliasing**

Continued . . .

Exclude Areas Using Selections

Sometimes, the elements you want *excluded* from editing are easier to define than the areas you want to edit, as in the case of a complicated object on a simple background. In that case, select the background elements first, and then invert the selection:

1. Use any combination of selection tools to select the background elements you do not ultimately want selected.

2. Click **Select** and then click **Inverse**, or press **SHIFT+CTRL/CMD+I**, to invert the selection. **SHIFT+F7** performs the same selection inversion. Everything that was selected is deselected, and everything that was deselected is now selected.

Change, Save, and Load Selections

Once you have created a selection, you can change it.

Modify a Selection

You can modify a selection in a number of ways: reposition it, resize it, expand or contract it, add to it, or subtract from it.

MOVE A SELECTION BORDER

To move a selection border:

1. Using any selection tool, click inside the active selection border.

2. Hold down the mouse button, and drag the border to a new position.

FEATHERING AND ANTI-ALIASING

(Continued)

FEATHER A SELECTION

1. To feather an existing selection, from the Application bar, click **Select | Feather**. When a selection tool is active, you can also access this command from the right-click context menu.

   –Or–

   To feather a new selection, select any of the **Lasso** or **Marquee** tools.

2. In the Options bar, type a **Feather Radius** value between 0.2 and 250 pixels. The larger the number, the more the edges of the selection will be softened.

ENABLE ANTI-ALIASING

When the correct selection tool is selected, click the **Anti-Aliased** check box on the Options bar.

FEATHERING AND ANTI-ALIASING EXCLUSIONS

- You cannot apply anti-aliasing to an existing selection.
- Images in GIF file format will not accept anti-aliasing or feathered edges. You must first click **Image | Mode**, and then convert the image from Indexed Color to Grayscale or RGB color mode.

TRANSFORM A SELECTION

You can transform a selection—making it larger or smaller, moving it…basically, anything you can do to an object on a layer, you can do to a selection. To transform an existing selection:

1. With any selection tool (such as the Lasso), right-click within the existing selection and choose **Transform Selection**. Or, from the Application bar, click **Select | Transform Selection**.

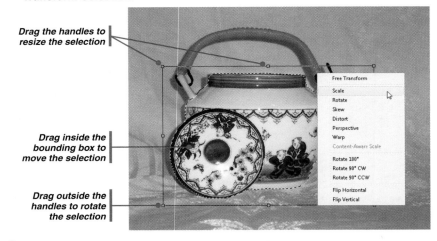

Drag the handles to resize the selection

Drag inside the bounding box to move the selection

Drag outside the handles to rotate the selection

2. The Free Transform bounding box with eight handles appears at the edge of the selection. Here are the functions you can perform by directly manipulating the bounding box and its handles:

- Drag the bounding box by any of its four edges to scale one dimension of the selection.
- Press and hold **CTRL/CMD+ALT/OPT** and drag on one side of the bounding box to scale one dimension of the selection—from its center equilaterally away or toward its center.
- Drag a bounding box edge while holding **CTRL/CMD+SHIFT** to skew (slant, italicize) the selection.
- Drag inside the bounding box to reposition the selection.
- Drag outside a corner bounding box handle to rotate the selection.
- Drag directly on a corner bounding box handle to scale the selection. To constrain the scaling, hold **SHIFT** while you drag.

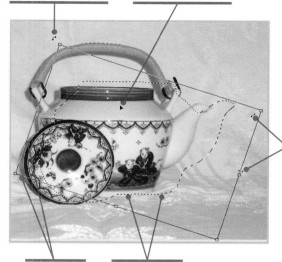

Outside the bounding box your cursor will morph into this to rotate the selection

Place your cursor inside the bounding box and drag to move the whole selection

Place your cursor over the handles of the bounding box to change the size of the selection in the direction you drag

Transform bounding box

Selection being transformed

Additionally, if you require precise selection transformation, use the Options bar's field to type degrees and/or amounts. You can also perform a distort (move the bounding box's corner handles independent of each other), perspective, and use the Warp Grid to treat the selection as though it's soft plastic by dragging within the Warp Grid. Mirroring the selection and rotating in 90-degree increments can also be done, but this requires that you choose a Transform mode first; right-click once the selection is in Transform mode and then choose a transformation type from the context menu.

ADD TO A SELECTION OR MAKE MULTIPLE SELECTIONS

To add to an existing selection or make multiple selections using any combination of selection tools:

1. Choose a selection tool from the Tools panel.
2. Hold down the **SHIFT** key, and make another selection.
3. Change tools at any time, and hold down the **SHIFT** key to continue adding to the current selection.

SUBTRACT FROM A SELECTION

To subtract from an existing selection:

1. Choose any selection tool from the Tools panel.
2. Hold down the **ALT/OPT** key, and drag with the selection tool over the area you want to subtract from the active selection.
3. Change tools at any time, and hold down the **ALT/OPT** key to continue subtracting from the current selection.

CONVERT A SELECTION TO A BORDER

You can create a border around any subject in an image from a selection you create. To convert an active selection into a border:

1. From the Application bar, click **Select | Modify | Border**.
2. Type the width of the border in pixels, and click **OK**. Photoshop creates a border selection centered about the original selection.

EXPAND OR CONTRACT A SELECTION

Sometimes, you might want a selection to be slightly larger overall. To expand a selection by a fixed number of pixels:

1. Click **Select | Modify | Expand**.
2. Type the number of pixels by which to expand the selection.
3. Click **OK**.

To contract a selection:

1. Click **Select | Modify | Contract**.
2. Type the number of pixels by which to contract the selection.
3. Click **OK**.

DESELECT OR RESELECT A SELECTION

To quickly deselect a selection, press **CTRL/CMD+D**. To quickly reselect a previous selection, press **CTRL/CMD+SHIFT+D**.

Crop to Fit a Selection

Cropping cuts off unwanted areas from the perimeter of an image. Photoshop has a Crop tool, but it is often easier to crop an image to fit a selection:

1. Choose a selection tool from the Tools panel.
2. Make your selection.
3. If necessary, move, resize, or rotate the selection by clicking **Select** and then clicking **Transform Selection**.
4. From the Application bar, click **Image** and then click **Crop**. The crop will be rectangular to fit the dimensions of the selection.

NOTE

You can crop an image to a nonrectangular selection as well, such as an elliptical selection. The image will be cropped to the smallest dimensions that include all selected pixels. The end result will still be a rectangular image and will include pixels outside of the selection.

NOTE

If a selection is active, pressing the **DELETE** key only deletes pixels within the selection. You can use selections to quickly erase large parts of an image. Using **BACKSPACE** also works.

Remove Fringe Pixels

When you copy the contents of an anti-aliased selection to a new layer or document, a fringe of the original background color is occasionally retained. The Defringe command replaces the color of edge pixels with colors found inside the selection. To remove a fringe:

1. Click **Layer | Matting | Defringe**. The Defringe dialog box appears.

2. Type the width in pixels of the edge pixels to be replaced. Typically, the default value of 1 works well.

3. Click **OK**. The colored halo disappears.

If the Defringe command replaces the color on too many or too few pixels, press **CTRL/CMD+Z** to undo the Defringe command and try again, this time specifying a different width.

Save and Load Selections

You can save selections and then load them again later in the session, easily reselecting the same area. Keep in mind that saved selections will not be saved with your image in all image formats. If you want to load a selection the next time you open an image, save the document in Photoshop (PSD) format or TIFF.

SAVE A SELECTION

With a selection active:

1. Click **Select | Save Selection**. The Save Selection dialog box appears.

2. Type a name for your selection.

3. Leave the other settings alone, and click **OK** to save your selection.

LOAD A SELECTION

To reload a previously saved selection:

1. Click **Select | Load Selection**. The Load Selection dialog box appears.

2. Click the **Channel** down arrow, and click your named selection.

3. Click **Invert** to invert, or reverse, the selection.

4. Leave the other settings alone, and click **OK** to load your selection.

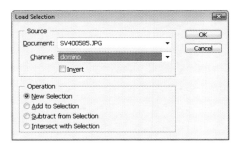

Selections are saved in your Photoshop document as new *channels* (images that store information, such as color and image masks).

Eye icon **Object on background image copied to a new layer**

Figure 5-8: You can copy a selection to another layer, which may be invisible to you until you click the eye icon in the Layers panel to make the background layer invisible.

Do Something with the Selection

You can subtract or eliminate an area of an image from its background to get the precise image you want. You can do it by copying to a new layer or to a new document or by using the Extract filter. In this case, you select the edges of the object—with many options for refining the area to be extracted—and then extract just the selected image.

Copy to a New Layer

To copy a selection to a new layer:

1. Use any combination of selection tools to select the elements you want to extract from the background.

2. Press **CTRL/CMD+J** to copy the contents of the selection to a new layer. Since the copy will be positioned on a new layer directly above the original, the results of this process will not be apparent at first. You can see it in the Layers panel, as shown in Figure 5-8.

TIP

Another way to copy the pixels defined by a selection to a new layer, with a selection tool active, is to right-click inside the selection marquee and then click **Layer Via Copy** from the context menu.

QUICKSTEPS

MOVING AND DUPLICATING

MOVE THE CONTENTS OF A SELECTION

With a selection active:

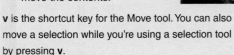

1. Select the **Move** tool from the Tools panel.

2. Drag within the selection to move the contents.

v is the shortcut key for the Move tool. You can also move a selection while you're using a selection tool by pressing **v**.

DUPLICATE THE CONTENTS OF A SELECTION

With a selection active:

1. Select the **Move** tool from the Tools panel.

2. Hold down the **ALT/OPT** key, and drag within the selection to duplicate the contents.

To see the copy by itself:

1. Open the Layers panel by clicking **Window | Layers**. The Layers panel is displayed.

2. In the Layers panel, click the **eye** icon to the left of the Background layer to hide the background layer. The new copy, without the background, becomes apparent.

Layers are covered in more depth in Chapter 6.

Copy to a New Document

Although Photoshop adheres to your operating system's convention of copying and pasting (in this case, copying and pasting image selections), you can ease the burden on the operating system of holding large chunks of data in system memory by using Photoshop's internal copying/pasting feature.

To copy a selected image area to a new document:

1. With a selection tool, right-click inside the selection marquee and then click **Layer Via Copy** from the context menu.

2. On the Layers panel, right-click over the title of the new layer (for example, "Layer 1"), not the layer thumbnail, and then click **Duplicate Layer**.

3. In the Duplicate Layer dialog box, you can name the layer in the **As**: filename (or leave it at its default name), and then in the Destination field, choose **New** from the drop-down list. You can name the document at this point, or leave it at the default name.

4. Click **OK** and a new document is created, the same size as the original photo, and there's nothing on the Clipboard to stress out your system or a potential receiving application.

5. If you want to trim this new document to scale to only the copied image area, hold **CTRL/CMD** and then click on the layer thumbnail on the Layers panel.

6. Click **Image | Crop**.

   –OR–

   If the selection is a relatively small image area, press **CTRL/CMD+K** to display Preferences if you're not certain Export Clipboard is checked in General Preferences. If it's not, check it and then close Preferences.

7. Press **CTRL/CMD+C**.

8. Press **CTRL/CMD+N** (**File | New**). Photoshop reads the Clipboard and offers a New Document size scaled to the copied image area; the Preset field confirms this. Click **OK**.

9. Press **CTRL/CMD+V** to paste the copied image area to the new document window.

EXPANDING SELECTIONS

The Grow and Similar commands expand the current selection, adding pixels of similar color to those pixels already selected.

Original selection |

EXPAND A SELECTION WITH THE GROW COMMAND

The Grow command expands the selection to include only adjacent pixels that fall within the Tolerance range

Continued . . .

TIP

Try using the Defringe command after using the Magic Eraser to clean up layer edges and make it easy to create a multilayer composite image.

Use the Magic Eraser Tool

The Magic Eraser tool works like a combination of the Magic Wand tool and the DELETE key. It selects an area of similar color and deletes it:

1. If the Magic Eraser tool is not selected, click the current **Eraser** tool icon in the Tools panel, and hold down the mouse button. The Eraser tool pop-up menu appears. Click the **Magic Eraser** tool.

2. You have these options on the Options bar:

   - **Tolerance**   The higher the value, the wider the range of colors erased. A good starting tolerance level is 32, which is also the default.
   - **Anti-Alias**   Click this check box to soften the edges of the selection.
   - **Contiguous**   Click this check box to erase only connected (*contiguous*) areas of the sampled color. If this is unselected, all occurrences of the sampled color will be deleted regardless of where they are in the image.
   - **Sample All Layers**   Click to sample the erased color in all visible layers of an image, not just the current layer.
   - **Opacity**   Drag the slider to vary how much of the color will be erased. The higher the Opacity, the more color is erased.

3. Click a color area in your image to delete all similar colors in the image. Figure 5-9 shows the original image, the image after two clicks of the Magic Eraser (set to a fairly high Tolerance), and finally a simple gradient fill placed on a layer behind the flower.

Figure 5-9: **You can click in the image to quickly erase pixels of a similar color.**

EXPANDING SELECTIONS *(Continued)*

specified in the Magic Wand tool Options bar. With a selection active:

From the Application bar, click **Select | Grow**. Similarly colored adjacent pixels are selected.

Selection expanded with the Grow command

EXPAND A SELECTION WITH THE SIMILAR COMMAND

The Similar command expands the selection to include any pixels throughout the image that fall within the Magic Wand's Tolerance range, whether those pixels are adjacent to the current selection or not.

With a selection active, from the Application bar, click **Select | Similar**. Similarly colored pixels are selected throughout the image.

Selection expanded with the Similar command

Use the Background Eraser Tool

The Background Eraser tool erases areas of similar color—it's like a manual version of the Magic Eraser tool. Use the Background Eraser tool to erase similar background colors you define around a foreground element. When you first click in the image using the Background Eraser tool, it samples the background color, the background is automatically turned into a layer, and you follow these steps and options to surround your foreground subject with transparency. Figure 5-10 shows the options on the Options bar when the tool is selected.

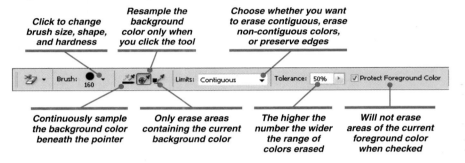

Click to change brush size, shape, and hardness

Resample the background color only when you click the tool

Choose whether you want to erase contiguous, erase non-contiguous colors, or preserve edges

Continuously sample the background color beneath the pointer

Only erase areas containing the current background color

The higher the number the wider the range of colors erased

Will not erase areas of the current foreground color when checked

*Figure 5-10: **The Options bar offers Tolerance and other settings to use on almost any sort of photo to remove the background pixels.***

1. If the Background Eraser tool is not selected, click the current **Eraser** tool icon in the Tools panel, and hold down the mouse button. The Eraser tool pop-up menu is displayed. Click the **Background Eraser** tool.

2. Click the **Limits** down arrow, and select an option:
   - Click **Contiguous** to erase only areas of the sampled color pixels that directly neighbor one another.
   - Click **Discontiguous** to erase any area matching the sampled color.
   - Click **Find Edges** to make it easier to guide the cursor along distinct edges in the photo. This option produces cleaner edges between color and transparent areas.

3. Click one of the Sampling buttons to the left of the Limits field:
   - **Sampling: Continuous**   As you drag to erase, the color you erase to continually updates, which is useful if the background has several different, distinct hues.
   - **Sampling: Once**   The background color targeted to erase is only sampled the first time you click in the background.

- **Sampling: Background Swatch**   The tool only erases the current background swatch you see on the Tools panel. You can hold **ALT/OPT** to temporarily toggle to the Eyedropper tool, click the background color (which sends the color to the foreground color swatch on the Tools panel), then press **X** to swap foreground/background colors, and you're all set to use this Sampling style. If you have a fairly solid background, this is a good Sampling choice.

4. Click in an area you want to erase to sample the background color.

5. Without releasing the mouse button, drag the tool over the background to erase pixels of similar color. You can see an example in process in Figure 5-11. Note that the foreground swatch on the Tools panel has been defined as the green of the apples and that Protect Foreground Color is enabled on the Options bar. This helps the tool distinguish between the Forest Green background colors and the lighter apple colors.

*Figure 5-11: **Erase the background colors while protecting the foreground colors.***

6. To erase multiple areas or multiple colors, repeat Steps 4 and 5.

*Figure 5-12: **Use the Background Eraser tool when you need manual control over deleting areas, with a little assistance from Photoshop.***

The payoff, naturally, is the ability to slip a new background beneath the image after the background has been completely erased. In Figure 5-12 you can see that a layer containing elements warmer in color than the original photo background is added behind the original, and the overall color cast of the photo is more eye-pleasing.

Paint Selections with Quick Masks

A Quick Mask is a selection that you paint on, usually with the Brush tool (see Figures 5-13 and 5-14). You can convert a current selection to a Quick Mask. A mask is a colored overlay that allows you to edit one selected part of the image and protect the rest of it. You can control the opacity of a mask to vary the intensity of the editing.

*Figure 5-13: **The mask defines the area to be protected; that is, the image not masked will be selected.***

*Figure 5-14: **The selection surrounds the image of Tank the cocker spaniel, which can be edited as with any selection.***

DECIDING WHAT YOUR QUICK MASK INDICATES

Adobe considers black to be "color," and by default, when you paint a Quick Mask overlay to define an area, the area is masked—protected from editing, and not available for editing ("selected"). However, you can work vice versa in Quick Mask (and other areas of Photoshop) and make the areas you paint selection areas:

- Double-click the **Edit In Quick Mask Mode** button on the Tools panel to open the Quick Mask Options dialog box. Here you have a number of customizable goodies that will make your Quick Mask work a joy to perform.

- Click the **Color Indicates: Selected Areas** button. Now whenever you paint, the area will have a selection marquee around it when you return to Standard mode.

- Click the **color swatch** to go to the Color Picker. You can define the visible Quick Mask overlay as any color you like, which is handy if, for example, you're creating a selection in an image that has a lot of red objects. Your solution for high visibility of the Quick Mask is to choose blue as the Quick Mask Color.

- Set the **Opacity** of the Quick Mask higher or lower, depending on how visible you want the underlying image to be.

Click **OK** and you're in Quick Mask mode. Click the **Edit In Quick Mask Mode** button to toggle back to Standard mode.

Work with Quick Masks

To select an area using a Quick Mask:

1. Click the **Edit In Quick Mask Mode** button 📷 in the Tools panel, or press **Q** to enter Quick Mask mode.

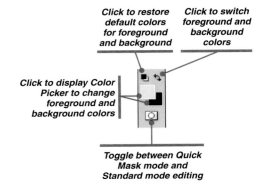

Click to restore default colors for foreground and background

Click to switch foreground and background colors

Click to display Color Picker to change foreground and background colors

Toggle between Quick Mask mode and Standard mode editing

2. Click the **Brush** tool in the Tools panel.

3. Press **D** to set the foreground and background colors to the default black foreground and white background.

4. With the Brush tool (or other paint application tool), paint over the areas you do not want selected; they are *masked*.

5. You can work with a Quick Mask in the following ways:

- To remove some of the masked area from the selection, click the **Swap Foreground And Background Colors** button, or press **X**, and paint (white) over the areas to be subtracted from the selected area.

- To add some additional area to the mask, press **D** to make the foreground color black, and paint over the areas to be added to the selection.

- Switch back and forth between the **Edit In Standard Mode** button, to see the marquee outline for a visual look-see, and the **Edit In Quick Mask Mode** button, to see the mask. You can press **Q** to quickly toggle between the two modes.

6. When you have the mask selection the way you want it, click **Edit In Standard Mode** to perform edits on the pixels that lie under the selection. Quick Mask mode is only for previewing a proposed selection area; you cannot edit image pixels in this mode.

QUICK**FACTS**

DOING JUST ABOUT ANYTHING TO A QUICK MASK

Although Quick Mask is nonprinting screen data, it is a real part of your document in the sense that most editing you can perform on an image, you can perform on the Quick Mask overlay. And this leads to some interesting effects possibilities. For example, you can apply the Filter | Blur | Gaussian Blur filter on a Quick Mask overlay to really soften it and thus create an extremely smooth selection to vignette a portrait photo. You can apply Quick Mask with the Pattern Stamp tool to create selections that fade in and out at intervals to make a selection that, when cut or copied, looks like distressed fabric. You can use the Gradient tool to create a transition from selected to masked to then blend the edge of a photo into a different photo.

There are 256 brightness levels you have at your disposal when creating a Quick Mask. Use intermediate levels of selection to create sophisticated and intricate compositions.

TOUCH UP A SELECTION WITH QUICK MASK

You can use Quick Mask mode in combination with other selection tools to select images more easily:

1. Use a selection tool, such as the Magic Wand tool, to create a rough selection. In this example we selected Tank, the cocker spaniel, with the Elliptical Marquee tool and then did an Inverse selection.

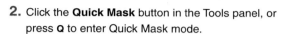

2. Click the **Quick Mask** button in the Tools panel, or press **Q** to enter Quick Mask mode.

3. Press **D** to set the foreground and background colors to black and white, respectively.

4. Select the **Brush** tool from the Tools panel.

5. Right-click the image and adjust the brush's size and shape.

6. Paint with the **Brush** tool to touch up the mask.

7. Press **X** to switch the foreground color between black and white. Black adds to the mask; white subtracts from the mask. Edit your mask as needed.

8. When the mask is complete, press **Q** again to leave Quick Mask mode and view your selection in Standard mode. Here, too, you can edit the image with white and black brush strokes, finalizing your selection before you perform other editing tasks, such as filling the background with white as shown here:

9. If necessary, flatten and save your image when the editing is complete.

EXPLORING THE ELEMENTS OF A PATH

A path is a vector graphic composed of geometrical primitives such as points, lines, curves, and polygons. There are three components to a Photoshop path:

- **The segment**   A curved path can change direction. Where it does this, we see an anchor point placed along the curve. In Photoshop, we break down an entire path into path segments, which begin and end at anchor points.

- **The anchor point**   A point in space where a path *might* change direction. An anchor point is not necessarily an indication of path direction change—a straight line can have any number of anchor points. A path that changes course, however, always must do so by passing through an anchor point. You reshape a path by relocating an anchor point.

- **Direction lines and points**   An anchor point that is intersected by a curve has *direction points* (handles) sprouting from direction lines connected to the anchor. Usually there are two direction lines that sprout from an anchor. You drag on the direction handles to steer the slope of the curve passing through the anchor point; one handle controls the previous path segment and the other controls the following segment. Shaping a curve using direction points is an intuitive art, but you can also drag directly on a path segment with the direct selection tool to create significant, less predictable path segment shapes.

Figure 5-15 shows examples of shapes that can be created with Photoshop's Pen tool(s), and the properties the components of the vector shapes.

Use Paths for Selections

Like type and Shapes in Photoshop, paths are vector data—not bitmap pixels—with one important distinction: vector paths don't print unless you fill them with pixels, and paths can be used as the shape for stroking with a brush, as well as defining an area you want to select. As vector data, paths are resolution-independent, so you can smoothly scale them, and you also can zoom into an area (even to Photoshop's maximum viewing of 3200% of the original), create a closed path, and edit an area smaller than a pixel!

Paths can be the most accurate, smoothest basis for creating a selection; to create a path, you use the Pen tool, of which there are the standard and the Freeform.

WORK WITH THE PEN TOOL

Closed and open paths are used in Photoshop to define selections—if a path is open and loaded as a selection, the selection auto-closes with a straight line between the first and last anchor points. Additionally, you can have a subpath within a path by creating a closed path, saving the path, and then drawing a closed path inside of the first one, which is useful for making donut selections. When you use the Pen or Freeform Pen tool, you have Add To, Subtract From, and other operation buttons on the Options bar. As you work, it might look as though you're intersecting paths, but when you load the paths and subpaths as selections, the selections have no overlaps but instead contain subtractions from the outermost path.

To trace a path along the edge of an image element:

1. Click+hold on the **Pen Tool** group on the Tools panel to reveal all the tools, and then click the **Pen** tool.

2. Click a point at the edge of a photo area where you want to start a selection.

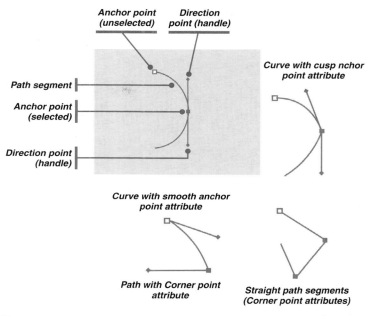

Figure 5-15: *Anchor points determine the shape of path segments.*

3. Click+drag at a tangent along the outline of the object you want to select. The click action sets an anchor point while the drag adjusts the curve of the path segment that precedes the anchor.

4. Repeat Step 3, click+dragging at points where the outline of the underlying object makes a change in direction (the apogee of a curve, the tangent point).

5. When you come to a corner—an area where the outline makes an abrupt turn—click, don't click+drag. This sets a corner-type anchor.

6. Click at the beginning point of the curve. This closes the curve. Figure 5-16 shows a partially complete path around a fairly complex shape.

7. You've created a Work Path, which is temporary and will be overwritten by any future path you draw unless you click the Paths tab on the Layers (grouped) panel, and then double-click the Work Path title. This brings up the Save Path dialog box where you save the work path by typing a name or simply clicking OK and letting Photoshop use the default path name.

Click+drag   Click+drag   Click   Click+drag

Figure 5-16: *Create different types of anchor by clicking and click+dragging with the Pen tool.*

NOTE

It can be visually frustrating to have a path displayed in your photo when you're trying to work on something other than the path! To hide paths, click on an empty area of the Path panel's list. To reveal—but not load—a path, click on its title.

8. If your path is perfect, it's time to load the path as a selection. If the path isn't perfect, read the upcoming section "Choose and Use the Path Tools You Need." To load a selection based on the shape of the path:

   ● On the Paths panel, click the **Loads Path As A Selection** button on the bottom of the panel. An alternative method is to **CTRL/CMD**+click the path thumbnail on the Paths list.

CTRL/CMD+
click to load

Load path as a selection

SKETCH WITH THE FREEFORM PEN TOOL

The Freeform Pen tool is used exactly like the Lasso tool—you sketch a selection area. However, the result is quite different; what you sketch is a path. The advantage to using this tool is that after sketching the area you want selected, you can refine the selection with the Direct Selection tool:

1. Drag the **Freeform Pen** tool to define a selection area.

2. Close the path at the beginning point; the cursor features a tiny circle to the bottom right of the pen that tells you when you're in proximity to the beginning point. Alternatively, you can leave the path open and the selection based on the path will auto-close in a straight line from beginning to end point.

3. Click the **Direct Selection** tool on the Tools panel.

Freeform
Pen tool

Direct
Selection tool

- Click once to choose the path. The anchor points are revealed.
- Click-drag an anchor to reposition it.
- Click-drag a direction point to alter the associated path segment.

CHOOSE AND USE THE PATH TOOLS YOU NEED

Although there are seven tools for creating and modifying paths, you really need to choose only the Pen tool and the Selection tool in your work, because you can use keyboard modifiers to choose the rest of the tools. Here is a list of the path creation and editing tools, what they do, and the shortcut keys for toggling to them so you don't need to reach for a different tool all the time during path creation:

- **Pen tool**   The basic path creation tool. Choose this or the Freeform Pen tool for 99 percent of all your path work.
- **Add Anchor Point tool**   Adds an anchor to an existing path when you click on the path. You don't really need this tool when you've checked the Options bar's Auto Add/Delete check box. With the Auto Add/Delete option turned on, clicking over a path segment with the Pen tool adds an anchor.
- **Delete Anchor Point tool**   Removes an anchor point along a path, thus reshaping the path a little. Similarly, with Auto Add/Delete enabled, clicking on an anchor with the Pen tool deletes the anchor.
- **Convert Point tool**   An invaluable tool for redefining an anchor point's attribute:
  - If you have a smooth anchor point that you want to make into a cusp point, click its related path segment to make every anchor point available for changing; then drag on the exposed direction point (handle) to convert the anchor's attribute and, at the same time, reshape the path segment.

- To convert an anchor to a corner attribute (removing the direction points), click once on the anchor point.

- To convert a cusp or corner anchor point to smooth, click-drag on the anchor point.

- If you're really into your work and don't care to switch from the Pen tool to the Convert Point tool, hold **ALT/OPT** and the Pen tool temporarily toggles to the Convert Point tool.

- **Direct Selection tool**   Selects components of paths. You use it to move anchor points, and when path segments are curved, you can drag directly on the curve to change its slope. The tool is located in the group directly below the Pen Tool group. The keyboard modifier to access the Direct Selection tool while using the Pen tool is to hold **CTRL/CMD**.

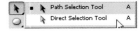

- **Path Selection tool**   Selects an entire path for repositioning. When you're working on a path (or it's simply selected), you can move it by pressing **CTRL/CMD+A** to select the entire path and then using the Direct Selection tool to move it; the Path Selection tool becomes unnecessary.

Chapter 6

Editing Layers and Selections

Layers and layer masks are the key to creating advanced effects, such as replacing backgrounds, combining photos, and making collages. They allow you to build complex compositions while still maintaining control of the individual elements. Better yet, they allow you to keep all your assets intact so you can change how you use them later. Think of layers as a combination of photographs and overhead transparencies that can be stacked up, one on top of the other, almost indefinitely. You can use a layer mask to hide all or part of a layer and then vary a layer's opacity to achieve the desired effect. You can use layer styles to create drop shadows and other effects.

WORKING WITH TRANSPARENCY

One of the big advantages of working with a stack of layers is that you can make all or parts of layers transparent, thereby revealing or hiding the images they contain. In this way, you build up an image, layer by layer. See "Work with Opacity and Fill" and "Work with Layer Masks" in this chapter to see how to use these tools to create and control transparency when you create layered images.

NOTE

When working on documents with multiple layers, you often need to temporarily hide individual layers. By doing so, you avoid having to sort through layers that are crucial to the document but that do not currently need editing. To hide a layer so that you can see only the visible layers, click the **eye** icon at the far left of the layer thumbnail in the Layers panel. The icon disappears and the layer is hidden.

To reveal a hidden layer, click the empty space at the far left of the layer thumbnail in the Layers panel. The eye icon reappears and the layer is revealed.

Work with Layers

As you work with an image, making changes to it, you can make the changes to other layers instead of to the original image, which is thereby protected from being altered as you experiment and edit the new image you're trying to create. This is referred to as *nondestructive editing*. Only when you merge the layers into one is the image permanently altered. As long as you retain the layers, you can always return to the original image.

There are several kinds of layers that you may be working with:

- **Background layer**   The original image containing the contents to be altered. It is always on the bottom of the stack of layers. You cannot change the opacity or blend mode of a background layer. You can, however, convert a background layer into a regular layer or make a copy of it, and then you can modify it and move it in the stack.

- **Adjustment layer**   A layer that changes the layers beneath it with color or tonal alternations, but without changing the actual pixels of the image layer. Unlike the background layer or another image layer, the adjustment layer doesn't contain recognizable image contents. Rather, it contains color or tonal changes. The adjustment layer is a mask that you paint on using black, white, and shades in between to hide or reveal the effect attributed to the adjustment layer.

- **Fill layer**   Fills a layer with a solid, gradient, or patterned fill. The fill layer itself contains the color, unlike the adjustment layer, which modifies other layers beneath it.

- **Layer group**   A group of linked layers. By linking several image elements, you can treat them as a single element. An image can be made up of several layer groups.

- **Masked layer**   Enables you to paint a selection, or mask, that alters the image by blocking out parts of the image or partially revealing the image (making it more or less transparent).

- **Clipping mask**   A layer beneath another layer whose nontransparent regions determine what is visible on the layer above it. It is a nondestructive arrangement and produces effects visually similar to looking at an image through a cut-out stencil.

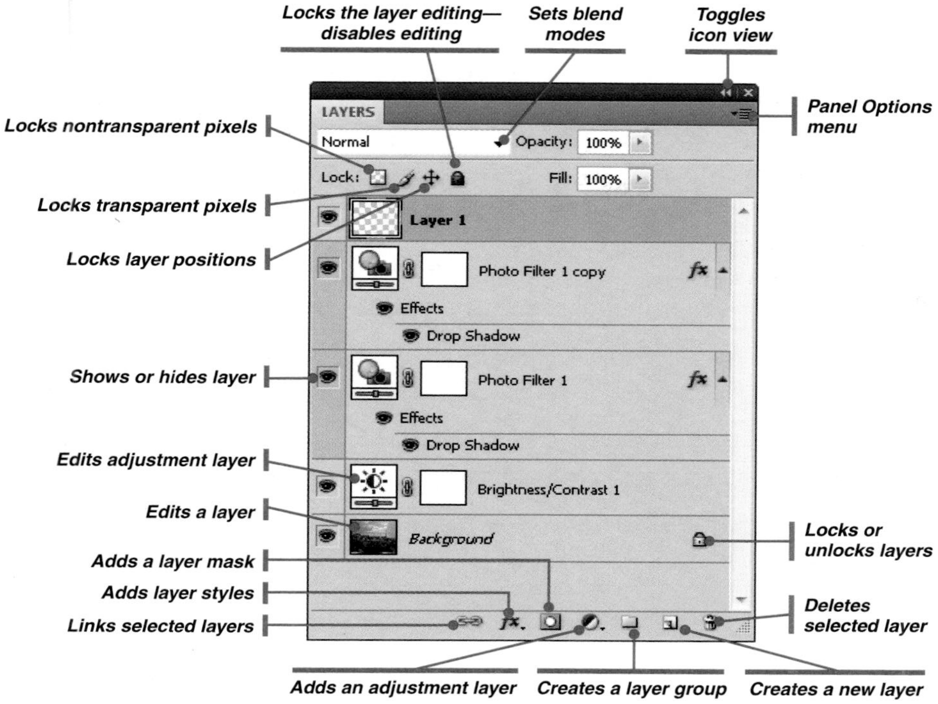

Locks the layer editing—disables editing
Sets blend modes
Toggles icon view

Locks nontransparent pixels

LAYERS

Panel Options menu

Normal ✓ Opacity: 100% ►

Lock: ☑ ✦ ✛ 🔒 Fill: 100% ►

Locks transparent pixels

Layer 1

Locks layer positions

Photo Filter 1 copy *fx* ▲

● Effects

🌑 Drop Shadow

Shows or hides layer

Photo Filter 1 *fx* ▲

● Effects

🌑 Drop Shadow

Edits adjustment layer

Brightness/Contrast 1

Edits a layer

Background

Locks or unlocks layers

Adds a layer mask

Adds layer styles

Deletes selected layer

Links selected layers

🔗 *fx.* 🔲 ⬭ 🔲 🔲 🗑

Adds an adjustment layer   Creates a layer group   Creates a new layer

Figure 6-1: **Use the Layers panel to control image layers.**

When you save a file in the PSD format, the default Photoshop file format, you can retain its layers—images, adjustment layers, masks, and so on. You lose the history (the Undo steps listed on the History panel) but retain the last-saved information of each layer. As a consequence, your PSD files may be very large. When you are finished with your editing, you may want to retain one version of your file in the PSD format so that you can return to it at some future time. For other uses, however, you will want to save the file to another format, such as JPG, TIFF, GIF, or PNG, formats in which your layers will be compressed into a single layer containing the image.

Use the Layers Panel

The Layers panel helps you manage the layers in an image. It enables you to identify, create, copy, delete, rearrange, and add special effects to your images. Figure 6-1 shows an example of the Layers panel.

Create New Layers

You can create layers in a variety of ways: by clicking a button in the Layers panel, by using a keyboard shortcut, or by using a menu command. When you create a new blank layer using a menu command, the New Layer dialog box appears, which enables you to create a clipping mask (the transparent pixels of the underlying layers are used to mask the new layer), specify the blend mode, and set layer opacity.

CREATE A NEW BLANK LAYER

To create a new blank layer, choose one of these options:

- Click the **Create New Layer** icon at the bottom of the Layers panel.
- Click **Layer | New | Layer**.
- Press **SHIFT+CTRL/CMD+N**.

NOTE

Hidden layers cannot be modified or copied.

TIP

To rename a layer, double-click the layer's name in the Layers panel and type a new name.

NOTE

If a selection is active, the Layer Via Copy command (**CTRL/CMD+J**) copies the selected portions to a new layer. If there is no selection, then the command copies the entire layer.

QUICKSTEPS

LINKING AND UNLINKING LAYERS

Layers that are linked move, rotate, and transform together. If you move the contents of a layer 50 pixels to the left, the contents of all layers linked to that layer will also move 50 pixels to the left. You can also link groups of layers. Linked layers can be unlinked, unlinked temporarily, and then relinked as needed to edit or view the effects.

LINK LAYERS

To link another layer to the currently selected layer, select the layers you want to link; this is done by holding **SHIFT** as you click neighboring layer titles on the Layers panel, or by holding **CTRL/CMD** to select noncontiguous layers. Then click the **Link Layers** icon at the bottom of the Layers panel. A chain icon appears to the right of each layer's name.

UNLINK LAYERS

Select a linked layer and then click the **Link Layers** icon at the bottom of the Layers panel. The chain icon disappears.

Shows these two layers are linked

Another type of link between selection and style

Click here to link or unlink selected layers

COPY AN EXISTING LAYER

You also can create a new layer by copying an existing layer. In the Layers panel, click the source layer. The cursor changes to a fist. Perform one of these options:

- Drag the layer to the **Create A New Layer** icon at the bottom of the Layers panel.
- Click **Layer | New | Layer Via Copy**.
- Press **CTRL/CMD+J**.

Photoshop creates a new layer that is an exact copy of the original. The new layer appears immediately above the source layer in the Layers panel.

CREATE A NEW LAYER FROM A SELECTION

You can create a new layer by copying only the selected portions of an existing layer. This is a useful way to separate a selected element or elements from the background while leaving your original image intact.

1. Use any of the selection tools to select the portions of a layer that you want to copy.
2. Click **Layer | New | Layer Via Copy**.

   –Or–

   Press **CTRL/CMD+J**.

Edit with Layers

You can add as many layers to a document as needed (as the amount of system RAM and scratch disk space you've allocated to Photoshop allows). Some commands, such as painting, can only be made to one layer at a time. Other adjustments, such as moving, applying styles, or transforming, can be made to multiple layers at a time. To identify which layers will be included in an edit, select layers, link, or group them. Here is how you can manipulate the layers, make the background layer editable, and add additional layers as needed.

UNLOCK THE BACKGROUND LAYER

The background layer in a Photoshop document is initially locked. You cannot erase it (other than painting over it with a background color). You cannot move, rotate, or resize it as you would a document layer (there are commands to rotate and scale a background that can be found in the Image menu); nor can you create a mask for it. To make these kinds of changes on the background, you must first turn it into a normal layer:

- Click **Layer | New | Layer From Background**. The background becomes a normal layer.

    –Or–

- Double-click the background layer thumbnail on the Layers panel, and then respond to the New Layer dialog box.

COPY MERGED LAYERS

You might want to copy a merged version of a layered document—a version that looks the same but does not contain multiple layers—to the Clipboard. Remember that the size of image files may cause this to be an unwise way of copying your images.

1. Select the entire document by clicking **Select | All** or by pressing **CTRL/CMD+A**.

2. Click **Edit | Copy Merged** or press **SHIFT+CTRL/CMD+C**. All layers in the document are copied to the Clipboard as a single layer.

When you copy the contents of the Clipboard to a new document, the contents appear as a new layer made up of all layers from the parent document (see Figure 6-2 and Figure 6-3). If the original layers had transparency, the transparent regions that did not overlap any opaque areas on other layers will still be transparent.

*Figure 6-2: **Before using the Copy Merged command, the document is composed of many layers.***

*Figure 6-3: **Copying the merged layers into a new document results in a single layer.***

COPY FROM ANOTHER APPLICATION TO A NEW LAYER

To copy an item from another application (for example, Microsoft Internet Explorer) to a Photoshop document:

1. Open an image in Photoshop.

2. Switch to another application, such as a web browser, and select and copy an image.

3. Return to Photoshop and click **Edit | Paste**. The new image is pasted into the Photoshop document on a new layer. **CTRL/CMD+V** is the keyboard shortcut.

If you need to copy text as editable text into Photoshop, click the Type tool on the Tools panel before pasting. Click an insertion point in your document, and then press **CTRL/CMD+V**. Reformatting your text is usually necessary, but this beats retyping a paragraph of text. If you choose to paste using a tool other than the Type tool, a new layer is created, but the pasted text is a bitmap, and not editable text.

The system clipboard typically doesn't handle transparency between applications. Usually, if you copy an image containing transparent regions and try to paste it into a Photoshop document, you'll get a black area instead of the original image transparency. You can copy and paste to new layers within Photoshop because Photoshop uses an internal clipboard, not your system's clipboard.

COPY A LAYER BY DRAGGING

You can drag layers directly from one Photoshop document to another. To copy a layer from one Photoshop document to another:

1. Open two images in Photoshop with the Layers panel open.

2. Click **Window | Arrange | Tile** to display both images at once.

NOTE

You cannot copy a layer to a background layer. You must first convert the background layer to a regular layer.

TIP

Before making changes, copy your work to a new layer. Make changes on the new layer, and if you don't like them, delete the layer.

3. Make sure the source document is selected. If it is not, you can just click its title bar.

4. Click the desired layer title on the Layers panel and drag it into the destination document. It will be added to the second document as a new layer.

Press and hold **SHIFT** as you drag a layer from one document to a different document window to make it centered in the receiving document.

REARRANGE LAYER ORDER

The order of layers in the Layers panel usually determines the final result, as shown in Figures 6-4 and 6-5.

To change the order of layers:

1. Click a layer title on the Layers panel.

2. Drag the layer up or down to a new position.

The original background layer is locked and therefore cannot be moved.

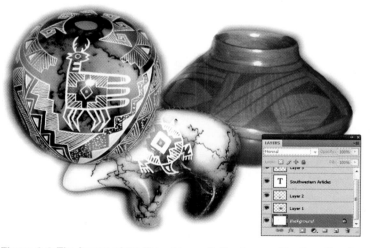

*Figure 6-4: **The image of the "bear" is partially obscured by the other layers when it is not the top layer.***

Southwestern Articles

Figure 6-5: **When the "bear" layer is moved, it appears as the top layer, no longer obscured by the others.**

![clock icon] **QUICKSTEPS**

MANIPULATING LAYER GROUPS

MOVE THE CONTENTS OF A LAYER GROUP

1. Select the **Move** tool from the Tools panel.

2. Click a layer group in the Layers panel.

3. Drag the image to move the entire layer group.

RESIZE A LAYER GROUP

1. In the Layers panel, click the layer group you want to resize.

2. Press **CTRL/CMD+T** to enter Free Transform mode, or click **Edit | Free Transform**.

3. Drag the handles to resize all layers in the layer group at once. Press and hold **SHIFT** while you drag to constrain the resizing to proportional resizing.

4. Press **ENTER/RETURN**, click **Commit** (the check button on the Options bar), or double-click the image to accept the changes.

DELETE A LAYER GROUP

1. Click a layer group thumbnail in the Layers panel.

2. Drag the layer group to the **Delete Layer** button at the bottom of the panel.

   –Or–

Continued . . .

DELETE A LAYER

To delete a layer:

1. Click a layer's thumbnail in the Layers panel.

2. Drag the layer to the **Delete Layer** button at the bottom of the panel.

   –Or–

1. Right-click the layer's name in the Layers panel, and click **Delete Layer**.

2. Photoshop asks you to confirm the deletion. Click **Yes**.

Consolidate Layers into Layer Groups

Layers can be grouped together into folders called *layer groups*. Layer groups help you keep multilayer documents organized. You can group parts of an image together so that they work as a single component of the image.

MANIPULATING LAYER GROUPS

(Continued)

1. Right-click the layer group's name in the Layers panel, and click **Delete Group**.

2. Photoshop asks you to confirm the deletion. You can choose between deleting both the group layer and its contents or only the group layer. Click **Group And Contents** or click **Group Only**.

DUPLICATE A LAYER GROUP

1. Click a layer group thumbnail in the Layers panel.

2. Drag the layer group to the **Create A New Layer** button at the bottom of the panel. Photoshop creates a duplicate of the layer group and appends the layer group name with "Copy."

   –Or–

   Right-click the layer group's name in the Layers panel, and click **Duplicate Group**.

TIP

Rename a duplicated layer group to reflect the duplicated group's intended purpose.

CAUTION

You may need to relocate your layer group to a different place in the stack in order to maintain the intended image effect.

With ambitious and complex compositions, you may have several groups. Although you cannot paint on a layer group, in most other ways, they act the same as individual layers. You can reposition, resize, mask, and hide all layers in a layer group at the same time.

Create a Layer Group

When you create a new layer group, you first create a blank folder into which you can drag other layers in the document. Creating layer groups when working with a multilayer document makes it easier for you to work within the Layers panel, since you can collapse any layer groups you are not currently editing to eliminate clutter and confusion in the Layers panel.

To create a new layer group:

● Click the **Create A New Group** icon at the bottom of the Layers panel.

–Or–

● Click **Layer | Group Layers**.

MOVE A LAYER INTO A LAYER GROUP

To move a layer into a layer group:

1. In the Layers panel, click an existing layer.

2. Drag it to the desired layer group.

FLATTENING AN IMAGE

When you *flatten* an image, you condense all layers in the document into a single layer. As a result, you can no longer edit the layers you created. Flattening an image is generally the last step prior to saving an image in a file format other than PSD for clients who don't own Photoshop or don't need editable layers in their work. If you intend to edit the image further in another session, do not flatten it. Save the document as a Photoshop (PSD) document. Doing so preserves all layers in the document for further editing.

To flatten all layers into a single layer:

- Click **Layer | Flatten Image**.

  –Or–

1. In the Layers panel, click the **Options** button. The Options menu appears.
2. Click **Flatten Image**.

TIP

If you want to work on a composition later, but need to send a copy of your work to someone, it's often a good technique to save your work as a PSD file, then click **File | Save As**, choose the file format you need in the Save As dialog box, choose a location for the copy, then click **Save**. You'll see that the As A Copy check box is automatically checked and a little caution icon appears at the bottom of the dialog box, telling you that the file format you chose necessitates that special Photoshop-specific features such as layers won't be saved. Your work is auto-flattened to conform to the new file format's structure.

REMOVE A LAYER FROM A LAYER GROUP

To remove a layer from a layer group:

1. In the Layers panel, within the layer group, click the layer that you want to remove.
2. Drag it to a position outside of the layer group.

Merge Layers

When you are finished editing several layers in a document, you can select them and then merge them into a single layer. When you merge selected layers, the other layers in the document are still editable. You can apply edits to the layer created by merging other layers. You can also select other layers in the document and merge them.

Merge a Layer with the Layer Beneath It

When you have edited two layers to your liking, you can select a layer and merge it with the underlying layer. This creates a new layer, which can be further edited.

1. In the Layers panel, select the topmost layer of the two layers you want to merge.
2. Click the **Options** button in the upper-right area of the Layers panel, and click **Merge Layers** from the flyout menu.

   –Or–

   Press **CTRL/CMD+E**.

Merge Linked Layers

To merge all linked layers into a single layer:

1. In the Layers panel, click one of the linked layers to select it.
2. Click **Layer | Select Linked Layers**.
3. Click **Layer | Merge Layers**.

   –Or–

QUICKSTEPS

CHECKING FILE SIZE

The file size for your image depends on the image size—specifically the number of pixels it contains. If you have many layers, depending on the number of pixels in each layer, your file size can become quite large. You may find that you need to reduce your file size to make editing easier, to make web page loading faster, or to reduce disk space.

To check your file size:

1. On the Status bar, click the right-pointing arrow in the lower-left corner of the document window. A context menu will display. **Doc: 8.18M/12.9M**

2. Click **Show** for a submenu.

3. Click **Document Sizes**.

The Doc Size will be displayed. It contains two numbers: the size on the left is the size of the flattened image; on the right is the size of the file with all its layers and channels.

TIP

Mask, don't erase. When you erase a pixel, it's gone forever; but you can always change a mask if you change your mind later—nothing is ever lost.

1. Click the **Options** button in the upper-right area of the Layers panel. The panel Options menu appears.

2. Click **Select Linked Layers**.

3. Right-click the selected layers and click **Merge Layers**.

Merge Visible Layers

To merge visible layers into a single layer, you first must hide the layers you don't want to merge:

1. In the Layers panel, click the **eye** icon for all layers you want to hide, or do not want to merge.

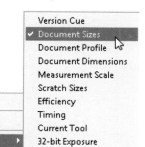

2. Click a visible layer to select it.

3. Click the **Options** button in the upper-right area of the Layers panel. The panel Options menu appears.

4. Click **Merge Visible**.

   –Or–

   Press **CTRL/CMD+SHIFT+E**.

   –Or–

   Right-click a layer title to access the merge commands from the context menu.

Work with Layer Masks

When working with layers, you may find that you want only part of a layer to show, or perhaps a layer to show only faintly in the background. In this case, you can use *layer masks*. A layer mask hides, or *masks*, part of a layer. Layer masks are by default black, white, and shades of black. Where the layer mask is black, the masked layer is not visible. If the mask is a shade of black (gray), the underlying mask is partially visible. If the mask is white, the layer is completely visible. You can add or subtract from a layer's visibility by painting on the mask with shades of gray to partially reveal areas on underlying layers, or with black to completely reveal areas of the underlying layer.

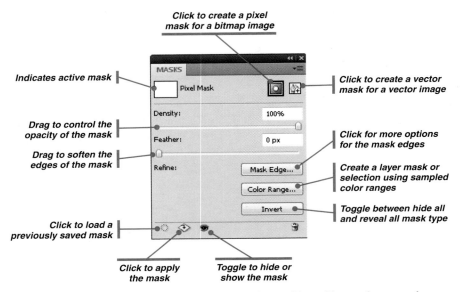

Click to create a pixel mask for a bitmap image

Indicates active mask

Click to create a vector mask for a vector image

Drag to control the opacity of the mask

Click for more options for the mask edges

Drag to soften the edges of the mask

Create a layer mask or selection using sampled color ranges

Click to load a previously saved mask

Toggle between hide all and reveal all mask type

Click to apply the mask

Toggle to hide or show the mask

Figure 6-6: **The Masks panel provides controls for working with your layer masks.**

Masks come in two types in Photoshop, but their use is the same:

- **Bitmap masks** Created with paint tools such as the Brush tool, and also by creating selections you then fill with foreground color.

- **Vector masks** Created using the Pen tools. They produce crisp edges (so feathering is best done using bitmap masks) and can be edited and moved using the selection tools on the Tools panel.

Create Layer Masks

You can create a layer mask from an image, from a Quick Mask, or from a selection. Figure 6-7 shows an example of a layer mask that shows part of the image as a background and hides part of it.

TIP

If the mask is not perfect, press **Q** to revert to Quick Mask mode, and then paint white over the areas you do not want to mask or black over those you do want to mask.

NOTE

Be sure that the mask, not the layer, is selected when you are working with the mask. Click on the layer mask thumbnail in the Layers panel to select the mask. When the layer mask is selected you will see a selection border around its thumbnail, or, in the Masks panel thumbnail, a "Pixel Mask" or "Vector Mask" notation confirms the selection.

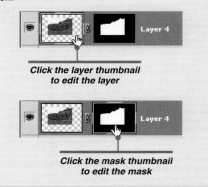

Click the layer thumbnail
to edit the layer

Click the mask thumbnail
to edit the mask

Figure 6-7: **Using layer masks, you can hide, obscure parts of, or reveal all of an image, such as this one where the background sky is hidden and the cliffs are dimmed using the Opacity setting.**

PAINT A LAYER MASK

Overall, layer masks without previous selections are created in two steps:

1. You create a mask that will either hide all or reveal all.

2. You refine the mask by painting the parts you want to be seen, seen partially, or hidden.

To either hide or show the whole layer, follow these steps:

1. Deselect any active selections so that none of the image is selected.

2. In the Layers panel, select the layer or group to be masked.

TIP

If at any time you want an onscreen preview of what is hidden and revealed with layer masks, press and hold **SHIFT+ALT/OPT** and then click the layer mask thumbnail on the Layers panel. The Quick Mask tinted overlay shows you where you've painted. **SHIFT+ALT/OPT**+click the mask thumbnail again to hide the Quick Mask indicator.

3. These are your options:

- To reveal the whole layer, either click the **Add Layer Mask** button at the bottom of the Layers panel, or click **Layer | Layer Mask | Reveal All**, or click the **Pixel Mask** button in the Masks panel. A new white mask for the selected layer is created, identified by the white icon to the immediate right of the layer image thumbnail.

- To hide the whole layer, either **ALT/OPT**+click the **Add Layer Mask** button at the bottom of the Layers panel, or click **Layer | Layer Mask | Hide Selection**, or **ALT/OPT**+click the Pixel Mask button in the Masks panel. A new black mask for the selected layer will be created, which you identify by the black icon to the immediate right of the layer thumbnail.

4. Select the **Brush** tool or other painting tool from the Tools panel.

5. Notice that the foreground and background colors are changed with active masks. If you want to change the mask colors, click the foreground or background thumbnails and select the image you want.

6. Paint the mask with the color you need for the effect you want, as shown in Figure 6-8.

Figure 6-8: ***Paint on a layer mask to reveal or conceal underlying layers.***

EDITING A MASK

The best thing about masks is that they aren't permanent. You can edit them at any time, hiding or revealing the underlying image.

EDIT A MASK WITH THE BRUSH TOOL

1. In the Layers panel, click the layer mask you want to edit.

2. Select the **Brush** tool or other painting tool from the Tools panel.

3. Select a foreground color: black to mask, white to reveal, or gray to partially reveal.

4. Paint to alter the mask.

ADD A SELECTION TO A MASK

You can expand a layer mask by selecting additional pixels to be masked and adding them to the layer mask:

1. In the Layers panel, click the layer mask you want to modify.

2. Use any selection tool to select an area you want to mask.

3. Press **D** to set the foreground and background colors to black and white.

4. Press **CTRL/CMD+BACKSPACE** to fill the selected area of the mask with black.

CREATE A NEW SELECTION FROM A MASK

In the Layers panel, press **CTRL/CMD** while you click the mask thumbnail. All unmasked pixels are selected.

CREATE A LAYER MASK FROM A QUICK MASK

Chapter 5 describes selecting using Quick Mask mode:

1. Select the layer image for which you want to create a Quick Mask.

2. Press **Q** to switch to Quick Mask mode.

3. Select a painting or drawing tool from the Tools panel.

4. Set the foreground color to black, and paint on the areas of the image you want to mask.

5. Press **Q** again to leave Quick Mask mode. An animated dashed outline (called "marching ants" by Photoshop pros) signifies the area to be masked.

6. In the Layers panel, click the layer to be masked.

7. Click the **Add Layer Mask** button (or press **ALT/OPT+** click **Add Layer Mask** to hide the pixels within the selection) at the bottom of the Layers panel. Photoshop creates a new layer mask from the selection.

CREATE A LAYER MASK FROM A SELECTED AREA

1. In the Layers panel, click the layer to be masked.

2. Use one or more of Photoshop's selection tools, such as the **Rectangular Marquee** or **Lasso** tool, to select the part of the image to be masked.

3. Click the **Add Layer Mask** button at the bottom of the Layers panel. Photoshop creates a new layer mask from the selection. Only pixels that were within the selection are now visible in this layer.

CREATE A NEW BLANK LAYER MASK

- Click the **Add Layer Mask** button at the bottom of the Layers panel.

  –Or–

- Click **Layer | Layer Mask | Reveal All**.

You can now paint in the layer mask with black or shades of gray to hide parts of the layer.

HIDE A LAYER WITH A NEW LAYER MASK

- Click **Layer | Layer Mask | Hide All**.

You can now paint in the layer mask with white or shades of gray to reveal parts of the underlying layer.

CREATE A GRADIENT MASK

1. Press **D** to set the foreground and background colors to black and white.

2. In the Layers panel, click the layer to be masked.

3. Click **Add Layer Mask** at the bottom of the Layers panel to create a new blank layer mask.

4. Select the **Gradient** tool from the Tools panel.

5. Right-click within the image to bring up the Gradient context menu.

6. If you hover the pointer over a gradient, a Tool Tip appears showing you that gradient's name. Click **Foreground To Background** from the presets menu.

7. Drag in the image from left to right or from top to bottom to create the background gradient, as shown in Figure 6-9. The areas of the gradient that are white reveal the underlying layer; black reveals the entire masked layer; while shades of gray partially reveal the underlying layer.

*Figure 6-9: **A linear gradient mask causes the top layer to fade in from left to right, giving the image depth.***

6. Choose a brush size and type that scales well to the areas you want to replace; right-click over the document and then choose from the brushes presets—click outside the document window to dismiss the pop-up preset box.

7. Stroke over the areas you want to replace. You'll see that light image areas don't change, but only the colors darker than your chosen color are replaced with…the lighter color!

QUICKSTEPS

REPLACING LIGHTER COLORS WITH DARKER ONES

Suppose you have a photo or a scanned image whose background is almost white, making a somewhat bland composition. You can add colors to the background without altering the foreground element when you use Darker Color mode on a layer. Here's how:

1. Choose a photo whose foreground subject is overall medium to dark in brightness, while the background is fairly light.

2. Click the **Create A New Layer** icon on the Layers panel, and then choose **Darker Color** from the blend modes drop-down list.

3. Click the **Brush** tool, and then right-click anywhere in the document window to choose an interesting brush from the pop-up panel. The maple leaf is used in this example because the color jitters and the stroke scatters when you use it. See Chapter 11 for the low-down on the Brushes panel.

4. Hold **ALT/OPT** to toggle to the **Eyedropper** tool.

5. Click over the *lightest* area of the foreground subject in the photo. By doing this, you assure yourself that when you paint on the Darker Color mode layer, only areas darker than the lightest foreground color will be colored over. This is an awesome technique for editing without using a selection!

Continued . . .

Use Color Burn and Linear Burn Modes

The Burn tool on the Tools panel (see Chapter 8) is the basis for Color Burn and Linear Burn blend and painting modes—you get a similar effect as using the Burn tool but you have the advantage of using a foreground color to refine the operation. Using Burn painting or layer blend mode:

- Color Burn decreases brightness and, depending on the color you use, increases contrast between the blend and the base colors. Using white as the blend color produces no change. If Overlay mode doesn't produce an increase in contrast and saturation, Color Burn is usually a satisfactory alternative.

- Linear Burn decreases brightness like Color Burn, but instead of increasing contrast, it further decreases brightness, producing an effect closer to Multiply mode. Using white in a Linear Burn blend produces no visible change.

REPLACING LIGHTER COLORS WITH DARKER ONES *(Continued)*

6. Click the **Set Foreground** color swatch on the Tools panel. In the Color Picker, feel free to adjust the hue and saturation, but don't drag up or down in the color field, as this changes brightness. Just drag the target circle directly left or right, and change the **Hue** slider's indicator. Click **OK** when you're finished, and check out Figure 7-9 as a reference.

7. Stroke over the layer; you do not have to stroke very accurately to replace the lighter areas with the darker color, while preserving details in the darker foreground; in Figure 7-9: a scan of an autumn leaf.

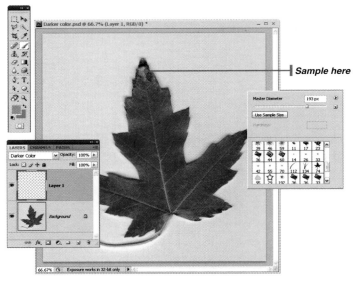

Sample here

Figure 7-9: *Keep your special effects work fresh and unique by choosing a novelty brush and interesting colors.*

Color Burn is quite useful in image retouching to put a tattoo on a model's forearm (or other anatomical area), to put makeup on a subject, and to put a logo on a textured product—all letting some of the base tonal values show through. In effect, you can paint into a photo instead of painting on to it. Figure 7-10 shows clown makeup applied to a clown's base white face color, using Color Burn and then Linear Burn. Notice the subtle yet distinct difference using the same layer colors: Color Burn retains more of the hue on a blend layer than Linear Burn. Where the clown makeup is decreased in saturation on the right of the layer, Linear Burn darkens more than it tints the clown's face. And yet the clown still looks happy.

Consider Color Dodge and Linear Dodge

Think of the opposite effect as Color Burn to better understand the Color Dodge blend modes. Dodging lightens areas and usually adds saturation; color dodging mixes a color into the overall recipe. Linear Dodge (Add) is useful for tinting the base layer while adding a little Screen function—lighter base layer areas become

QUICK**FACTS**

USING HARD LIGHT TO RETAIN BLEND COLORS

Hard Light mode is one of many variations on the result of putting a colored gel in front of a spotlight. Hard Light primarily uses the brightness of colors used on a blend layer or brush in this blend mode; if your blend color is brighter than 128 on the 0–255 scale Photoshop uses, Hard Light bleaches and tints the underlying layer(s)—when you use a color darker than 128, you'll get a Multiply, staining sort of effect.

Keep in mind that painting with pure black and white in Hard Light mode results in pure black or white.

Here's a good example of the difference between applying Screen mode and Hard Light in a composition: the sun illustration in Figure 7-11 is on top of a light cloud background, and like the kid's halo effect discussed earlier, yellow was Gaussian blurred to create some illumination behind the sun layer. In Screen mode, you can hardly see the yellow in the sunburst. However, in Hard Light mode, the sunburst layer is easy to read for color, and produces a much better effect.

TIP

If you want an effect close to but not exactly the same as Hard Light, use light colors and use Color Burn instead. The effect of these two blend modes is related.

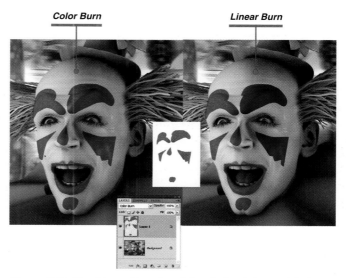

Figure 7-10: **Use Linear Burn for duller tinting jobs, and Color Burn for a more pronounced coloring effect.**

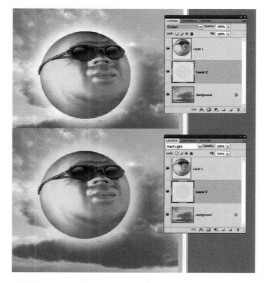

Figure 7-11: **Use Hard Light to emphasize and tint a color you need to add to your composition.**

washed out. Use the Dodge blend modes with deep saturated colors (such as R:15, G:0, B:126, an ultramarine color, good for sky areas) when you want to tint the base layer but *don't want to decrease the brightness* of any underlying layer area.

Know When to Use Overlay and Light Blend Modes

On the blend mode menu, the group of modes beginning with Overlay and ending with Hard Mix all produce different blend effects but are based on a similar idea—the Overlay and Light modes affect the base layer as though you're looking through colored gels or lenses.

Let's say you have an assignment where you're asked to bring out a little color, add a little contrast, and warm *parts* of the image *slightly*: this is not impossible, and it's not even difficult if you paint on a layer that's in Overlay blend mode:

1. Click **Create A New Layer** from the Layers panel to add a new layer to the document, and then choose **Overlay** from the modes drop-down list on the Layers panel.

2. Depending on the original brightness of the photo, use the **Eyedropper** tool and click the **Set Foreground** color swatch on the Tools panel, and then pick a medium bright, slightly warm color in the Color Picker. In Figure 7-12, Red: 95, Green: 92, Blue: 71 is chosen to add a little less blue to the paint color, to better warm up the underlying image.

3. Click the **Brush** tool and stroke over only the areas that need contrast and a little warmer, more intense colors. To back off the effect, drag the **Opacity** slider or scrubby slider (drag over the label "Opacity") to the left.

The other Light blend modes are of limited use in day-to-day assignments; they're of more use in creating special effects than in practical blend operations:

- **Soft Light**   Creates the effect of a soft spotlight, but the effect is faint even if you paint with pure white. If you want to direct the viewer to a specific image area, paint in Overlay mode instead.

- **Vivid Light**   Decreases contrast if the blend color you use is greater than 128 (out of 255), and increases contrast if the blend color is darker than 128. Hue and saturation are not used in determining the result colors, so feel free to experiment with these two properties when you use the Color Picker. You might find that Vivid Light is of limited use in photo retouching.

> **TIP**
>
> Remember, Overlay mode screens underlying areas whose pixel brightness is higher than 128 on the 0–255 scale, and multiplies pixel colors darker than 128. If you're not getting the effect you seek, try one of the other Light blend modes; or use a different brightness blend color.

Original   Overlay area   R:95, G:92, B:71

*Figure 7-12: **Use Overlay blend mode to emphasize color and contrast.***

- **Linear Light**   Similar to Vivid Light: using light blend colors increases the resulting brightness, while using dark blend colors decreases brightness. Linear Light is useful for simulating *Day for Night* photography—put medium blue on a Linear Light layer with a daytime photo beneath, and you'll get a very credible version of the same scene taken at midnight!

- **Pin Light**   A combination of Lighter Color and Darker Color blend modes. If the blend color is lighter than 128 on the 0–255 scale of brightness, underlying pixels darker than the blend color are replaced, while lighter pixels remain unchanged. But if you use a dark blend color, pixels on underlying layers that are lighter than the blend color are replaced, while the darker pixels do not change. It can be considered a "special effects" mode that you won't use often in day-to-day retouching.

- **Hard Mix**   Changes all underlying colors to primary and secondary colors, and includes pure black and white. It's quite useful for posterizing all or only part of an underlying image layer. Here you can see the same vintage auto composition, with 60% gray applied on a Hard Mix mode layer. When you add color to a Hard Mix layer, depending on the color, you can cycle the underlying image colors.

TIP

To preview a lot of different Hard Mix possibilities, use a medium gray, and then use the Hue/Saturation (**CTRL/ CMD+U**) Adjustment, then check Colorize to tint the gray. Then, before you click **OK**, drag the **Hue** slider to the left and right. In the document window, you can preview the variations you can achieve and decide on one before exiting the adjustment.

60% Gray

Explore the Difference Blend Mode

In the Difference blend mode, each color channel of the blend layer is mathematically subtracted from the color channel of the base layer's colors. The blend process looks at all the document's color channels; the blend color is then subtracted from the base or the base is subtracted from the blend layer—depending on which layer has the greater brightness at any given pixel.

This mode is not intuitive; however, you can produce very surreal imagery if you:

- Remember that Hue, the distinguishing property in a color, travels around the traditional color wheel starting at red (0 degrees) and increasing clockwise—yellow is at 90 degrees, add 180 to arrive at yellow's color opposite (blue) at 240 degrees, and continue until you arrive back at red at 360 degrees. The process is *difference*—delta, change—not exactly subtraction. So, for example, a base color of magenta (300 degrees) and a Difference blend color of green (120 degrees) results in a cyan-blue, a 180-degree difference in hue.

- Use Figure 7-13 as a cheat sheet. It provides many common Difference combinations and features a traditional color wheel. As you can see, the result color usually lies between the base and difference color around the wheel.

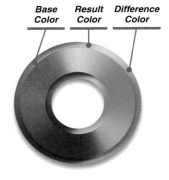

Base Color **Result Color** **Difference Color**

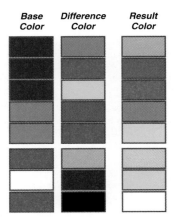

Base Color **Difference Color** **Result Color**

Figure 7-13: **Difference blend mode calculates the difference in hue between the layer in this mode and the layer(s) beneath it.**

TIP

If you own Photoshop CS4 *Extended*, you can easily make dramatic video clips by changing the position of the blend layer's contents or the base layer's visual content over time.

If the two colors are exactly the same, the result—your view of the composition—will be black, no difference. If the two colors are on exactly opposite sides of the color spectrum, the result will be white.

As shown in Figure 7-14, the glass of the blender is blue and the bananas outside of the glass area are completely unsaturated, color neutral, white in some areas. But where the bananas coincide with the blue glass, the result is yellow, the difference between white and blue.

*Figure 7-14: **Create dramatic changes using Difference blend mode and different base and blend colors.***

NOTE

In Figure 7-14, notice that the bottom layer's background is apparently unaffected by the Difference layer's color content. All underlying layers are affected by the top layer's blend mode; however, the background behind the blender's glass was selected and tinted a neutral color, so the audience doesn't see any effect. Read Chapter 5 to learn how to work with the contents of a selection you create.

QUICKFACTS

UNDERSTANDING EXCLUSION MODE

You can create an effect similar to Difference mode with Exclusion, which lowers the contrast of the affected layer(s), but still produces the psychedelic inversions of Difference mode. Blending with white inverts the base color values, and blending with black produces no change.

NOTE

Saturation is the presence of hue, so you cannot expect Hue blend mode to add color to areas that lack saturation.

Work with HSL Blend Modes

The remaining blend modes on the drop-down list on the Layers panel are terrific for performing significant edits to images, and they are quite straightforward. Hue, Color, and the other modes covered in the next sections only modify *one* color attribute based on the HSL color model—such as saturation. In contrast Color Burn or Overlay alter both saturation *plus* brightness, begging some guesswork on the user's part.

CREATING EFFECTS WITH HUE BLEND MODE

The Hue blend mode will do absolutely nothing to underlying layer image areas that have no Saturation, but has a great effect on areas with adequate saturation and medium brightness. Hue blend mode is therefore ineffective at hand-tinting grayscale images, but you can turn this to your advantage when you have a photo with a combination of saturated and dull image areas.

Figure 7-15: *Use Hue blend mode to replace saturated colors with different hues.*

The design possibilities for Hue blend mode are only limited to your imagination: you can change the color of leaves in a nature scene while leaving dull tree bark and rocks unchanged. You can also *remove* the saturation from image areas if you paint with white on the Hue blend layer:

1. Choose an image that has both unsaturated areas and colorful areas.
2. Click the **Create A New Layer** icon on the Layers panel to create a new layer on top of your original photo.
3. Choose **Hue** from the blend mode drop-down list on the Layers panel.
4. Click the **Gradient** tool on the Tools panel, then on the Options bar, click the **presets** pop-up arrow and click the **Spectrum** preset gradient. 
5. Click the **Radial Gradient** style button to the right of the presets pop-up, drag the cursor from the area in your photo where there is little saturation to an area of more colorful visual content, and then release the mouse button. If you're unhappy with the result, repeat this step: you don't have to erase your current layer or create a new one. When a gradient has no transparency in it, you overwrite the layer's pixels. Figure 7-15 shows a beautiful, dreamlike image as a result of using Hue blend mode in combination with an appropriate photograph.

NOTE

You don't have to use the Gradient tool to use Hue blend mode; it's just fun to do! Use the Brush tool, the Clone Stamp, or any other paint application tool you like to create changes via Hue blend mode.

COLOR BLEND MODE

Color blend mode is perhaps the best all-purpose feature for hand-tinting photographs; unlike Hue, Color mode tints every underlying image area, including areas that have no saturation. The only caveat with working with Color mode is that *the amount of saturation* you use when defining a color to use with this mode has an impact on how vivid the result color is. The other deciding factor is the brightness of any given pixel on the base layer: generally, a medium tone takes the Color mode the best—light areas can produce pastels (or no color at all) and, similarly, dark or black areas will not result in a colorized photo.

Here is a white on white composition; through careful lighting, there are a lot of shades of black in this image, which means most of the image can be manually colorized.

To colorize an image—that is, to add color to an image using the Color blend mode:

1. Click the **Create A New Layer** icon on the Layers panel to add a layer to your photo.

2. Choose **Color** from the Layers panel's blend mode drop-down list.

3. Click the **Set Foreground** color swatch on the Tools panel to display the Color Picker.

4. Choose a color, but do not fully saturate it. Somewhere between the left and right of the color field is a good choice for brightness and saturation. Choose an appropriate hue using the slider, then click **OK**.

5. Click the **Brush** tool on the Tools panel and set the size to scale with your photo using the controls on the Options bar (or right-click in the document window to choose a preset from the pop-up menu).

6. Paint away, changing hues from the Color Picker when appropriate. You can see the choice of green in Figure 7-16, and the result in the document window. It's brighter than one would expect; this is a function of both the brightness on the bottom layer's pixels and the choice of saturation for the color.

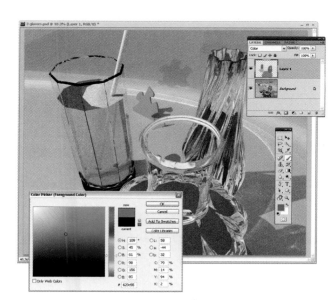

Figure 7-16: **Choose a duller color than you anticipate to keep the Color blend layer's output looking natural.**

CORRECT PHOTOS WITH SATURATION

Saturation blend mode produces results depending on the saturation value of the color you apply; it makes no difference what *hue* you apply, so you can, in practice, apply saturated green to a blue sky and the sky would remain blue.

When you apply a highly saturated color, you increase the native saturation of colors on the base layers; applying gray, black, and white removes the saturation from underlying image areas.

Here is a picture of a cookbook cover; the image was saved in CMYK mode and, as a result, the colors are duller than those that could be shown in monitor RGB mode.

To bring out the saturation in the image:

1. Add a new layer to the document by clicking the **Create A New Layer** button on the Layers panel.

2. Choose **Saturation** from the blend modes drop-down list on the Layers panel.

3. Click the **Set Foreground** color swatch on the Tools panel, and then drag the marker in the color field to the right, and then upward to increase the brightness of the color. Click **OK** to set the color and return to the composition.

4. Click the **Brush** tool on the Tools panel.

5. Stroke over the areas in which you want to increase the saturation.

6. Optionally, if you want to play down certain overly saturated areas, choose white in the Color Picker and then stroke over these areas.

USING LUMINOSITY MODE

The Luminosity blend mode is one of the few blend modes that is better used to paint with than to assign to a layer blend mode. This is because you will have more control and visual feedback. Luminance doesn't touch the hue or saturation of the underlying pixels; you use it to apply shading to a photo as you'd use the Dodge and Burn tools on the Tools panel.

One suggestion is to create several shades of black and save them to the Swatches panel so you can quickly choose different ones. Then paint using Luminosity mode, varying your foreground color via the Swatches panel, and you can quickly fix the tones in a photo.

As shown in Figure 7-17, the food on the cookbook cover looks a lot more appetizing; although some of the background was stroked over with white, it doesn't become white, but instead grayscale. Use this trick to make certain areas of a color image grayscale, imitating the special effect used in the classic motion picture *Pleasantville*!

Figure 7-17: **Use Saturation blend mode to increase or remove saturation.**

Use the Paint-Only Blend Modes

There are two modes reserved for painting; you won't find Behind or Clear on the Layers panel's drop-down list. They're good modes and here's how to use them.

Paint with Clear

Essentially, the Clear painting mode is an Eraser tool, with the advantage of being able to use it with any painting tool: the Clone Stamp, the Paint Bucket tool, and the Gradient tool can all be used to produce wild, interesting effects.

However, the more straightforward use of the Clear painting mode is to just use the Brush tool. You can vary a "buildup" of opacity on an image layer by stroking at partial opacity: set the Opacity for Brush tools on the Options bar.

Here you can see an eyesore in an otherwise beautiful image in the process of being removed.

To use Clear painting mode:

1. Double-click the background layer title on the Layers panel, and then click **OK** in the New Layer dialog box. The normal image is now a layer image, and Clear paint mode will now be available on the Options bar when a painting tool is chosen.

2. Choose a painting tool (the Clone Stamp, the Brush tool, or others) and a size for it from the Options bar, and then stroke over the area you want to make clear (delete).

   - If you overdid an area, press **CTRL/CMD+Z** to undo the step.
   - If you overdid the Clear painting a little, but want to retain a little transparency, press **CTRL/CMD+SHIFT+F** to fade the last editing move you made. Alternatively, use a low Opacity for the brush, such as 40%, and then repeatedly stroke over an area to gradually build up an area of transparency on the layer.

NOTE

Your current foreground color makes absolutely no difference when you paint in Clear mode.

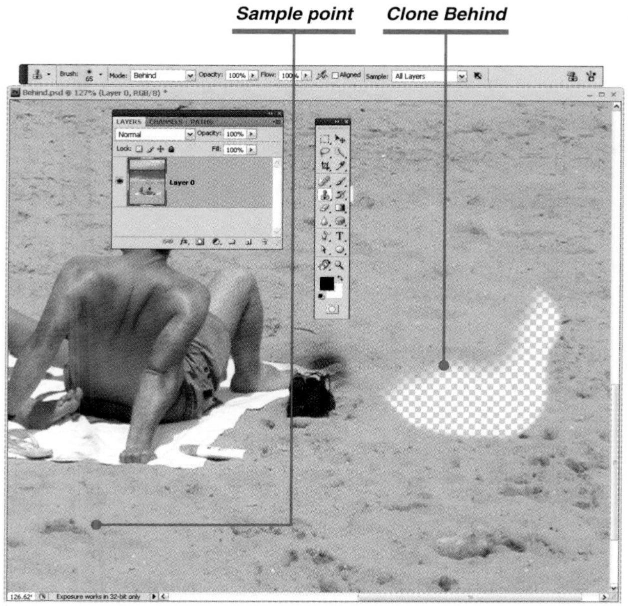

Figure 7-18: *Use Behind mode on a layer transparency to retain the original image pixels, and to add new opaque ones only to transparent areas.*

NOTE

When you're done with your mode blend work, you can make your layered image a normal one by right-clicking the bottom layer title and then clicking **Flatten Image**. The photo can now be saved to any file format, not just Photoshop's native PSD.

GET BEHIND YOUR WORK

Behind painting mode treats an image layer as though it is a two-sided sheet of acetate, and you're only painting on the back side. Use it when you need to replace an area on a layer you've erased (or painted in Clear mode), and you don't want to alter any surrounding pixels.

To paint behind a layer (using the Clone Stamp tool is the best use of Behind when photo restoring) you:

1. Choose a painting tool; in this example, choose the **Clone Stamp** tool from the Tools panel.

2. **ALT/OPT+**click an area of the image you want to use as a replacement for the current hole in your layered photo.

3. Choose a brush size from the Options bar and then choose **Behind** from the **Mode** drop-down list on the Options bar. For a scene such as that shown in Figure 7-18, it's best to uncheck the **Aligned** box on the Options bar before you begin. By doing this, every time you release the mouse button, the sample origin point snaps back to its first sampled position in the document, thus avoiding inadvertently sampling over something you don't want for cloning.

4. Stroke over the area you want to mend. It's fast and produces great, undetectable editing. However, this is Behind mode, so if you make a mistake, you can't paint over *your* error—it's *behind* mode. You need to be prepared to press **CTRL/CMD+Z**, or switch to Normal paint mode to finish your work.

Chapter 8

Making Local Adjustments with the Tools Panel

Photoshop contains several tools that you can use to directly change the color of the pixels in images. If you want to perform color editing using brush strokes, you can use the Brush tool. If you want to fill areas of an image, you can use the Gradient tool to add gradations to an image, or the Paint Bucket tool to create new colors and patterns within selections. Tools like the Eraser tool, Blur tool, Sharpen tool, and Smudge tool change image areas by erasing them, softening them, sharpening them, or smudging them, respectively. Along with the painting tools, Photoshop CS4 provides many presets for brush tips, gradients of color, color swatches, patterns, and more, so that your opportunities for varying your images are extraordinary. Plus you can create your own presets.

8

Work with Paint

Painting is how we change the color in images; it reassigns the color value of pixels in images. As you have seen in other chapters, by using tools such as the Brush, Pencil, Eraser, Gradient, Pattern, Smudge, Blur, Sharpen, and Stamp tools, you can repair images, create new images, and create masks to protect image areas as you edit images. If you have a digital stylus or are adept at drawing with a mouse, you can use the Photoshop brushes to paint inside a document and add artistic splashes of color. You can also create a stylized work of art by painting on a separate layer with an underlying image as a template. This chapter explores painting in detail.

Use the Brush Tool

You use brushes in Photoshop for many things: creating selections, specifying how a path guides a paint stroke, and so on. You also use the Brush tool to create an artistic daub of color in a document and to paint stylized strokes of color in a document. The foreground color is what is painted on the image. To use the Brush tool:

1. Click the **Set Foreground** color swatch on the Tools panel, and choose a color from the Color Picker.

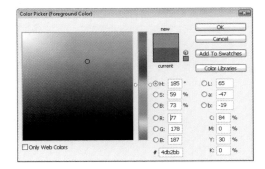

2. Select the **Brush** tool.

3. In the Options bar, click the down arrow to the right of the current brush tip to reveal the Brush Preset Picker, which gives you these options:

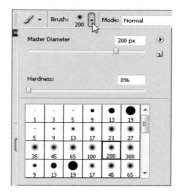

- Drag the **Master Diameter** slider to specify the size of the brush tip in pixels.
- Drag the **Hardness** slider to specify a value. Choose a low value for a soft-edged brush; choose a high value for a hard-edged brush.
- Drag the scroll bar to reveal thumbnail images of available brush types. The thumbnail represents the shape of the brush nib you stroke with. Click a brush tip thumbnail to replace the current tip.

4. In the Options bar, specify the **Mode**, **Opacity**, and **Flow** options for the brush. See the "Using Mode, Opacity, and Flow" QuickFacts.

5. Click the **Airbrush Capabilities** button to enable airbrush capabilities.

6. Drag inside the document to create the desired brush strokes.

CHANGE BRUSH TIP GROUPS

Photoshop supplies a library of preset brush tips you can use to create calligraphic brush strokes, watercolor brush strokes, and facsimiles of objects such as grass. The default brush group is powerful, but if you want more options, you need look no further than the Brush Options menu or the Preset Manager:

1. Select the **Brush** tool.

2. Click the down arrow to the right of the current brush tip to reveal the Brush Preset Picker.

TIP

Use the airbrush feature to "spray" paint over the area according to the Opacity and Flow options. The paint will build up—increase in opacity and spread outward—if you keep the cursor in one spot while holding the mouse button, just as a regular paint spray gun does.

TIP

You can restore the default foreground and background colors (black and white) by clicking the small icon to the left of the color swatches or by pressing **D**.

USING MODE, OPACITY, AND FLOW

When you choose a Brush tool, you have these options for refining the stroke of the brush:

| Mode: | Normal | ▼ | Opacity: | 100% | ▶ | Flow: | 84% | ▶ |

- **Mode** Establishes how the paint will blend with an image's pixels. Chapter 7 covers blend modes in detail. Normal is the default Mode setting.
- **Opacity** Sets the coverage of color you apply to an image or image layer; the higher the number, the more opaque the paint stroke will be. The default is 100%, which is completely opaque; 0% is completely transparent.
- **Flow** Measures how fast the paint will flow from the brush. Its effect is to build up a layer of paint as you press and hold the brush over an area, similar in effect to decreasing the Opacity for a brush. It will build the layer of paint up to the value of Opacity, unless you release the brush and apply it again over the same place. Then it will apply it again up to the value of the Opacity. The default Flow value is 100%.

TIP

Press **B** to select the Brush tool. Press **B** again to switch to the Pencil tool. Press **B** once more to switch to the Color Replacement tool, before finally pressing **B** to return to the Brush tool again.

3. Click the right-pointing arrow in the upper-right corner of the Brush Preset Picker, to display the Brush Options menu, and select a brush group as shown in Figure 8-1.

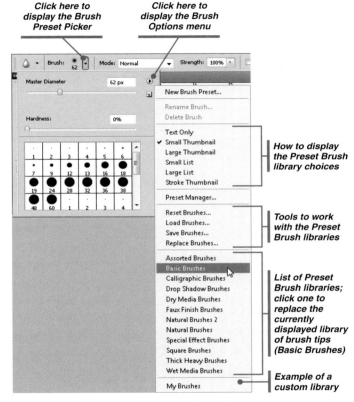

Figure 8-1: **In addition to the brush tip options you see on the main list, there are many other interesting groups that ship and install with Photoshop.**

See the Chapter 1 section "Change the Brush Tool Options" to learn some basics about changing brush tool options.

CREATE A CUSTOM BRUSH

If you like diversity, you can modify a brush preset. You can also create a brush from an image or from a portion of an image. After doing either, you can save the brush preset for future use. Here's the short overview of how to do it:

1. Open an image that contains an area you want to use for a brush preset.
2. Using one of the selection tools, select the area of the image you want to define as the brush tip. You can also select the entire image (press **CTRL/CMD+A**).
3. Click **Edit** and then click **Define Brush Preset** (you may need to click **Show All Menu Items** to see it). The Brush Name dialog box appears.

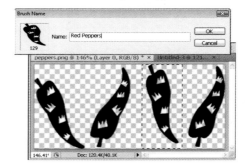

4. Type a name for the preset.
5. Click **OK** to add the preset to the Brushes panel using the selection area as the tip size.

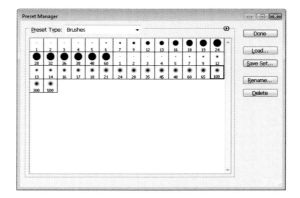

*Figure 8-2: **The Preset Manager is where you manage the contents of the preset libraries.***

TIP

From the Brushes panel you can rename brushes by double-clicking the brush thumbnail and typing a new name.

TIP

To change the size of a chosen brush tip using the keyboard, press the **RIGHT BRACKET** key ( ]) to increase the brush tip size; press the **LEFT BRACKET** key ([ ) to decrease the tip size. Hold down the applicable key until the brush is the desired size.

QUICKSTEPS

USING THE PRESET MANAGER

In Photoshop CS4 you can access several libraries of presets: Brushes, Swatches, Gradients, Styles, Patterns, Contours, Custom Shapes, and Tools. All of these libraries can be accessed and managed with the Preset Manager, shown in Figure 8-2. This chapter provides additional information on using individual preset libraries such as Brushes and Patterns, and subsequent chapters cover other preset libraries. Here is a quick overview of how to use this feature.

1. To display the Preset Manager, click **Edit | Preset Manager**.

Continued . . .

USING THE PRESET MANAGER

(Continued)

2. Click the **Preset Type** down arrow and click the library you want to use.

3. Click the **Options** right-pointing arrow for a pop-up menu. You have these options:

   • To change the size of the thumbnail, choose **Text Only, Small Thumbnail, Large Thumbnail, Small List** (which contains both a small thumbnail and the name of the preset), or **Large List**.

   • To restore the default presets, click **Reset Preset Type**. If you've created custom presets and have not saved them, *don't do this*—your unsaved presets will be deleted.

   • To replace the current pattern with a custom one, click **Replace *Preset Type***, select the preset file you want, and click **Load**.

4. Click the name of the preset library you want to work with. A dialog box will ask what you want to do. Click **OK** to replace the current pattern with the selected one. Click **Append** to add the selected pattern to the current one.

When you have selected the preset you want, you can manage the contents with these options:

   • **Load**   Adds a new preset to the active library. The preset must have been previously created and saved.

   • **Save Set**   Saves the selected preset in the default folder.

   • **Rename**   Changes the name of the selected preset.

   • **Delete**   Deletes the selected preset.

Work with Custom Brush Presets

Photoshop CS4 comes with many preset brush tips, which are arranged in libraries, as shown previously in Figure 8-1. Before you stroke with a brush in a document, you first select a brush tip. If you need to change Preset Brush libraries to get the exact brush tip you want for a brush stroke, you can easily do so. If you don't find the one you need, you can create your own, as described previously in "Create a Custom Brush." When you add several custom brushes to an existing library, you may find that the sheer number of presets makes finding a specific brush a difficult task. You can create a custom library just for your brushes.

CREATE A CUSTOM BRUSH LIBRARY

To create a new brush library for your own use:

1. Select any **Brush** tool. You can delete the brushes you don't want later.

2. In the Options bar, click the down arrow to the right of the current brush tip to reveal the Brush Preset Picker.

3. Click the right-pointing arrow in the upper-right corner to open the Options menu, and click **Save Brushes**. The Save dialog box appears.

4. In **Save In**, type a filename for the new brush library.

5. Click **Save**.

6. At this point, after saving an existing library under another name, delete all but one of the presets that are duplicates of the original library. You must retain at least one preset in a library.

7. Next add at least one of your own custom brushes or frequently used brushes, and then delete the last original remaining preset. If you have additional brushes for this library, add all that you want.

8. Save your custom library again.

Figure 8-3: **You create and display your own custom Preset Brush library with the Preset Manager or the Brush Options menu.**

DISPLAY A CUSTOM BRUSH LIBRARY

You can either add one custom library's brushes to the currently displayed library brushes or replace one library with another:

1. Select any **Brush** tool.

2. In the Options bar, click the down arrow to the right of the current brush tip to reveal the Brush Preset Picker.

3. Click the right-pointing arrow to open the Options menu.

   - To add to the currently displayed library, click **Load Brushes**.

   - To replace the currently displayed library, click **Replace Brushes**. The Load dialog box appears, as shown in Figure 8-3.

4. Select the brush library you want to display and click **Load** or **Replace**.

DELETE A BRUSH

1. Select a **Brush** tool.

2. Click the down arrow to the right of the current brush tip to reveal the Brush Preset Picker, and select the thumbnail of the brush you want to delete.

3. Click the right-pointing arrow in the upper-right corner to display the Brush Options menu, and click **Delete Brush**. The Delete Brush dialog box appears.

4. Click **OK** to delete the brush.

Erase Pixels

Because Photoshop is both an image editing program and a painting program, you have a selection of three Eraser tools:

- **Eraser tool**   Erases foreground pixel colors to the current background color swatch you have defined on the Tools panel, and to transparency when used on an image layer

- **Background Eraser tool**   Erases parts of a layer to transparency while preserving the edges of an object in the foreground

- **Magic Eraser tool**   Erases pixels similar in color to transparency

USING THE ERASER TOOL

What happens when you stroke with the Eraser tool depends on the type of layer you're working with. If a layer's transparency is locked, the pixels are changed to the background color; similarly, a typical photo that only has a background layer listed on the Layers panel is erased to the current background color swatch. If the layer is unlocked, the pixels are changed to be transparent. Figure 8-4 illustrates this.

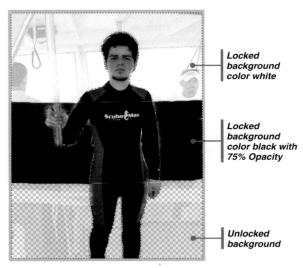

Locked background color white

Locked background color black with 75% Opacity

Unlocked background

Figure 8-4: *The Eraser tool changes the pixels of an image to the background color or to transparent.*

1. Select the **Eraser** tool.
2. In the Options bar, click the **Mode** down arrow, and click **Block** for rectangular or larger erasures, click **Brush** (the default mode) to perform erasures that require intricacy and an anti-aliased edge, or click **Pencil**, which offers shaped tips but aliased, hard edges, good for coarse area erasing. Block mode has no additional options.
3. Specify the brush size and tip if you've selected Brush or Pencil mode.
4. Specify the **Opacity** if you've selected Brush or Pencil mode.
5. Specify the **Flow** if you've selected Brush mode.
6. Drag inside the document to erase pixels.

NOTE

To undo edits instead of erasing the background of a document, click **Window | History**, set the point at which you want to erase to by clicking one of the boxes at left (don't click the title on the History Panel list; this changes the *document* history), check the **Erase To History** box on the Options bar, and then use the Eraser tool.

Figure 8-5: **The Background Eraser tool tests for color as it erases image pixels to transparent.**

USE THE BACKGROUND ERASER TOOL

The Background Eraser tool considers the color it is erasing and makes similar colors transparent. The locked status of the layer does not matter. In Figure 8-5, you can see that by choosing Contiguous, the integrity of the selection edges is maintained. The pixels are tested to see if the color matches that in the "hot spot" of the brush. If it does, the pixels are erased to transparent. So in this case, the dissimilar colors in the image are not affected. You can make them transparent by going over them again, as is seen in the left leg and arm of the background man in Figure 8-5.

1. Select the **Background Eraser** tool.

2. In the Options bar, click the down arrow to reveal the Background Eraser Settings dialog box. You have these options:

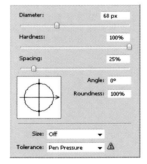

- Drag the **Diameter** slider for the size of the eraser.

- Drag the **Hardness** slider to set the sharpness of the edge of the eraser.

- Drag the **Spacing** slider to set how close together each application of the eraser will erase the image (whether there will be spaces between the erasures).

- Type in an **Angle** setting or drag in the thumbnail diagram to alter the angle of the eraser tip (this is only applicable when the Roundness is less than 100%).

- Type the **Roundness** setting for the percent of roundness that the eraser shape holds.

- If you're using a digital stylus, click the **Size** and **Tolerance** down arrows, and click **Pen Pressure** or **Stylus Wheel**, depending on the type of digital stylus you're using. Click **Off** if you're not using a digital stylus.

3. In the Options bar, shown in Figure 8-6, click the **Limits** down arrow to select any of the following options:

- **Discontiguous**   Erases pixels of the sampled color wherever they occur under the brush

- **Contiguous**   Erases pixels of the sampled color that are connected to each other

- **Find Edges**   Erases pixels of the sampled color that are connected to each other while preserving the integrity of edges

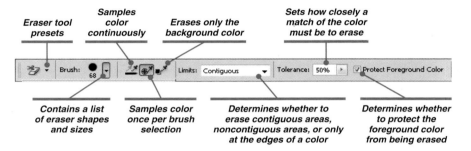

*Figure 8-6: **The Erase Background tool Options bar has options for sampling color; defining limits of the erasure, tolerance, or selection ability of the erasure; and whether to preserve the foreground color during the erasure.***

4. Type a value in the **Tolerance** text box. Specify a low value to erase areas similar to the sampled color; specify a high value to erase a broader range of colors.

5. Click the **Protect Foreground Color** check box to prevent the tool from erasing pixels of the foreground color.

6. In the Options bar, choose one of the following options:

- **Once**   Erases only areas of the sampled color that you first click

- **Continuous**   Samples colors under the Eraser tool continuously as you drag the tool across the document

- **Background Swatch**   Erases only pixels of the current background color

7. Drag the tool across the area you want to erase.

USE THE MAGIC ERASER TOOL

The Magic Eraser tool erases pixels based on color. If the layer is locked for transparency, the background color is used to erase. If transparency is unlocked, pixels are made transparent.

TIP

To prevent erasing an area such as a silhouette of a building or a line of trees, click the **Set Foreground** color swatch, and use the **Eyedropper** tool to sample the color you want to protect. Click the **Protect Foreground Color** check box for the Background Eraser tool prior to dragging the tool along the border of the area you want to preserve.

1. Select the **Magic Eraser** tool.

2. In the Options bar, shown in Figure 8-7, you have these choices:

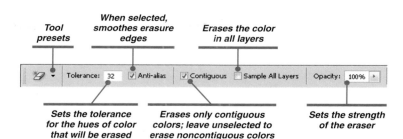

Tool presets

When selected, smoothes erasure edges

Erases the color in all layers

Sets the tolerance for the hues of color that will be erased

Erases only contiguous colors; leave unselected to erase noncontiguous colors

Sets the strength of the eraser

*Figure 8-7: **The Magic Eraser tool Options bar allows you to refine the tool when selecting what will be erased.***

- Type a value in the **Tolerance** text box. Specify a low tolerance to erase pixels similar in color to the first pixels you click with the tool; specify a high tolerance to erase a wider range of colors.

- Click the **Anti-Alias** check box (selected by default), and Photoshop smoothes the edges of areas you erase.

- Click the **Contiguous** check box (selected by default) to erase only areas of contiguous pixels (pixels that directly neighbor one another) containing the sampled color. Deselect the option to erase all areas of pixels of similar color to the pixel you click over.

- Click the **Sample All Layers** check box to erase similar colors on all visible layers in the document.

- Type a value in the **Opacity** field. The default value of 100% erases pixels completely. Specify a lower value to partially erase pixels.

3. Drag the tool over the area you want to erase.

TIP

When using the Magic Eraser tool, in addition to dragging, you can just click on the background image to create a layer out of the background layer. The pixels corresponding to the Options setting are automatically erased.

Use Other Adjustment Tools

In addition to painting tools, Photoshop CS4 provides several other tools for modifying images. You can adjust areas of an image or edges with Sharpen, Blur and Smudge tools, use the Gradient or Paint Bucket tools to create or replace color, and use the Dodge, Burn, and Sponge tools to adjust light or saturation.

FINE-TUNING WITH THE SHARPEN, BLUR, AND SMUDGE TOOLS

When you edit an image, you often want to touch up small areas. For example, you can bring out an edge of an object that's slightly blurred with the Sharpen tool. You can also smudge or blur an area that you want to de-emphasize. Since these tools use the same brush tips as the painting tools to change image areas, you have available controls such as opacity of the brush, brush size, mode, strength, and so on.

1. Select the **Sharpen**, **Blur**, or **Smudge** tool from the Tools panel:

- Click **Sharpen** to increase contrast between dissimilarly colored pixels in an area, making the edges sharper.
- Click **Blur** to soften or blur the area stroked.
- Click **Smudge** to drag color from one area to another (much like smearing wet paint) as you stroke, evening out blemishes.

2. In the Options bar, specify the values in the **Brush Size**, **Brush Tip**, **Mode**, and **Strength** fields.

3. Drag the tool over the area you want to touch up.

TIP

When you use the Smudge tool, it normally uses the color beneath the brush tip where you make your initial click point to smudge. If you click the Finger Painting option, the foreground color will be used to smudge.

You will also see how to create patterns from images or select Pattern Presets from a library, to create stylized art from images using the Art History Brush, and crop images.

Remove Fringe Pixels

When you copy the contents of an anti-aliased selection to a new layer or document, a fringe or halo of the original background color is often retained. The Defringe command replaces the color of edge pixels with the color of pixels inside the selection (or inside the edge of nontransparent pixels on a layer). To remove a fringe:

1. Click **Layer | Matting | Defringe**. The Defringe dialog box appears.

2. Type the width in pixels of the colored halo to be replaced. For a photo that's approximately 2500 pixels on a side, usually 1-pixel width will do the trick, 3 pixels at most.

3. Click **OK**. The colored halo disappears.

If the Defringe command replaces the color of too many or too few pixels, press **CTRL/CMD+Z** to undo the Defringe command and try again, this time specifying a different width.

Use the Gradient Tool

Use the Gradient tool to apply a blend of two or more colors to a background layer or to a selection. Figure 8-8 shows an example of a gradient fill. You can select a gradient preset or create a custom gradient.

APPLY A GRADIENT FILL

To apply the gradient, you select the pattern and then drag the pointer across the area you want to fill:

*Figure 8-8: **A gradient fill can create interesting effects.***

1. Select the layer to which you want to apply the gradient fill. You can also use one of the selection tools to select the area to which you want to apply the fill.

2. Select the **Gradient** tool.

3. In the Options bar, shown in Figure 8-9, click the **Gradient Picker** down (menu) arrow, and select one of the presets.

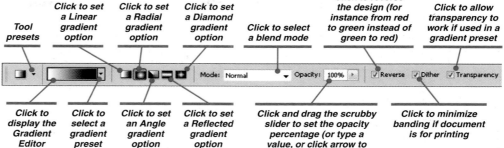

Figure 8-9: **The Gradient Options bar displays ways to vary the effects of a gradient fill.**

4. In the Options bar, click the appropriate options to select one of the following gradient types:

- **Linear**   Creates a fill that blends colors in a straight line from the starting point
- **Radial**   Creates a circular fill that radiates from the starting point outward
- **Angle**   Creates an angular fill in a counterclockwise direction from the starting point
- **Reflected**   Creates symmetrical linear fills on either side of the starting point
- **Diamond**   Creates a diamond-shaped fill that radiates from the starting point outward

5. Specify a blend **Mode** and **Opacity**.

6. Click the **Reverse** check box to reverse the order in which the gradient colors are applied.

7. Click the **Dither** check box to create a smoother blend of colors without distinct bands.

8. If the preset gradient you chose contains transparency, click the **Transparency** check box to include the transparency on a layer when you use the Gradient tool. With Transparency unchecked, all areas of the layer (or selection) are filled with the gradient pattern; transparent areas are filled with the closest nontransparent color in the gradient blend.

9. Click inside the document where you want the gradient fill to start, and then drag to create the fill.

NOTE

To select a different library of Gradient presets, click the Gradient Picker for the Gradient Editor dialog box. Then click the right-pointing arrow for the Options menu located in the upper right of the Presets thumbnail display box. On the lower half of the menu are the Preset library names.

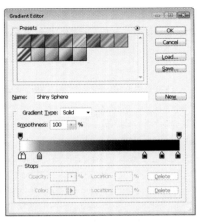

Figure 8-10: *The Gradient Editor is used to modify and customize gradient-fill presets.*

EDIT A GRADIENT

You can alter the presets or create a custom preset by saving it under a new name:

1. Select the **Gradient** tool and select a gradient, as outlined previously.

2. Click the **Gradient Picker** (second button from the left, as shown in Figure 8-9) in the Options bar to open the Gradient Editor dialog box, shown in Figure 8-10.

3. Click a Presets thumbnail to set the values for the color bar.

4. Click **New** and name the preset so that you duplicate, and don't overwrite, the existing preset you chose.

5. Click the **Gradient Type** down arrow, and click either **Solid** or **Noise** (which creates scores of color bands, not individually editable, but visually interesting). If you choose Noise, new options appear.

6. If you choose a gradient type of **Solid**, drag the sliders on the color bar above the Stops area:

   - Drag the **top** sliders (*pins*) to move the opacity stops. As you drag the stops, you determine where the opacity appears in the gradient. To add another opacity stop to the color bar, click the top edge of the color bar; the pointer will change from an eyedropper to a hand, indicating the point at which you click to add the stop. As you select or move the opacity sliders above the color bar, the opacity stops beneath it become available. All new stops you add default to the opacity of a stop you've previously clicked on.

   - To duplicate an opacity stop, press **ALT/OPT** and drag. You can drag the duplicate through other opacity stops when you reposition the duplicate.

   - Vary the opacity for a selected stop by clicking the stop, clicking the **Opacity** down arrow, and then dragging the slider to the percentage you want. To delete an opacity stop, select the stop and click **Delete**. Alternatively, you can drag a stop away from the color bar and it disappears.

   - Drag the **bottom** sliders to move the color stops. As you drag the stops, you determine where the color appears in the gradient. To add another color stop to the color bar, click the bottom edge of the color bar (the pointer will morph from an eyedropper to a hand, indicating you can insert a stop) where you want the stop inserted. Beneath the color bar, the color stops become available when you move or select a color stop.

   - Color stops have similar behavior to opacity stops: press **ALT/OPT** and drag to duplicate an existing one. Deleting stops can be accomplished by dragging the stop away from the color bar.

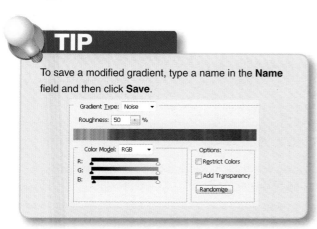

To save a modified gradient, type a name in the **Name** field and then click **Save**.

- Vary the color for a selected stop by clicking the stop, clicking the **Color** down arrow, and clicking **Foreground**, **Background**, or **User Color**. To delete a color stop, select the stop and click **Delete**.

7. If you have chosen a gradient type of Noise:

- Click the **Roughness** down arrow, and drag the slider to set the amount of random color bands you want.

- Click the **Color Model** down arrow, and click **RGB, HSB,** or **LAB**. Beneath the color model, three smaller color bars appear:

- Drag the sliders on the color bars to determine where the color or opacity stops appear in the gradient. For example, you can limit a noise gradient type to grayscale by choosing LAB as the color model and then dragging the sliders for both the A and B channels to the center of their color bars. The narrower the range you determine with the sliders, the less of the color component is featured in your custom gradient. Dragging a slider skews that amount of color component to become less predominant in the final gradient. Dragging the L color channel slider's white slider to the left, for example, favors darker tones in the final gradient—white is moving toward black in the mix.

- Click the **Restrict Colors** check box to decrease the number of colors in a noise gradient.

- Click the **Add Transparency** check box to add random bands of transparency to the gradient. You have no options for determining precisely where the transparent regions are generated.

- Click **Randomize** to display a random version of the noise-based gradient. If one is generated that looks appealing, save it. Chances are good you'll never rediscover a random setting!

8. Click **OK** to apply the changes.

Use the Paint Bucket Tool

Use the Paint Bucket tool to replace areas of color with a different color. You can determine the extent of the color replacement by specifying a Tolerance value:

1. Click the **Set Foreground** color swatch and select a color from the Color Picker.

2. Select the **Paint Bucket** tool.

QUICKSTEPS

USING THE DODGE, BURN, AND SPONGE TOOLS

There are times when you want to lighten or darken areas without affecting the whole image. You can use the Dodge tool to lighten an area, or the Burn tool to darken it. The Sponge tool increases or decreases the saturation of an image. (See Chapter 7 for how to use the Color Dodge and Color Burn effects using layer blend modes.)

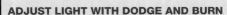

ADJUST LIGHT WITH DODGE AND BURN

1. Select the **Dodge** or **Burn** tool from the Tools panel:

    • Click **Dodge** to lighten an image area.

    • Click **Burn** to darken an image area.

2. In the Options bar, you have these choices:

    • Specify the shape, hardness, and diameter of the tip by clicking the **Brush Preset Picker** down arrow. Choose a preset and then modify its size and hardness using the sliders or the number fields.

Continued . . .

3. In the Options bar, click the **Set Source For Fill Area** down arrow, and click **Foreground** to fill the tool with the foreground color; or you can click **Pattern**. If you click Pattern, the Pattern field becomes available. Click the down arrow to the right of the current pattern preview, and select a preset.

4. Click the **Mode** down arrow to choose a blend mode, and click the **Opacity** down arrow to set the opacity for the Paint Bucket tool.

5. Type a value in the **Tolerance** text box. This value determines how closely pixels must match the color of the pixel you initially click over before an area is filled. You can specify a value between 0 and 255. Type a low value to fill pixels that are similar in color; type a high value to fill pixels with a wider color range.

6. Leave the **Anti-Alias** check box selected to ensure smooth blending of adjacent pixels.

7. Leave the **Contiguous** check box selected to fill contiguous pixels of similar color. Deselect the option to fill all similar pixels within the image.

8. Click the **All Layers** check box to apply the fill to pixels of similar color in all layers.

9. Click inside the area you want to fill.

Create and Manage Patterns

You can create patterns by sampling an area from within an image. After creating a pattern, you can apply it as a fill using the Paint Bucket tool, as a new pattern-filled layer via **Layer | New Fill Layer | Pattern**, with the Pattern Stamp tool, or by clicking **Edit | Fill | Pattern**.

CREATE A PATTERN

1. Open the desired image.

2. Select the **Rectangular Marquee** tool, and select the pixels you want to use as the basis for your pattern. Generally, if your sample contains little distinct detail but instead is diffuse, like the rhododendron shown in Figure 8-11, the pattern is much less likely to visibly repeat.

3. Click **Edit Define Pattern**. The Pattern Name dialog box is displayed.

4. Type the name you want for the pattern and click **OK**.

USING THE DODGE, BURN, AND SPONGE TOOLS (Continued)

- Click the **Range** down arrow and select **Midtones** to alter the middle tones, **Shadows** to alter the dark pixels, or **Highlights** to alter the light pixels of an area.

- Click the **Exposure** down arrow and drag the slider to the percentage of what's best described as "intensity" of Dodge and Burn.

- Click the **Airbrush** tool to enable the ability to concentrate the effects by holding without dragging the cursor.

- Select the **Protect Tones** check box to maintain the level of saturation in areas you dodge or burn. Without this option checked, it's quite easy to increase saturation to an unrealistic (and unappealing) degree when you use the Toning tools. Pixel brightness is usually irrevocably tied to pixel color.

3. Drag the tool over the area you want to touch up.

ADJUST SATURATION WITH THE SPONGE

1. Select the **Sponge** tool from the Tools panel.

2. In the Options bar, click the **Mode** down arrow:

- Click **Saturate** to increase the distinct hue in areas you stroke over.

- Click **Desaturate** to reduce distinct hues. If you scrub over an area several times with the Sponge tool, eventually you'll get grayscale image areas.

Continued . . .

Figure 8-11: **Create a pattern to add to your pattern library.**

5. The pattern will be added to the current active pattern library. If you click the Pattern presets, you'll see the new pattern appended to the bottom of the list.

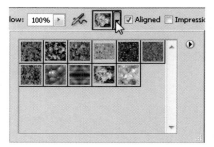

USE THE PATTERN PRESET MANAGER

You can find and manage your patterns using the Preset Manager. You manage your pattern libraries from the Pattern Preset Picker panel. To load a library of patterns:

1. Click the **Pattern** tool, and then on the Options bar, click the **Pattern Preset Picker** down arrow. The currently selected presets are displayed.

2. Click the **Options** menu right-pointing arrow and click **Preset Manager**.

3. Follow the guidelines in the "Using the Preset Manager" QuickSteps earlier in this chapter.

USING THE DODGE, BURN, AND SPONGE TOOLS *(Continued)*

3. In the Options bar, click **Flow** to control how fast the Sponge tool decreases or increases saturation.

4. In the Options bar, specify the values in the **Brush Size**, **Brush Tip**, and **Strength** fields.

5. Drag the tool over the area you want to touch up.

Original

Find the image state in the History panel that you want to paint

Click the Set Source For The History Brush

*Figure 8-12: **The original image with and without a filter before the Art History Brush is applied.***

Use the Art History Brush

The Art History Brush, as its name suggests, makes somewhat stylized artwork out of photographs, based on a state (a point in time) you find on the History panel. The Art History Brush examines the colors and general geometry of the scene as it existed at a point on the History panel, and then randomizes the original colors, using geometric variations you set using the Style presets on the Options bar drop-down list. Further randomization and modification is achieved through the Painting Area slider, which determines the size and number of individual strokes the brush applies, Tolerance slider, which when set at 0 enables you to modify the entire image, while setting it at a higher value increases the tolerance so that some strokes may not result in a change, and the Opacity and blending Mode. To get the best artistic effect using this brush, use the following points as recommendations:

- Apply a filter to your original image, ideally one that creates a lot of pleasing color changes in your photo. Because the Art History Brush doesn't change original colors, the filter can add a dramatic modification to the original. Bas Relief, Water Paper, and even Image | Adjustments | Gradient Map can prep your work well for the Art History Brush, as shown in Figure 8-12.

- Choose a tip for the Art History Brush that has some texture, and possibly some Jitter in it. The Chalk 44 Pixels tip in the default collection of Brushes can serve you well; you add texture as you add abstraction.

- Set the History panel (click **Window | History**) to an early point in the changes you make by clicking the box to the left of the state's title. You can use the original image, or a state between multiple filter applications.

- Work a little with one style; then change styles as a specific area calls for it. Use your artistic eye. The Tight Long style actually works well in Figure 8-13; a combination of the right filters, the right History state, and not overdoing it can result in an eye-pleasing variation on your photographic work.

Figure 8-13: *You can create stylized artwork by painting inside an image with the Art History Brush.*

Crop a Photo with the Crop Tool

Use the Crop tool to trim an image to the desired size. You can make a freehand selection, or you can specify the resolution and size of the area to which the tool will crop.

1. Open the image you want to crop and click the **Crop** tool.

2. Drag diagonally inside the image to define the size of the cropped image. Photoshop displays a cropping rectangle inside the image. Eight sizing handles appear on the perimeter of the rectangle, as shown in Figure 8-14.

Figure 8-14: *Adjust the cropping rectangle to the desired size.*

3. If the cropping rectangle is not sized as desired, do one of the following:

   ● Drag a corner handle to resize the width and height of the cropping rectangle. Press **SHIFT** to resize proportionately.

   ● Drag the middle handle on the left or right border to change the width of the cropping rectangle.

   ● Drag the center handle on the top or bottom border to change the height of the cropping rectangle.

   ● Drag inside the cropping rectangle to move it to a different position.

   ● Drag outside the cropping rectangle to rotate it in a free-form manner.

4. Press **ENTER** or click the **Commit** button on the Options bar to crop the image.

Create Vector-Shaped Shapes

You can use the Shape tools to add vector-based shapes to a document. Shapes act as masks for pixels on a layer, which can be modified when converted to vector paths. You also have the option not to draw vector shapes on layers at all, but instead to draw shapes as paths and also as an ordinary collection of pixels—you click one of the option buttons for shape creation at the left of the Options bar when the Shape tool is selected.

Use the Shape Tools

You have six Shape tools from which to choose: Rectangle, Rounded Rectangle, Ellipse, Polygon, Line, and Custom Shape. You specify the settings for each tool in the Options bar (see Figure 8-15). For example, when you create a shape using the Rounded Rectangle tool, you can specify the radius of the rectangle's corners. When you select the Custom Shape tool, you can select a preset shape.

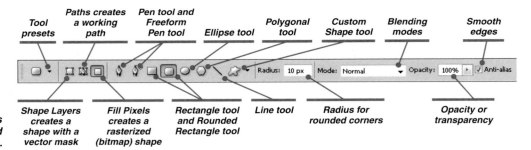

Figure 8-15: The Shape and Pen tools Options bar has features for customizing the way you add predefined geometry to a composition.

Here is how you use the Shape tools:

1. Select one of the **Shape** tools.
2. In the Options bar, click one of the following buttons to define the type of shape:
   - **Shape Layers**   Creates a shape on its own layer. You can create shape layers with Shape tools or Pen tools. Shape layers are often used for creating graphics. If you look at a selected shape layer in the Paths panel, you'll find that it contains both a fill layer with the shape color and a linked vector mask defining the shape path.

TIP

When you use a Shape tool, hold down the **SHIFT** key while dragging to create a rectangle or polygon of equal width and height or to create a circle.

QUICKSTEPS

CONVERTING PATHS

You can create an intricate path with the Pen tool and then convert it to a selection. Trace the shape you want to select, and then convert it to a path:

1. Select the **Pen** tool from the Tools panel, and click it around the shape you want to select, creating a path.

2. Click **Window** and then click **Paths**. The Paths panel is displayed.

3. Click the **Options** button in the upper-right area of the Paths panel, and click **Make Selection**.

4. In the Make Selection dialog box, select these options:

   - Create a feathered effect by entering the **Feather Radius** in pixels.

   - Click **Anti-Alias** to smooth the selection edges.

   - Click **New Selection** to create a new selection; click **Add To Selection** to add to an existing selection; click **Subtract From Selection** to decrease an existing selection by this new one being defined; or click **Intersect With Selection** to create one selection with the intersecting points on the new selection being defined.

5. Click **OK**.

- **Paths**   Creates a working path that can be used to make a selection, create a vector mask, or fill or stroke the path with a color or a gradient. You can create raster graphics with paths, and you can save them.

- **Fill Pixels**   Creates a rasterized (bitmap) shape. The shape is not vector-based, but as you paint, the pixels in the image are changed.

3. If you have selected the Fill Pixels option, specify the **Mode**, **Opacity**, and **Anti-Alias** options for the shape you are about to create. The Anti-Alias option prevents jagged edges at the border of the shape.

4. Specify other options for the shape you have selected—they vary.

5. Click the down arrow on the Options bar next to the Custom Shape tool icon to reveal a menu that enables you to specify geometry options for the tool. Here you can see the options for the Rounded Rectangle tool. Note that you can specify the exact size of the shape.

6. Drag diagonally inside the document to create the shape. If you've specified the size of the shape, click inside the document.

Edit Shapes

If you create a shape using the Shape Layers or Paths option, you can edit the shape by adding, converting, moving, or deleting points, as outlined in Chapter 5:

1. Select the **Direct Selection** tool.

2. Select the shape you want to edit to reveal the points used to create the shape.

3. Select the applicable tool to edit the points as needed.

When a path is selected with the Path Selection tool or Direct Selection tool, all anchor points are displayed.

Chapter 9

Restoring and Repairing Images

For a lot of us, Photoshop and digital photography came a little too late for us to archive everlasting digital photos of our parents, grandparents, and other loved ones. Fortunately, if you still have a snapshot and read Chapter 2 on scanning (and have access to a scanner), you not only can archive your heirloom photos, but also make significant improvements to their appearance. This chapter shows you how.

Repair a Photograph

Figure 9-1 shows a good example of a bad image. In addition to the poor scan, which includes dust and a crooked baseline, the original photo suffers from flash photography fall-off and soft focus, and the years haven't improved the photo either. If you have a similar photograph, the following sections take you step by step through the Photoshop remedies that will cure this valuable heirloom image.

QUICK**FACTS**

PREPARING VINTAGE PICTURES FOR SCANNING

Although you probably know how to use your scanner, there are a few things to consider *before* you scan your one-and-only 1928 photo of your grandmother:

- Without ruining them, try to clean your precious photos as thoroughly as possible. The less garbage on a photo, the more detail is revealed for scanning, and the less work is required to restore the photo. Take the photos out of glassine holders; don't scan through a surface but instead scan the photo itself. Additionally, remove any photo corners—anything that increases the height of the photo will prevent the lid of the scanner from closing completely, letting light leak into your scan. A scanner is a camera in many ways; remember what happened to a roll of film in your old camera when you didn't close the back completely?

- To wipe photographs (don't use fluids of any kind that might melt the photo emulsion), buy a pack of lens-wipe cloths from the photo supply store. Specially treated cloths have antistatic properties, helping to remove lint and dust, and these cloths are made of long-fiber fabric, the type that doesn't leave fibers as you clean.

- Clean the *platen*—the glass plate above the scanning mechanics that you rest the photos on. Use a long-fiber cloth; *don't* use paper towels, which are short fiber and shed all over anything you wipe. It's up to you whether to use glass cleaner. Typically, the platen doesn't have a special coating, but if you use window cleaner, make sure you don't leave streaks, and that the platen is completely dry before scanning.

Continued . . .

Figure 9-1: *The photo is aged, it was taken with a cheap camera, and the scan was performed ineptly.*

Labels on figure: Scratches · Dust · Flash fall-off · Sepia aging · Baseline is crooked

Straighten a Scanned Photo

Although it's best to get a scan straight in the scanner, a slight crookedness can happen sometimes. To straighten a crooked photo:

1. With the image open in the workspace, click the **Layers** panel on the docking strip to open it.

2. Double-click the layer thumbnail. The New Layer dialog box opens, shown in Figure 9-2, asking you to name the new layer; accept the default name and click **OK**. You'll notice that the layer titled "Background" is now renamed and it no longer has a locked icon on it. This means it can be rotated now.

3. Press **CTRL/CMD+R** to display the rules, and then drag a guide out of the top ruler to the top edge of the photo, and then drag a guide from the left ruler so that it meets at the upper-left corner of the photo. You'll want to zoom into the corner before you add

PREPARING VINTAGE PICTURES FOR SCANNING *(Continued)*

- Get an inexpensive measuring triangle (try the stationery department at the supermarket) to ensure that the photo you place on the platen is parallel to the platen. This isn't always possible if one of your ancestors got creative and trimmed the photo with a fancy border, but if it's just a rectangular photo, try to ensure that it's at a perfect 90° angle to the platen. Photoshop can rotate a photo, but rotation changes the original pixels in the picture and inevitably degrades image quality.

- If your scanner supports it, scan at 48 bits instead of the usual 8. The more scanned visual information you have, the easier it will be to precisely restore the photo. Also, scan at a high resolution such as 600 pixels/inch. If the result is a 25MB file, that is completely okay; restoring vintage photos is time consuming and should be done only once, on a high-resolution copy.

*Figure 9-2: **Turn a normal photo into a layer document to gain access to more of Photoshop's editing features.***

the guides; you can use your mouse scroll wheel to zoom—push the wheel toward your screen and away from yourself to zoom in.

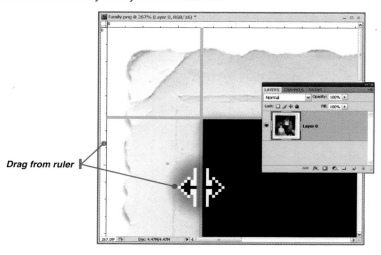

Drag from ruler

4. Press **CTRL/CMD+T** to put the layer photo into Free Transform mode and then drag the center of rotation icon in the center of the bounding box to the point where your guides meet.

5. Hover over a corner bounding box handle until it turns into a bent-arrow cursor and then drag until the bottom of the photo is aligned with the guide, as shown in Figure 9-3. Then either click **Commit Transform** (the check icon on the Options bar) or press **ENTER** to finalize the rotation.

Figure 9-3: *Rotating an image to de-skew it is a simple Photoshop feat.*

Crop Away Superfluous Photo Areas

Cropping a photo is simple: click the **Rectangular Marquee** tool, drag a selection, and then click **Image | Crop**. However, judging where to crop, what remains, and what you crop away is an artistic call. Remember: the more excess you trim from your work, the less retouching you'll need to perform. This means, for example, a distracting painting on the wall, a lamp, and even a family member who is partially out of frame and as such unrecognizable.

Here's a creative decision you might need to make; the little girl on mom's lap is partially out of frame. However, the picture (not the family itself) would benefit if the girl was cropped out:

1. Click the **Rectangular Marquee** tool and drag an area that includes what you want shown in the finished photo. If necessary, to reposition the marquee, drag inside the marquee. Pull guides from the rulers if you want to previsualize the crop.

2. Click **Image | Crop**.

3. Click **File | Save As**, and then save the image to a folder using a name other than the original. Choose PSD as the file format.

Restore a Photograph

Now that the scan itself looks better, it's time to concentrate on improving the visual content of the scan, the photograph. The following sections walk you through various features in Photoshop used to enhance what your family remembers in the photo, but can't see due to hidden and missing image details.

Improve Image Focus

Although it's impossible to command a software application to put something into a photo that wasn't originally there, you can "enhance" focus in a photo using any of the Filter | Sharpen commands. In particular, Smart Sharpen is useful on scans of older images, to allow you to better see the dust and scratches that need to be removed:

1. Click **Filter | Sharpen | Smart Sharpen**.

   ● Use the zoom in button (+) below the preview area to zoom to an area where you can best evaluate the amount of edge detail you want to apply.

   ● To sharpen edges, drag the **Amount** slider to the right. Usually, the default amount of 100% will serve you well. If you begin to see harshness where there should be smooth skin tones, drag the slider left.

   ● To make the filter search pixels neighboring an edge to emphasize edges, drag the **Radius** slider to the right. Typically with large photos, an amount of 1–3 pixels will do; high amounts can actually result in less-visible edge sharpening. To compare the proposed sharpening to the original, click-hold your cursor (a hand cursor) in the preview area—this shows the original. Release the mouse button to return to the Smart Sharpen preview.

   ● Choose the defect that best fits your image from the **Remove** drop-down list. Gaussian is the default, but Lens Blur may work better on vintage snapshots taken with a relatively inexpensive camera lens.

   ● Click the **More Accurate** check box.

2. Click **OK** to apply the Smart Sharpen filter.

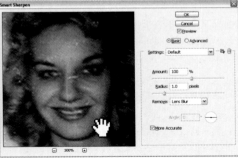

Figure 9-4: Use Smart Sharpen to bring out detail that the camera might not have adequately captured.

As you can see in Figure 9-4, the Smart Sharpen filter reveals a lot more image detail than the original at left.

Remove Dust and Scratches

There are two techniques for reducing—and even occasionally removing—dust acquired from the scanner and the photo, as well as scratches; the Dust & Scratches filter can be used when you have dozens of images to fix, while a manual approach lies with the Healing Brushes on the Tools panel.

USE THE DUST & SCRATCHES FILTER

The Filter | Noise | Dust & Scratches filter is very potent and works its magic by seeking out pixels whose color value is exceedingly off the norm of its neighboring pixels. Here's how to use this filter:

1. Click **Filter | Noise | Dust & Scratches**.

2. Click the zoom in button (**+**) below the preview image and then drag in the image until you can see an area that can show the filter's results.

3. Drag the **Radius** slider, which the filter uses to compare any given pixel to its neighbor, resulting in smoother transitions of the corrected pixels. Try starting with 1 or 2 pixels; you can use a fractional amount such as 1.3 pixels for images that are large in resolution, because occasionally a fractional amount gives you exactly the filtering you need.

4. Drag the **Threshold** slider to specify how many brightness levels (0–255) in the image are affected by the filtering. At high Threshold levels, the Dust & Scratches filter decreases the overall effect—for example, a value of 255 produces no filter effect.

5. Click **OK** to apply the filter.

 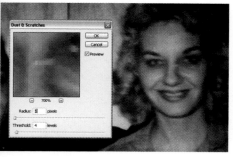

Figure 9-5 shows a close-up of the family photo at left and the result of the Dust & Scratches filter at right. Clearly, this filter is not a panacea for all images; the focus that was gained by Smart Sharpen is lost due to the Dust & Scratches filter. The solution for this and many other photos is the manual approach, covered in the next section.

*Figure 9-5: **The Dust & Scratches filter smoothes images, so its best use is on photos with good, crisp focus to begin with.***

WORK WITH THE HEALING BRUSHES

The Healing Brushes perform a lot of the function of Photoshop's Clone Stamp tool, but they're a little more intelligent and don't require you to constantly resample an image area. The difference between the two brushes is

- The Spot Healing Brush does not provide results as quickly as the regular Healing Brush, but it can be used very effectively to remove spots of dust in areas that do not have a lot of visual detail. With this tool you also have the option to create a texture based on the area where you first click; you click the **Create Texture** button on the Options bar, then click an image area to instruct Photoshop to sample it, and then apply it as you drag into the area that needs repair. Therefore, your technique with Spot Healing is to scout down an area that needs repair, begin your stroke just outside of it, drag into the area, and then release the mouse button.

- The (regular) Healing Brush requires that you initially **ALT/OPT**+click a sampling point before you stroke, but it's excellent for cloning good, large, recognizable areas into bad ones.

Follow these steps to use the Healing Brush:

1. Zoom into an area that needs healing.
2. With the Healing Brush chosen, right-click in the document window to bring up the brush options. Depending on the area you want to heal, drag the **Diameter** slider to increase or decrease the size of the tip and drag the **Hardness** slider left to decrease the hardness of the tip to about 50%.
3. **alt/opt** +click *near* a good area, outside of a scratch area. Then release **ALT/OPT** and make a brisk, definitive stroke over the scratch.

Figure 9-6 shows a before image at left, and the results achieved with the Healing Brush in less than 10 minutes.

Use the Smudge Tool

The Smudge tool is great for repairing image areas that contain little or no visual detail. It drags pixel color values from one area to another, which causes blurring, but if there's no visual detail to begin with—such as a shadow or highlight area—you can repair areas and remove spots at lightning speed.

1. Choose the **Smudge** tool from the Focus Tools group on the Tools panel.
2. Right-click in the document window and then click the **Brush** down arrow to choose a small tip for the Smudge tool.
3. Drag the **Master Diameter** slider to set the brush size in proportion to the area you want to smudge, and on the Options bar, click the **Strength** slider to an average of 50%.
4. Zoom into the area you want to correct.

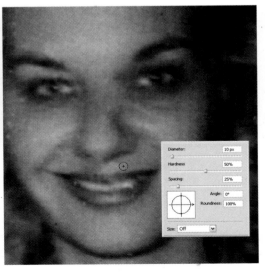

*Figure 9-6: **Use the Healing Brush to fix photo scratches.***

TIP

Various modes are available for the Smudge tool, accessed via the Options bar. You can, in practice, choose Lighten blend mode and then only the pixel tones that are lighter than the target area for retouching are smudged into this area. See Chapter 7 for details on blend modes.

5. To move a good area into one that needs correcting, drag from the good area into the bad one. As you can see here, because of the camera's flash, mom's left canine tooth appeared to be a fang. This is easily corrected with the Smudge tool, moving a darker area into the highlight area.

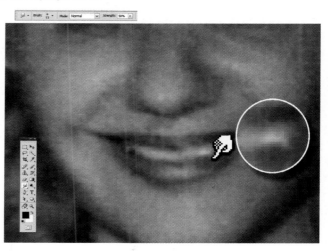

Fix Flash Reflections

Another show-stopper in older family photos was the use of a flash; in the photo shown in this chapter, the flash is particularly evident because mom and dad are quite far apart and the wood paneling reflected a hideous highlight. This sort of thing is quickly fixed by adjusting the levels of brightness where the flash produces a hot spot. You use a combination of tools and features, first for selecting the offending area, and then for correcting it.

EDIT A SELECTION USING QUICK SELECTION AND QUICK MASK

You use the Quick Selection tool when you want to select an area by stroking over it, instead of using a selection tool such as the Lasso. This tool allows you to be very precise in your selection, and the Quick Selection tool helps by making assumptions about what you want to select. The Quick Selection tool might not always precisely select an area you want (the tones in neighboring areas might be too similar) but you can manually refine a Quick Selection.

You can add or subtract from the selection as you paint by pressing **ALT/OPT** to switch from one mode (add or subtract) to the other. Alternatively, use the buttons for switching selection operation with the Quick Selection tool on the Options bar.

Quick Mask mode is also used in the steps to follow. See the "Using Quick Masks to Paint Selections" QuickFacts to learn about the Quick Mask process.

1. Choose the **Quick Selection** tool, and then make a brisk stroke over the area you want to select. Make sure the **Add To Selection** button is chosen on the Options bar (it is by default). Then make additional strokes if necessary until the area is selected.

2. Click the **Edit In Quick Mask Mode** button on the bottom of the Tools panel. The selection (by default) turns a bright red. If the outside and not the inside area of your selection turns red, press **CTRL/CMD+I** to invert the Quick Mask. You can also reset the Quick Mask selection by double-clicking the **Quick Mask** button and then clicking **Color Indicates Selected Areas** (but don't do this while you want the Quick Mask to be active).

3. Click the **Brush** tool, and then press **D**, then **X**—you're painting with white now, which adds to the size of the selection, removing the Quick Mask as you paint.

4. Set the **Opacity** to about 50% on the Options bar.

5. Right-click in the document, and then choose a large brush tip such as 200 pixels.

6. Stroke over the edges of the Quick Mask until it fades slightly. Figure 9-7 shows the edges of the Quick Mask being reduced in opacity. Less opacity means that the area is "less selected"—in short, the editing will be subtle and blend well with the original areas.

7. Click the **Blur** tool, choose a brush about 200 pixels in diameter, and drag the **Strength** slider on the Options bar to 100%.

8. Stroke around the edges of the Quick Mask until you can see that they're soft, preventing any edges in your selection work.

9. Click the **Quick Mask** button to toggle back to Standard mode and the selection marquee.

10. Choose any geometric selection tool (such as the Lasso tool), and then right-click inside the selection marquee and choose **Layer Via Copy** from the context menu. The layer containing the area to be fixed is now on its own layer (to prevent accidental editing of the background image) and is now the current editing layer.

*Figure 9-7: **Anything you can do to pixels in an image you can do to a Quick Mask.***

WORK ON THE LAYER AREA WITH THE BURN TOOL

1. To correct our flash reflection, we are choosing certain qualities that you may need to accommodate your own specific task. Click the **Burn** tool on the Tools panel, on the Options bar click **Shadows** from the Range drop-down list, set the **Exposure** to 30%, and uncheck **Protect Tones**—the tones are exactly *what* you want to change. Choose a large brush—100 to 200 pixels in diameter will do the trick.

2. Click, don't drag, over the washed-out area until you can see more detail and so that overall it looks similar in tone to the rest of the background photo. Figure 9-8 shows the work in progress.

3. The color of the burned area will change; that's a result of using the Burn tool. To desaturate the colors, click the **Sponge** tool in the Toning Tool group on the Tools panel.

4. Choose **Desaturate** from the drop-down box on the Options bar, leave **Vibrance** checked, and then, with a large brush, stroke over the content on the layer until it loses most of its unique color and blends into the rest of the background photo. See Figure 9-9.

5. Consider using the **Eraser** tool to clean up any unwanted edges on the layer. Then right-click on the **Layer 1** title (not the thumbnail image) on the Layers panel and click **Flatten Image**.

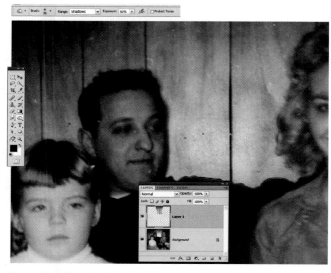

*Figure 9-8: **Use the Burn tool to bring out detail in washed-out areas.***

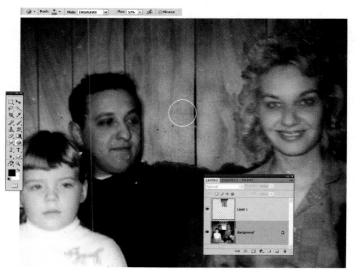

*Figure 9-9: **Use the Sponge tool to de-emphasize colors.***

EDITING AN OLD B&W PHOTO IN RGB MODE

There is often important visual detail in black and white photos that time fades. However, some of the detail still exists in one or more of the individual colors channels. This detail can be brought out using techniques demonstrated in the "Reveal Hidden Detail" section later in this chapter. This is why you should scan a vintage B&W photo in RGB mode, and only when you're finished editing should you convert a copy of your work to grayscale.

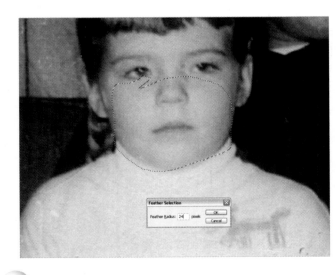

Feather Selection

Feather Radius: 24 pixels

OK
Cancel

TIP

Press **F8** to display the Info panel whenever you need to measure an existing selection. The bottom-right area on the panel tells you the X (width) and Y (height) measurements.

Put a Smile on a Face

Altering reality is just as important as improving upon reality when you're restoring images. With some care and artistic sensitivity, you can improve the expression of a subject in only a few steps using Photoshop's Liquify filter:

1. Click the **Lasso** tool and create a selection around the area of a face you want to change, such as the mouth. You're doing this to confine your editing to this area, preventing accidents.

2. Right-click within the marquee selection, and then click **Feather** from the context menu; doing this creates a smooth transition between areas you'll edit and the original photo areas.

3. Type a value that's in scale to the overall size of the photo. For example, this scan is about 24MB and the child's lower face area is about 300 pixels in width, so a Feather of 24 pixels works.

4. Click **Filter | Liquify**.

5. Zoom into the untinted area of the photo for a good look at what you're going to do. Liquify displays Quick Mask instead of your marquee selection, and the edges of the image preview are not at the photo's edges, but instead at the point where the feathering ends. If you find this distracting, uncheck the **Show Mask** check box (or you can change the color of the mask).

6. Click the **Forward Warp** tool at the top of the vertical toolbox. This tool moves pixels, but unlike the Smudge tool, it retains image focus. Set the **Brush Size** under Tool Options to scale with the selected photo area; 55 pixels in this example image is fine.

7. Use **Brush Density** to set the softness of the tip, the amount of edge feathering. 50 is a good choice for subtle retouching.

8. Set the **Brush Pressure** to 100; this controls the speed, the flow of the brush as you retouch.

9. Check the **Show Mesh** check box; when you make alterations, the mesh overlay serves as a visual guide.

10. Drag ever so slightly beginning at the corner of a lip, moving up and away from the point where you begin. Don't overdo it!

11. Repeat Step 10 with the other corner. If you've overdone the edit, you can undo by pressing **CTRL/CMD+Z**. However, a better alternative is a partial, manual undo: click the **Reconstruct** tool and then tap, don't drag, on an area you want to restore. The Liquify effect is shown in Figure 9-10; click **OK** when you've finished to apply the effect.

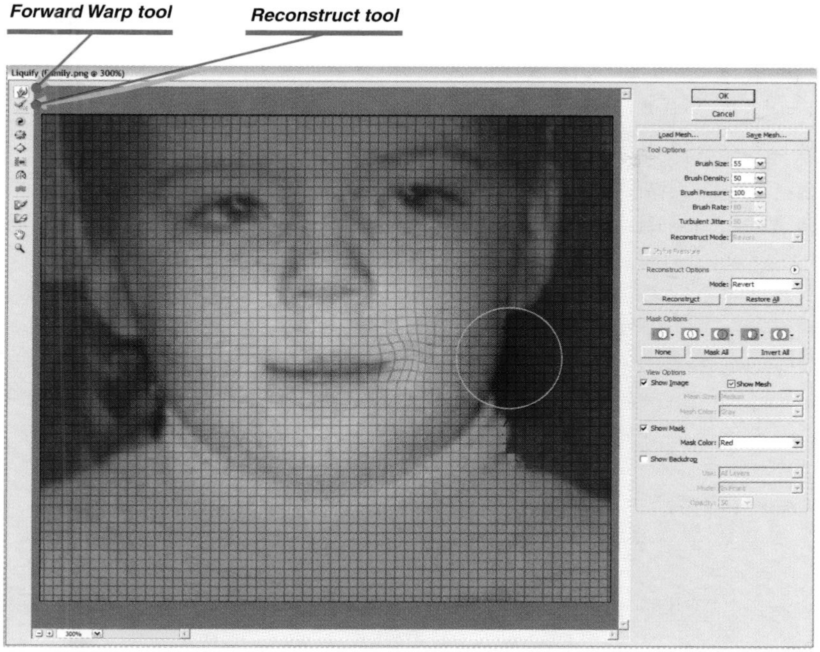

Forward Warp tool   **Reconstruct tool**

Figure 9-10: *A little use of the Liquify filter can produce amazing results.*

Remove a Family Member in Front of a Different One

When you have a group photo, many times one member is partially hiding another toward the back. If you want the photo to show the person in back rather than the person in front, you are confronted with one of the most difficult retouching assignments. Fortunately, Photoshop, and the way human beings are designed, makes this possible. Naturally, when someone completely hides another person in the back, there's nothing to copy of the individual in the back row—but this seldom happens, and there's usually at least half of the person in back in the clear to copy.

The following steps show how to duplicate, mirror, and then use the mirrored copy of someone to reconstruct the person, hiding the individual in the front of the photo. Thank goodness mankind is bilaterally symmetrical!

1. Click the **Zoom** tool and zoom into the subject behind the one you want to remove. Look for areas that are good source areas in the back subject to use to cover the front subject.

2. Click the **Quick Mask Mode** button. You'll want to select areas while you paint in the next step, not mask areas, so if Quick Mask is set up for Color Indicates: Masked Areas, double-click the **Quick Mask Mode** button on the Tools panel and change the setting in the Options box before continuing.

3. Click the **Brush** tool.

4. You need to select (by painting with Quick Mask) the opposite area that needs to be replaced in the photo; in this example, a copy of mom's right arm will serve as a duplicate for her hidden left arm. Choose a hard brush for the Brush tool to accurately define the silhouette edge of the area—an arm, a hand—that you need to duplicate.

5. Stroke with the Brush tool to trace the inside edge of the area. Then choose a larger brush with a soft edge and begin filling in the interior of the area you want to copy.

Hard edge

Soft edge

*Figure 9-11: **The mask should be crisp around the edge of the person, but soft in the interior.***

6. Reduce the **Opacity** of the Brush tool on the Options bar and finish stroking over areas that should blend into the original photo. See Figure 9-11.

7. Click the **Edit In Quick Mask Mode** button to toggle to **Edit In Standard Edit Mode**, and then press **L** (a keyboard shortcut to the Lasso tool).

8. Right-click inside the selection and then choose **Layer Via Copy** from the context menu.

9. Press **CTRL/CMD+T** to put the layer's contents (the copied background-person areas) into Free Transform mode.

10. Press **V** (Move tool), right-click inside the Free Transform bounding box, and then choose **Flip Horizontal** from the context menu, as shown in Figure 9-12.

11. Drag the copy to the appropriate position in the image, lining it up with the area of the foreground person you want to hide. Then click the **Commit** check mark on the Options bar to confirm the transformation when you've got the positioning correct.

TIP

If copying and mirroring areas of a background person doesn't completely hide the unwanted foreground person, you can simply paint over areas of little visual detail. Click the **Eyedropper** tool, sample a color of a background area—a solid shirt or dress, for example—and then click the **Brush** tool and paint over the foreground areas to complete the retouching illusion. The same is true of extreme highlight and shadow areas; these, too, can be painted over to complete a retouching assignment because they contain little or no visual detail, but only color.

*Figure 9-12: **You can often copy and flip body areas as replacement areas.***

MAKING FIXES WHEN AREAS SHOULDN'T BE MIRRORED

There are certain areas—mom's ring finger, for example—that don't copy and mirror logically; people don't usually wear a wedding ring on both hands! Fortunately, there is not a significant difference in size, and usually not in position, between one's middle and ring finger. So if you need to duplicate and flip someone's left hand (who is visibly married), select and then copy the middle finger, scale it if necessary using Free Transform, reposition it over the offending ring finger, and then right-click for the context menu and click **Merge Down** to complete the edit.

Reveal Hidden Detail

Particularly with color scans of faded black and white photos, there might be some texture in a scarf or a pattern in a dress you were certain was there. The visual detail might not be missing but instead simply hidden under 40 years of rotting photo emulsion. Play detective and check out the individual color channels:

1. Press **F7** if the Layers/Channels/Paths grouped panel isn't onscreen.
2. Click the **Channels** panel, and then one at a time, click the **Red**, then the **Green**, then the **Blue** Channel title to display each channel in the document window. You're looking for the channel that has the most detail and contrast in the areas that are faded in the RGB composite channel.
3. Click the **RGB** composite channel title to return to the composite (the normal) view of the image.

To restore the image detail, you need to first select the affected area, and then adjust the levels of the selected area. Be aware that the result of the following steps will tint the area to which you reveal detail, and should only be used with color scans of black and white images that ultimately are converted to Grayscale mode.

1. Click the **Quick Selection** tool, and then make a brisk stroke over the area to which you want to bring out detail and texture. If the marquee selection extends outside the desired area, click the **Subtract From Selection** button on the Options bar or hold **ALT/OPT**, and then stroke over the area to be subtracted.

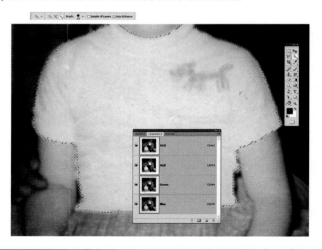

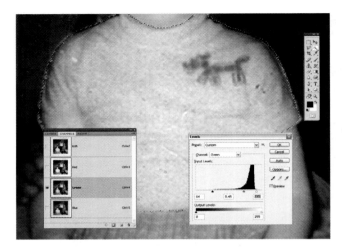

*Figure 9-13: **Reassign brightness values within the selection to add detail to the selection.***

2. Switch back to Standard mode and then, on the Channels panel, click the title of the channel that shows the most contrast and detail, in this example, the Green channel.

3. Press **CTRL/CMD+L** to display the Levels command.

4. You need to alter the Levels so that the black, midpoint, and white points all lie somewhere around the area on the histogram where pixels actually exist. Drag the Black Point (at left) input slider to the right. Then, drag the Midpoint slider to the left to open the midtones or to the right to create more contrast. Finally, drag the White Point slider to the left until you can clearly see the texture in the selected area. Click **OK**, and then press **CTRL/CMD+D** to deselect the marquee. As you can see in Figure 9-13, much more detail has been revealed in the little girl's sweater.

5. Return to the RGB view of the photo by clicking the **RGB** channel at the top of the Channels panel. Save your work now.

You will indeed see color casting in the color composite, RGB view of the photo now. This is okay, however; the finished image will be black and white, disregarding the colors you now see in the photo.

Even Out the Overall Photo Tones

In your own work, and certainly in this example image, overall lighting can look awkward, particularly when a camera flash was used. If your photo has a hot spot in a corner or the center, with steep fall-off toward the edges, one quick fix is to use Quick Mask mode and the Gradient tool to create a "reverse fall-off" in a selection, and then use Levels to correct the image:

1. Double-click the **Edit In Quick Mask Mode** button on the Tools panel.

2. In the Quick Mask Options box, click the **Color Indicates Selected Areas**. Photoshop considers black to be a color. Click **OK** and you're now editing in Quick Mask mode.

3. Click the **Gradient** tool.

4. Choose a style from the Options bar that best describes the exposure fall-off problem:

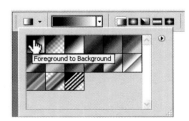

- If one side of the photo is darker than the other, click the **Linear Gradient** style button.

- If the center of the photo is well exposed but light falls off at the edges, click the **Radial Gradient** style button.

5. Press **D** (default colors) and then click the first gradient preset by clicking the down arrow to the left of the linear gradient button.

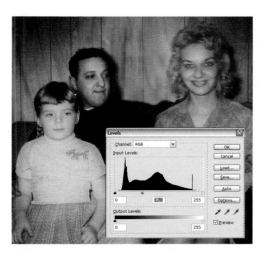

Figure 9-14: Use Quick Mask mode in combination with a gradient to even out a photograph's exposure.

6. Drag, beginning at the point that requires the most editing, to the point you don't want edited at all.

7. Return to Standard mode, press **CTRL/ CMD+H** to hide the marquee, and then press **CTRL/CMD+L** to display Levels.

8. Drag the Midpoint slider to the left until the overall photo looks as though the lighting is uneven, as shown in Figure 9-14. Click **OK**, and save your work.

Remove the Color

The Black and White adjustment goes far beyond a simple image mode conversion: this feature can emphasize or reduce any of the primary and secondary hues to grayscale, while still leaving your work in RGB color mode. This is a boon to photographers working with vintage photos that contain a lot of sepia aging; you increase the amounts of red or yellow and you brighten the photo while you remove colors and color casting. Additionally, you can tint the photograph (some customers actually *like* sepia tone images!); here's how:

1. Click **Image | Adjustments | Black & White**.

2. Drag to the right the sliders that are appropriate for the hues in the image that look too dark. For example, in Figure 9-15, the sepia tone family photo looks brighter and has better contrast by increasing the values for yellow and red (the components of the sepia tones).

3. Optionally, click the **Tint** check box, and then choose a **Hue**; a burgundy-tone image can be quite attractive. Drag the **Saturation** slider left or right to decrease or increase the tint effect, and then click **OK** to apply your settings.

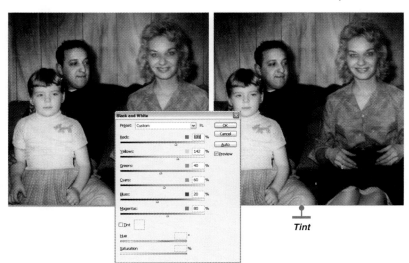

Figure 9-15: Use the Black and White adjustment to remove color-casting from a color scan of a black and white photo.

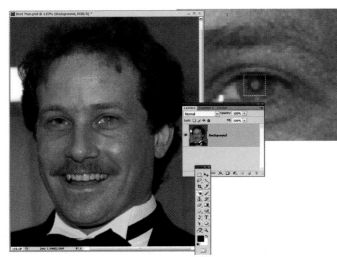

Figure 9-16: **Use the Red Eye tool to remove the result of an ill-placed camera flash.**

The options on the Options bar for the Red Eye tool do not produce a noticeable difference with most images.

The Red Eye tool doesn't work on pet photography. Cats, for example, who frequently exhibit a greenish pupil, do so because of a second eyelid reflecting a flash, and this has nothing to do with a retinal reflection. The Red Eye tool is for human photography correction.

Remove Red Eye

When a flash is too close to the camera lens, often the subject receives the dreaded "red eye" effect; the blood-rich pupil in the person's eyes reflects into the lens. Photoshop has a very simple and effective tool to remove red eye, which you use as follows:

1. Zoom into the subject's eyes area (see Figure 9-16).

2. Use the **Red Eye** tool (in the Healing Tools group on the Tools panel) in one of two ways:

   • Click over the pupil

   • Marquee select the pupil area

There's a distinct, visible advantage to marquee selecting. First, you constrain the tool's effect to the subject's eye region; suppose, for example, your subject was caught being showered with brightly colored confetti. The Red Eye tool only recognizes red, so in such a situation, it could remove red eye and also any red confetti in the photo! Second, any highlight that was in the subject's eye is preserved as red eye is removed. So marquee drag around a person's right eye and then his left eye.

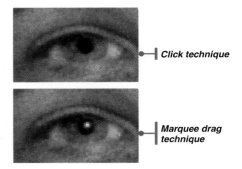

Click technique

Marquee drag technique

Chapter 10

Using Filters

A *filter* in Photoshop is a routine the program performs that alters the pixels in an image, usually in an inspiring, artistic way, over which you have a varying degree of input, depending on the filter. There are over 100 filters available in most image modes on the Filter menu; obviously, this chapter can't possibly document over 100 filters. The good news is that many of the filters are self-explanatory; they're predictable, and invite experimentation on your own. The best news, though, is that this chapter contains a potpourri of creative uses for some of Photoshop's most dramatic filters; with a few manual techniques described in the sections to follow, you'll be able to take an average snapshot and make it more visually interesting. You'll also be able to take a great photo and make it out of this world!

CHANGING ORIGINAL IMAGE DATA

Regardless of the effect a filter creates, all filters produce a similar side effect: they change original image data. Whether it's the Watercolor preset filter or the elegant Liquify command, the resulting image is an abstraction of the original photo. Therefore, you should only use a filter if it's your intention to remove or replace original data. Additionally, there is no real "instant art" filter, although you can indeed make a visually boring piece more interesting in two or three steps. Just remember that the more work you put behind tweaking a filter's settings, the better the chances you'll be happy with the results—and the results will make your work more outstanding and harder for someone else to imitate.

TIP

If you cannot see all these filters (see if Other is on the bottom of the list), click **Show All Menu Items** to extend the list.

Sift Through the Filter Menu's Organization

Toward the top of the Filter menu is the Filter Gallery, a very useful organizer of many of Photoshop's filters (covered in the following section). If you're cruising the main Filter menu, the individual filters are arranged in a somewhat arbitrary order; however, within this huge list the filters can be broken down into the following categories by their intended use:

- **Preset special effects** These include the Artistic subcategory, along with Distort, Sketch, and several others which do not appear in sequential order on the Filter menu. These filters offer a limited number of variations you set by dragging sliders, and they all provide quick transformation of designs and photographs into simulations of traditional media such as watercolors and charcoal. Several of the cooler ones are documented in this chapter.

- **Photographic filters** These include blurring, sharpening, removing dust and scratches (Noise), and the filters in the Other submenu. Although these filters can be used to create fancy special effects, their true forte is image *correction*, not enhancement or stylizing.

- **The heavy-duty filters** Liquify and Vanishing Point—at the top of the Filter main menu—perform the most substantial alterations to images. These filters have their own interfaces, and these filters are part of what makes Photoshop several cuts above an average image-editing program.

- **Third-party filters** If your Filter menu list ends at Other, you haven't bought or installed a third-party filter such as those available from Auto F/X, Richard Rosenman, Alien Skin, Corel's KPT suite, or other vendors. If you have a third-party filter installed, it should be listed below Other and you should read the documentation for its use.

Explore with the Filter Gallery

The best place to start investigating the Artistic, Distort, Sketch, and other submenus on the Filter menu is with the Filter Gallery. The Filter Gallery isn't simply an organizer like Adobe Bridge; you can apply one or more filters in

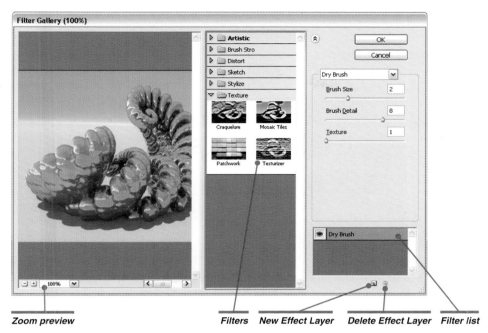

Zoom preview   **Filters**   **New Effect Layer**   **Delete Effect Layer**   **Filter list**

Figure 10-1: In the Filter Gallery, you expand folders and choose which filter(s) you want to apply to your workspace photo.

a single filtering session using the Filter Gallery. Additionally, if you choose, for example, **Filter | Artistic | Rough Pastels**, the Filter Gallery will appear anyway…so let's start here.

When you click Filter | Filter Gallery, the interface that pops up looks like Figure 10-1. You can resize the interface by dragging the window edges, and then make a comparison of your original document window and a proposed filter effect, but you cannot access the workspace while in the Filter Gallery box. The following list provides an explanation of how to identify the interface elements and put them to the smartest use:

- **Zoom preview**   Click the + or – button to zoom in or out of the preview window. Click the **down arrow** to choose from a preset viewing resolution. When the preview extends beyond the window, you can drag in the window to pan your view.

- **Filters**   To see the filters within a named filter category, click the right-pointing arrow to expand the view. To select a filter, display its controls, and see a preview, click a filter thumbnail. The filter title appears on the Filter list.

- **Filter list**   This area of the interface identifies the filters you've clicked and can be reordered, and their effects can be hidden by clicking the eye icon, exactly as you do on the Layers panel.

- **New Effect Layer**   After you click a filter to propose to apply it, you can add another filter by clicking this icon. However, you need to click this icon, then click the top entry on the Layers list, and choose a *different* filter; every click on this icon adds the last filter you chose.

- **Delete Effect Layer**   To remove a filter you've added to the list, click its title on the list first to highlight it, and then click the **Delete Effect Layer** (trash) icon.

QUICKSTEPS

CREATING A MULTI-FILTER EFFECT

You can preview, and then create, a unique effect by applying two filters simultaneously in the Filter Gallery. Just be aware that the order in which the filters are applied affects the outcome of the filtered image:

1. Click **Filter | Filter Gallery**.

2. Click the right-pointing arrow of the category (the folder) of the filter you want to apply first.

Continued . . .

CREATING A MULTI-FILTER EFFECT

(Continued)

3. Click the thumbnail of the filter to add it to the Filter list and to preview its effect on your image.

4. Drag the sliders left or right to change the settings for the filter. There is no particular order for adjusting the sliders; you just drag one, then another, then lessen the first parameter—working back and forth until you see an effect in the preview window you like. Different filters have different slider parameters.

5. If you want to compare the original to the filtered effect, click the eye icon to the left of the filter title in the Filter list to hide the effect; click a second time to restore its visibility.

6. To add a second filter, click the **New Effect Layer** icon (the dog-eared page icon) to add the same effect, and then with this new effect layer highlighted, click a different filter thumbnail to change it to your selected one, and then adjust its parameters by dragging the associated sliders (see Figure 10-2). To achieve the exact effect you desire, you might need to work back and forth between the first filter's sliders and the second filter's sliders. You can always tell which filter is the current one you're adjusting: the filter title on the list is highlighted and the title bar on the Filter Gallery interface tells you which filter is selected for modification.

7. Play with the order of the effects as they'll be applied. Click+drag a filter title on the list up or down to rearrange them; the top filter is always applied last, but for example when Cutout is applied *after* the Poster Edges filter, it can produce a nicer image than vice versa. Click **OK** to apply your filter combo.

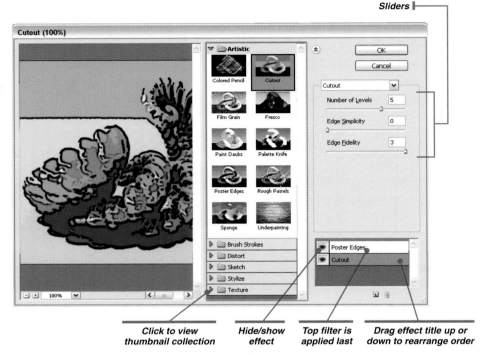

Sliders

Click to view thumbnail collection   *Hide/show effect*   *Top filter is applied last*   *Drag effect title up or down to rearrange order*

Figure 10-2: Add a filter by clicking the New Effect Layer icon.

Use Color Swatches for Some Filters

Almost the entire Sketch filter category is governed by the foreground and background color swatches on the Tools panel. Unfortunately, you might not know in advance which filter you're going to use, and you might have defined swatches in a previous Photoshop session that will produce hideous results. Here's a photo of some daisies, and clearly the foreground and background color swatches have been defined for a garish, festive design. To its right is what happens when the Bas Relief filter is applied. The good news is that you can preview this and other filters in the Filter Gallery interface, and click Cancel if you're about to commit a crime against art!

Actually, you can use the swatch colors needed by some filters in a creative way; here is the same daisy photo, and the same Bas Relief filtering, except you perform the following:

1. Before selecting a filter, click the **Set Foreground** color swatch, and choose an eye-pleasing and appropriate foreground color in the Color Picker (then click **OK**).

2. Click the **Set Background** color swatch, and, similarly, choose a nice background color—your best choice is one that has tone contrast with the current foreground color. If you chose a bright yellow foreground color, try a deep color for the background.

3. Now you're all set to apply Bas Relief, Photocopy, or any other filter that uses the color swatches. Click **Filter | Filter Gallery** and make your selection.

Clearly, the daisies look more aesthetically pleasing with the light yellow/deep green color combination now.

Use Smart Filters

If you want to take the power of Photoshop filters into your own hands and direct where and how much a filter is applied to a photo, laborious selecting,

1
2
3
4
5
6
7
8
9

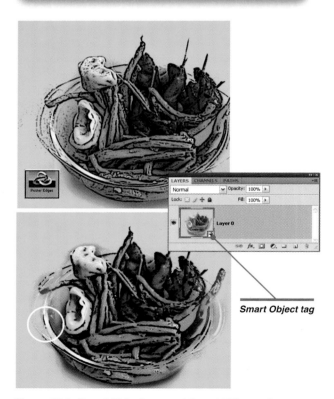

Smart Object tag

Figure 10-3: Smart Objects accept Smart Filters, whose results can be manually edited in the filtered image.

feathering, and copying to a new layer is not necessary—you can convert a layer to a Smart Object and then all filters are applied as Smart Filters:

- A Smart Object is an image area on a layer that you cannot directly edit but can do a lot of creative things with, such as applying Smart Filters. To make a layer into a Smart Object layer, right-click the layer title on the Layers panel and then click **Convert To Smart Object** from the context menu. A Smart Object icon is inserted on the layer thumbnail in the Layers panel.

- A Smart Filter is the same as the filter you choose on the Filter menu, except it adds a masking layer to the Layers panel, which you then edit to hide and reveal certain image areas. When the mask is highlighted on the panel, you paint with dark foreground tones in the document to hide effect areas (revealing the original photo), and use lighter tones to restore the visibility of the effect.

Here is how to create a Smart Object, apply a Smart Filter, and then edit the Smart Filter to create a manual, visually stunning composition:

1. Load an image you'd like to stylize. In the figures shown in this section, a bowl of Szechuan dumplings looks colorful, but the edges could use some emphasis using the Artistic Poster Edges filter.

2. On the Layers panel, right-click the layer title and click **Convert To Smart Object** from the context menu. The Smart Object icon will be inserted in the layer thumbnail.

3. Click **Filter**, click a down arrow to expand the category of filter in which there is one you think appropriate to apply to your image, and then click the filter. Note that the majority of filters are unavailable for Smart Objects.

4. Experiment with the parameter sliders for the filter. In Figure 10-3, Poster Edges—with a medium Edge Thickness and a high Edge Intensity—helps define the similar bright color areas of the food; it cleans up the photo as a graphic, but there are areas that also get blotchy and unappetizing. This is why a Smart Filter is appropriate here. Certain filtered areas can be erased.

5. Click **OK**.

6. Click on the **Smart Filters** thumbnail on the Layers panel. Notice that the foreground/background swatches on the Tools panel are now in grayscale. The swatches will return to your last-used colors when you return to editing a layer and not a layer mask. Click the **Brush** tool and choose a size from the Options bar appropriate for removing small imperfections created by the filter you applied.

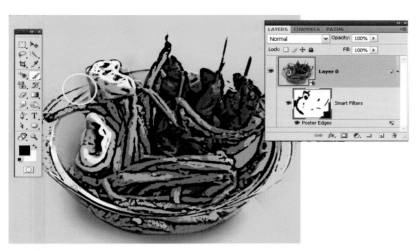

Figure 10-4: Hide areas of the filtered photograph by stroking with the foreground black swatch color.

7. Black hides the filter effect and white restores the effect. Stroke black over areas the filter created that you feel are wrong. As you can see in Figure 10-4, the unappetizing black flecks in the dumpling have been removed by stroking with black over these areas. The thumbnail is updated on the Layers panel to show where you've removed the filter's effect.

8. You can print your completed image now, or save to Photoshop's PSD file format to keep your editing work on the Smart Filter mask intact. To make a copy of your work to share with friends (who don't own Photoshop), click **File | Save As**, choose any file format you like from the **Format** drop-down list, choose a folder, and then click **Save**. Note that a caution icon is displayed for most file formats, and that the **As A Copy** check box is checked. The copy is saved as a flattened image with no masking, Smart Filter, or other Photoshop proprietary data. The copy is not loaded in Photoshop and your document in the workspace is still the original file.

Flatter Your Subject

One of the hardest portrait photography subjects is an elderly person. Try as you might with soft, warm lighting and perhaps even makeup, when you get over 60, it's just hard to disguise wrinkles and liver spots. The condition of a subject's skin—and this goes for teenagers with adolescent blemishes, too—greatly affects the overall photograph, and the Dry Brush filter can help soften or even eliminate skin problems. To flatter the portrait of a subject:

1. Click **Filter | Artistic | Dry Brush**.

2. Drag the **Brush Size** to its minimum of 0.

3. Drag the **Brush Detail** to its maximum of 10. The smaller the Detail value, the more random strokes are applied. The goal here is to soften the harsh details, not to make the image an obvious attempt at a painting.

4. To get a sharper focus in images, increase the **Texture** value.

5. If Dry Brush doesn't provide you with a more aesthetically pleasing image, try Watercolor and then Paint Daubs. Figure 10-5 shows a before and after on a distinguished, 60-ish gentleman, and clearly the image is sharper, contrast is better, the colors are warmer, and age lines have been reduced.

TIP

You can also edit a Smart Filter mask using the Gradient tool and other paint-application tools.

TIP

Watercolor tends to make an image less bright. Using the Hue/Saturation adjustment (**CTRL/CMD+U**) to increase saturation before using Watercolor helps to retain more of the original image's visual integrity…and traditional watercolors are usually brighter than their photographic equivalents.

Figure 10-5: Some of the Artistic filters can be used to reduce original image details and make a portrait more flattering to the subject.

Figure 10-6: Use the Photocopy filter to create stylized line art from photographs.

Create a Cartoon from a Photo

Making a photograph look like a hand-illustrated cartoon printed in the Sunday funnies requires the use of two filters:

- The best filter to make a line drawing from a photograph is **Sketch | Photocopy**, although occasionally you can use the Threshold Adjustment layer with success.

- **Pixelate | Color Halftone** does a splendid job of making solid colors into coarse, halftone screened image areas, completing the illusion.

To make a really good cartoon from a photo, the photo itself should be cartoonish, as is the case with the example image here.

To make a photo into a cartoon:

1. With the image open in the workspace, make sure the **Set Foreground** color swatch is black and the **Set Background** color swatch is white on the Tools panel. Photocopy uses the Tools panel color swatches.

2. Click **Filter | Filter Gallery**, and then click **Photocopy** in the Sketch folder.

3. Drag the **Detail** slider, a contrast control, to about 11 for good black and white balance.

4. Drag the **Darkness** slider, which controls brightness, to 48 for the best-looking ink sketch. Ease up on both Detail and Darkness with photos that have a lot of shadows and contrast. In Figure 10-6, you can see that the photograph is flatly lit, providing a lot of edge detail for the filter. Click **OK** to apply the filter.

5. Double-click the background layer title on the Layers panel to turn the document into a layered image. Accept the default name in the New Layer dialog box; click **OK**.

6. Click the down arrow on the Layers panel and then click **Multiply** blend mode.

7. Click the **Create A New Layer** icon on the Layers panel; this will be the layer for painting color into the cartoon composition, the target layer for the Color Halftone effect.

8. Drag the new layer title on the Layers panel list to below the original layer.

Figure 10-7: Color in the areas below the Photocopy filtered layer to prep the layer for the Color Halftone filter.

Figure 10-8: Use two or more filters in succession to make unique, stylized interpretations of your photographs.

9. Press **F6** (**Window | Colors**) or click the Swatches icon on the docking strip if it's on the strip. With the **Brush** tool chosen, click a flesh tone on the **Swatches** panel and paint on the bottom layer in the area corresponding to flesh areas on the top layer.

10. Continue filling in the bottom layer with bright colors. Because the top (Photocopy filtered) layer is in Multiply blend mode, your view of your work is completely unobstructed, as shown in Figure 10-7.

11. Click **Filter | Pixelate | Color Halftone**. A small dialog box appears; the Filter Gallery does not display this filter, nor is there a preview in the document window.

12. Depending on the size of your image and how subtle the effect should be, type a value in the **Max Radius** field—for example, use 6 for images that are about 4MB in file size. Click **OK** to apply the filter.

13. Optionally, consider adding some humorous text. See Chapter 11 for the details on working with the Type tool. Figure 10-8 shows a finished cartoon panel. The image can be flattened now, or you can click **File | Save As**, and save a copy to a file format such as JPG that you can e-mail to the undeserving subject!

Choose from Photoshop's Blur Filters

The most common blurring filters to use in everyday work are Blur, Blur More, and Gaussian Blur on the **Filter | Blur** menu (see Figure 10-9):

Original

Blur

Blur More

- If your image is less than 1MB in file size, and you need to slightly unfocus an image area, plain Blur is your ticket.

- Blur More performs four times the strength of the Blur filter; both filters create greater similarity between neighboring color pixels.

- Gaussian Blur is used for extremely intense blurring effects. Unlike Blur and Blur More, Gaussian Blur uses a weighted distribution curve to reassign pixel color values. Think of a bell-shaped curve—Gaussian blur produces an effect that is most intense at the center (of the bell) and tapers off, in a curve, to the outskirts of the bell shape.

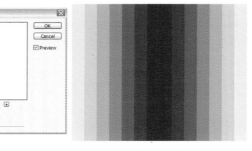
Gaussian Blur

Figure 10-9: Blurring reduces the color differences between neighboring pixels.

Put Blurring to Practical Use

There are quite a few things you can do with Photoshop's Blur filters, particularly when you've copied or cut an image area to its own layer, to add motion, depth of field, and other enhancements to your imaging assignments. The following sections show you how to make an average photo into an outstanding one through the creative use of the Blur filters.

CREATE REALISTIC SHADOWS IN COMPOSITIONS

Suppose you've copied an image area to a new background and, so that the object looks as though it's in the scene and not simply on top of a background, it needs a shadow casting onto the scene below it to photorealistically anchor it. For example, assume you have a multilayer composition in which a foreground object has a sharp shadow but the background objects' shadows are soft. To make all shadows similar in such a scene:

1. Select the object in the image (a bowling ball, in the example shown in Figure 10-10, is simple; you use the Elliptical Marquee tool), and then press **CTRL/CMD+C** to copy it to the clipboard.

2. In the document that has the background you need, press **CTRL/CMD+V** to paste the object as a new layer.

3. Create a new layer below it for the shadow. Think about the direction of the shadow; it should be in the opposite direction from the scene's light source. If, for example, there is illumination from the top left, a shadow should be cast from the object toward its bottom right.

4. Use a selection tool to create the shadow shape. Again, in this example, the Elliptical Marquee tool was used for the ball shape.

5. Fill the selection with a deep foreground color. Ideally, it shouldn't be pure black but instead should contain some of the scene's ambient color, which in this example is bluish.

6. Put the layer into **Multiply** blend mode on the Layers panel's drop-down list. Depending on the background scene's lightness, anywhere from 35% to 80% opacity for this layer will work.

7. The critical eye will see that the surface and the lighting in this bowling ball composition calls for a little softness around the edge of the fake shadow created for the ball. It is seldom that a shadow's edge is crisp; outdoor lighting sometimes produces a sharp shadow, but this is indoor lighting in this scene, so one solution is to use the Gaussian Blur filter to make the shadow fit into the scene better.

8. Click **Filter | Blur | Gaussian Blur**.

9. Click in the document window, on the edge of the shadow shape, which pinpoints the area in the Gaussian Blur preview window so that you get a good idea of the proposed filter effect.

10. If necessary, click the **+** button below the preview window to zoom into the area you'll filter.

11. Drag the **Radius** slider to the right until your eyes tell you it's the right amount of blurring, then click **OK** to apply it, as shown in Figure 10-10.

Figure 10-10: *Soften a shadow when it's called for, to match a shadow you create with its new environment.*

"Nuance" is a very important quality in your work, and Photoshop provides subtlety in editing that helps you achieve this quality. The shadow now looks correct for the scene; the surface the bowling ball appears to be resting on is diffusely lit and not perfectly smooth. And the shadow reflects these photographic traits.

USE LENS BLUR

The Lens Blur filter was created primarily for professionals who work with 3D modeling applications such as Vue, AutoDesk Maya, and Cinema 4D. These programs can write a depth map—a grayscale image that corresponds to the RGB image pixel for pixel—that indicates the closeness of objects to the camera as white or light shades, and distant objects as dark or even black. When added to the RGB image as an alpha channel, Lens Blur can create a depth of field effect similar to using your camera's narrowest f-stop in the rendered model image, creating a more believable simulation of a real-world scene.

However, as you'll soon learn in the following QuickSteps, the Lens Blur filter can be used for other purposes, specifically to reduce or eliminate halftone dots in a scanned newspaper clipping or other printed material.

Use Radial Blur

A very common photographic effect professionals use to force the audience to pay attention to the star of a scene is called *rack zooming*, done by keeping the camera shutter open while a motorized zoom operates. The Radial Blur filter—like many of the filters in Photoshop—is best used on an object on its own layer, thus ensuring that a rack zoom effect you create directs the audience

NOTE

Even if you have no knowledge or use for a modeling program, Lens Blur can be used effectively on a photograph to create vignette blurring, a common stylizing effect you might see in wedding photography. You create an alpha channel in the photo, and then use the Radial mode of the Gradient tool to create a central white area in the alpha channel progressing to black at the document edges. The white area of alpha will keep the corresponding center of the photo in focus, tapering off to a blur at the edges of the photo, where the alpha channel is black.

QUICKSTEPS

USING LENS BLUR TO PLAY DOWN HALFTONING

When you look at an old halftoned newspaper photo, you see that the line screen value is crude compared to that of today's newspaper photos and that the dots used to represent continuous tones really detract from what the dots are supposed to represent—a handful of huge black circles to portray a person's face is difficult to make out! And squinting at the halftoned photo usually compensates a little. Similarly, you can use the Lens Blur to degrade a scanned halftone photo so the dots aren't quite so apparent—a simulated "squint," in a manner of describing the effect:

1. Click **Filter | Blur | Lens Blur**.

2. Set the Depth Map **Source** to **None** (you don't need or want alpha channel information here).

3. Set the Iris **Shape** to **Triangle**. This is the key that appears to work; blurring rectangular pixels with a triangularly shaped iris performs halftone dot averaging in a way that tends to avoid harsh artifacting.

4. Drag the **Radius** slider to the right until the preview window shows decent focus but softer halftone dots that appear to merge together.

5. Use the Specular Highlights **Brightness** slider (in this use of Lens Blur) to add contrast in the highlight regions of the scan if necessary.

6. Don't use Noise at all; just click **OK**.

Figure 10-11 shows an enlargement of a halftoned rock band poster from decades ago, and without the original image, it would be nice to soften the harsh halftone dots to add visual warmth to the scan.

Figure 10-11: *Lens Blur can play down halftone dots while retaining edge sharpness in a way the other Blur filters do not.*

with precision and perfection. Radial Blur has two settings: Spin, which looks nothing like rack zooming but can be used very effectively for making leaves in a scene appear to be blowing and flying, and Zoom, which does the rack zoom effect quite well.

ZOOM AN OBJECT AT THE CAMERA

Figure 10-12 shows a vintage auto that has been separated from a fairly boring background (Chapter 5 describes how to use the Pen tool to create a crisp selection such as this one). The car currently has a new, more interesting background than its original surroundings; to duplicate a layer to a different document, you can click **Window | Arrange | Float All Windows**, then drag a layer's title on the Layers panel into the other document window. This is the setup for creating a zoom-style Radial Blur to focus on the car (or other foreground object) while making the background speed away from the viewer.

CAUTION

Scanning published halftoned photos is your own business, but publishing someone else's published work violates copyright laws. Use care and ask permission when duplicating and editing published works.

Figure 10-12: *Keep the object of interest on its own layer when applying Radial Blur to the background photo.*

To "zoom" the background and create a stunning, action-packed composition:

1. Click the background layer title on the Layers panel list to select it for editing.

2. Click **Filter | Blur | Radial Blur**.

3. In the Radial Blur dialog box, click **Zoom** as the Blur Method.

4. Drag the slider to an amount proportional to your composition's dimensions and the amount of effect you want. The example image here is 1024×768 pixels, and 32 as the amount works well.

5. Under Quality, choose **Good**. Actually, the effect is less dramatic if you choose Best, and Draft produces some harsh artifacting.

6. Your final step is to direct the center of the zoom. In Figure 10-13, the car is positioned in the vertical center of the background, but horizontally it's low. Drag in the proxy box to set the center of the effect. Then click **OK** to apply the filter.

Drag to position center

Figure 10-13: *The Radial Blur Zoom setting is great for suggesting speed in an image.*

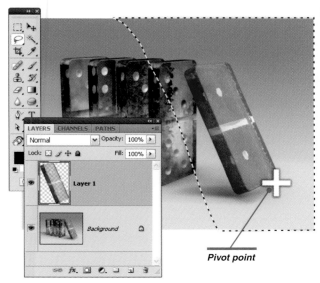

Figure 10-14: Create a selection marquee around the object to confine the blur to a specific area.

Pivot point

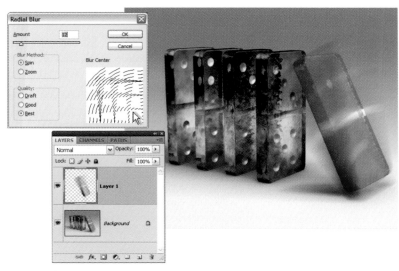

Figure 10-15: By creating a selection, you confine the Radial Blur to just the selected area.

CREATE SWOOPING MOTION BLUR

Another Radial Blur type, Spin, can be used to suggest motion in a back and forth direction and not *into* an image, as Zoom does. Let's suppose you want to suggest a lateral motion blur, a spin along the width and height of a frame, but not *into* the frame. Leaves blowing in the autumn, a hammer striking a nail, or, in this example, the first domino falling in a row are all scenes ideal for some Spin Radial Blur action.

Although the proxy window in Radial Blur specifies the effect for all of the image, you can create a selection to "guide" the Spin blur applied to an object on a layer, and the beauty of this is that *you can select transparency in addition to* the object on a layer—and the Spin effect calculates the entire selection area. Here's how to control the selection area and create the Spin effect:

1. Create a selection around an object to isolate it from the original background.

2. Duplicate the object to a new layer in a different document.

3. With the **Lasso** tool, drag a selection around the object, taking into account the object's pivot point, as shown in Figure 10-14. Here, the selection is created, so when the Radial Blur dialog box is displayed, it's very obvious where the pivot (the point of least blurring for Spin) will happen: toward the bottom, a little right of a vertical center.

4. Click **Filter | Blur | Radial Blur**.

5. Click **Spin** for Blur Method and **Best** for Quality to ensure a smooth blur. Good, when used in this example, doesn't produce a very pronounced motion effect.

6. Drag the **Amount** slider anywhere from 6 (a mild breeze) to 20 (an elephant falling down!).

7. Drag in the proxy window to the location you decided on for the pivot point for the object, and then click **OK**. Figure 10-15 shows the finished effect, beautiful and dramatic. Because the effect is confined to the selection you dragged, the object appears to be moving within a very limited image area.

Sharpen Photos

Although blurring can produce realistic photo effects, its converse, sharpening, does *not* restore image detail or add data to an image. Filters *remove* original picture data, but you can often improve the appearance of a picture by modifying data. The following sections take you through two of the strongest sharpening filters, their recommended use, and how *not* to attempt to sharpen an image.

USE SMART SHARPEN

Figure 10-16 shows a photo of a clock and a close-up that reveals not only that the image is blurred, but also why: it's not poor focus but rather that the photographer moved when the shutter was open. This makes the photo flaw an ideal candidate for the Smart Sharpen filter, which has an option for motion blur.

When you have a photo that's slightly blurred from camera motion, and there are clear signs in the photo of the direction of the motion (such as lettering, spokes on a wheel, and so on), here's how to compensate:

1. Click **Filter | Sharpen | Smart Sharpen**.

2. Click the **Advanced** button, and then choose **Motion Blur** from the **Remove** drop-down list.

3. Look carefully at the document or in the preview window (where you can zoom your view); set the **Angle** by dragging the wheel icon to the degree that shows the most "smearing" in your photo.

4. To control how far the filter will search from each pixel to create more contrast, drag the **Radius** slider to the right.

5. Drag the **Amount** slider to the right until you notice an improvement in focus *without introducing artifacting*. Hold your cursor in the preview window, then release the mouse button to make a before and after comparison as you adjust the Amount.

Figure 10-16: The Smart Sharpen filter has options for both lens and motion blur corrections.

EXPLORING ADVANCED SMART SHARPEN SETTINGS

The other settings and other tabs in Smart Sharpen are worth a little more exploration. You also have Lens Blur and Gaussian in the Remove drop-down. Both of these corrections will introduce a mild embossing around object edges in the photo, Gaussian more so than Lens Blur. So if your scene is intricately detailed, you might notice the faint emboss effect. But if your scene has broad areas of solid color, avoid these Remove types.

The Shadow and Highlight tabs can be used to reduce artifacting. If you set the Tonal Width very high and then drag the Fade Amount to 100%, what you're doing is removing the Smart Sharpen from the Highlight areas on the Highlight tab, and the image's shadow regions using the Shadow tab's controls. Additionally, the Radius slider is again used to determine how closely you want the filter to search from a specific pixel outward to a neighboring pixel of different color. Then Smart Sharpen increases the pixel color difference.

6. Click **OK** to apply the filter once you're satisfied with the settings you've made.

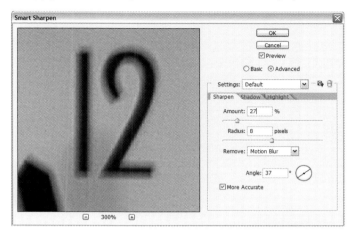

USE UNSHARP MASK

The Unsharp Mask does indeed sharpen images; the name comes from a chemical darkroom technique of exposing photographic paper through an underexposed, blurred positive film copy of the negative, sandwiched with the original negative. The results are often quite good, and if you can't get where you want to go with Smart Sharpen, Unsharp Mask would be your next choice. However, some embossing is introduced to strengthen object edge details, but Unsharp Mask can also introduce less artifacting than Smart Sharpen. Follow these steps to evaluate how well Unsharp Mask works on the same problem photo you used Smart Sharpen on:

1. Click **Filter | Sharpen | Unsharp Mask**.

2. Set the **Radius** amount before you do anything else. You determine this amount by the size of your photo and how far the blurriness travels, measured in pixels. Generally, for 1024×768-pixel images that have slight blurring, start at .5 pixels Radius, and for larger photos try 1 to 2 pixels.

3. Set the **Amount** to 100 and then back it down until the image looks sharper but doesn't have any visible embossing.

Unsharp Mask   *Smart Sharpen*

This book's bonus chapter, "Tricks of the Trade," covers the Vanishing Point filter. See the "Online Extra!" QuickFacts in the Introduction of this book for details on downloading the chapter.

Part of facial heaviness in typical photography is due to flash photography. The camera adds anywhere from 10 to 15 pounds to a person, particularly when a flashbulb flattens the depth of a portrait photo. That's why if you met a runway model or movie star you'd think they look a little too skinny: they diet for the camera.

4. Threshold determines the number of levels (tones) in the image you want to affect. Higher values produce less sharpening; try 0 to begin with. Hold your cursor in the preview window, and then release to compare the original to the Unsharp Mask version. Whether you use Smart Sharpen (with possible noise artifacting) or Unsharp Mask (which might introduce an embossing effect) is a matter of personal aesthetics. The clock image in this example appears to enjoy a better restoration using Smart Sharpen.

Do Plastic Surgery with the Liquify Filter

The Liquify filter has been used on every third greeting card in stores to make cats with eyes the size of saucers and a guy who looks like he's about to swallow his own head. However, Liquify has serious and aesthetic uses; it treats the canvas as though it's malleable plastic, and plastic surgery is the example shown in this section.

Figure 10-17 shows a fellow whose nose is aquiline but strays to his right a little too much for movie star quality. Also, his smile has distorted his cheeks and neck so his face appears heavier than it really is.

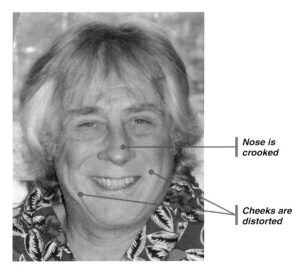

Nose is crooked

Cheeks are distorted

Figure 10-17: You can make an average person look like a movie star via the Liquify filter.

IDENTIFYING THE TOOLS IN LIQUIFY

Liquify has its own interface and its own tools. Here's a guide to what the tools do:

- **Forward Warp** Pushes pixels in the direction in which you drag.

- **Reconstruct** Reverses—undoes—things you've done with the Forward Warp and other modification tools.

- **Twirl Clockwise*** This tool is invaluable to putting a small smile on the corners of people's lips who didn't care to smile during the photographic session. The way you use the tool is to click or click+hold—don't attempt to drag the tool—just a touch to dramatically transform an image. Twirl Clockwise also has a hidden Twirl Counterclockwise option, accessed by choosing Twirl Clockwise and then holding **ALT/OPT**. There is no counterclockwise tool per se.

- **Pucker** Like the Twirl tool, you click+hold, don't drag, to shrink an area from the outside of the tool's onscreen cursor toward the center crosshair.

- **Bloat** To enlarge an area (very common on commercial greeting cards), click+hold with the tool.

- **Mirror** Useful for making a face more symmetrical or creating water reflections. Drag with the tool to create reflected areas perpendicular to the direction of your stroke. Unless used with artistic sensitivity and precision, it can be a Fun House Mirror tool, and overall not an everyday cosmetics tool.

Continued . . .

Subtlety is the name of the game in photorealistic retouching. You don't want too large a Liquify brush, and your strokes should be short, definitive ones. Let's take a trip through the Liquify filter's interface now and retouch someone (see Figure 10-18):

1. Click **Filter | Liquify**.

2. Click the top tool at left, the **Forward Warp** tool.

3. Click the **Brush Pressure** down arrow to choose how fast an edit is achieved: 50 is a good value to begin with—computers in general are quite powerful these days, and if you're editing, for example, an 11-megapixel photo, you might want to increase the Pressure. Pressure works with or without a pressure-sensitive digitizing stylus.

4. Click the **Brush Density** down arrow to choose the fall-off (the feathering) of a brush. 100 is a good value for very subtle edits with all the tools in Liquify.

5. To straighten a nose, use a large brush size; 250 pixels in diameter works well with this 768×1024-pixel photo. Although the cursor in the image window looks mighty large, there's a good reason for working large for this specific task. At small sizes, you indeed move small areas, but you want to *partially* move areas surrounding the fellow's nose to keep the overall integrity of the face.

6. Put the center crosshair of the cursor on the side of the nose you want to move, and then drag left ever-so-slightly. If you go too far, press **CTRL/CMD+Z**—the Reconstruct tool isn't always necessary. Work a little at a time up the length of the nose to straighten it and move it toward the correct direction.

7. Click the **Pucker** tool to fix facial distortion of cheek areas. You can increase the **Brush Size** for this task; about 300 works well, and a **Brush Rate** of about 20 will make your edits predictable and refined.

8. Click, don't drag, on one of the cheek areas that appears too large. Now try click+holding on a different area. The Pucker tool doesn't use a drag; you click or click+hold to work its magic.

9. Pucker is also useful for "squaring" a man's rounded chin, making it more angular. Click repeatedly along the chin area to shape it. As you can see in Figure 10-18, the fellow still looks like himself—his friends will recognize him in the photo—but the Liquify cosmetics have simply made a good picture look better.

IDENTIFYING THE TOOLS
IN LIQUIFY *(Continued)*

- **Push Left** Very similar in effect to the Forward Warp tool. To move pixels to the left, drag up; drag down to move pixels to the right. Clockwise and counterclockwise strokes increase/decrease the size of areas over which you stroke, but if you're inexperienced with Liquify, it's more predictable to use Pucker and Bloat to achieve these effects.

- **Turbulence** Adds a touch of randomness to areas you drag over. Note that right when you choose the tool, there is a Jitter control; this controls how tightly (low values) or widely (high values) the tool's randomness is applied. Turbulence is good for displacing water and making campfires look more like blazing infernos. It's usually not an appropriate tool for any portrait photography.

- **Freeze Mask** Paint with this tool to protect an area from changes you then make with other tools.

- **Thaw Mask** Erases frozen areas of the image.

- **Hand and Zoom** Perform the same functions as the tools on the Tools panel in the main Photoshop interface. Use them to navigate the document while in Liquify.

Additionally, there are two buttons at the right of the interface, Reconstruct and Restore All. Reconstruct is a global step-by-step "undo tool;" click once to undo an edit, click several times to step backwards in your editing. Restore All is a "revert" button; clicking it undoes all changes you've made.

Pucker tool

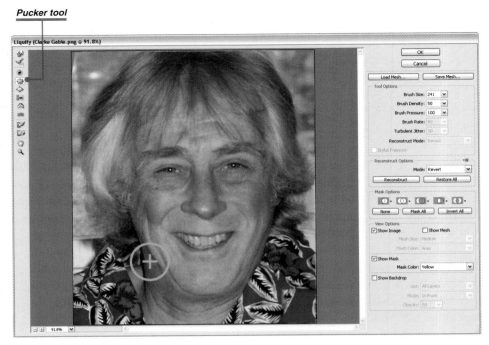

Figure 10-18: **A little Liquify goes a long way toward successfully glamorizing an average portrait photo.**

- Forward Warp tool
- Reconstruct tool
- Twirl Clockwise* tool
- Pucker tool
- Bloat tool
- Mirror tool
- Push Left tool
- Turbulence tool
- Freeze Mask tool
- Thaw Mask tool
- Hand tool
- Zoom tool

Use Lighting Effects

The Lighting Effects filter cannot change the lighting in a scene; for example, if you want to turn an overcast day into a sunny autumn afternoon, nope, uh-uh. However, what Lighting Effects *can* do is render a spotlight or a directional light, one or more, with gel options, onto an image to achieve an effect like museum lighting on paintings and sculptures. You can achieve a mood and even apply a texture while you light to simulate anything from bas relief to a plaster mold. You'll find it by clicking **Filter | Render | Lighting Effects**.

One of the secrets to creating a relief image—using the Texture Channel controls in Lighting Effects—is to actually blur a copy of one of the image channels, red, green, or blue, whichever contains the most tonal variation. The Texture Channel feature is called *bump-mapping* in other design applications, and the smoother the transition between light and dark areas of the channel, the more evident and smooth the resulting embossed image will be. Follow these steps to create a dramatic, museum-type lit scene of a photo. In this example, a photo of a sculpture is used, and it makes a lovely filtered image, but feel free to choose an interesting subject of your own.

1. Click the **Channels** panel of the Layers/Channels/Paths grouped panel. Look at each color channel in the document window by clicking its title on the Paths panel, and then decide which channel has the most tonal detail.

2. Drag this channel's title onto the **Create New Channel** icon at the bottom of the panel; Photoshop duplicates the channel. You *can* use an existing channel in Lighting Effects, but this duplicate channel will be filtered before entering the Lighting Effects filter, destroying it as a useful color composite channel within the image itself. Click the **RGB** channel title now to return to the normal view of your document.

3. Click **Filter | Blur | Gaussian Blur**. Blur the channel by about 2 to 4 pixels, depending on the size of your image; type this amount in and then click **OK**.

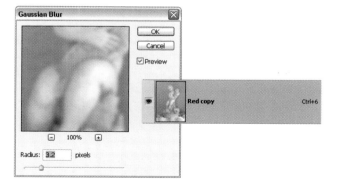

4. Click **Filter | Render | Lighting Effects**. In the Lighting Effects dialog box, shown in Figure 10-19, the default Spotlight is active, and this is fine to both shade the photo and apply a little embossing effect.

UNDERSTANDING YOUR LIGHTING EFFECTS OPTIONS *(Continued)*

- In **Properties**, you have controls for determining how your scene reacts to the lights. The **Gloss** slider produces highlights in the scene when dragged toward Shiny, and the **Material** slider is dependent upon scene shininess and will vary the scene from bright highlights (Plastic) to more subtle ones (Metallic), which tends to take on highlight color that's the same hue as the image area color.

- **Exposure** can help adjust the *overall* brightness of the scene; you can brighten and dim the scene without affecting the shapes cast by the lights in your setup. Ambience works similarly to the Exposure control. You can add or subtract from the overall image's brightness while keeping your lights in the scene at the same intensity. Ambient lighting is called *indirect lighting*, light that bounces from a wall or other semi-reflective surface into a scene.

- In the proxy window, you have your light(s). Click **Preview** to see it reflect your changes. You will see a single Spotlight in the scene when first using this filter; this is the default setup when you enter the filter interface. The direction handle for spotlights serves two purposes. You drag the direction handle clockwise or counterclockwise to point your spotlight, and you drag away from the proxy window or toward it to shape the spotlight to tall or squat. You drag the light source control to move the spotlight. There are three other controls, used to shape the light and work symmetrically—if you drag one handle, its opposing one drags in an equal and opposite direction.

Continued . . .

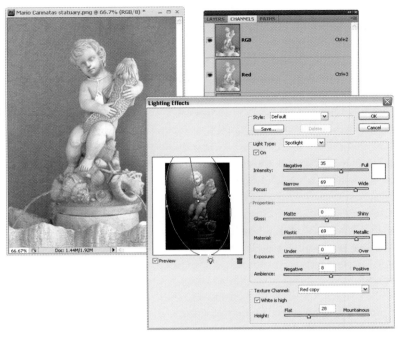

Figure 10-19: Lighting Effects creates textured embossing effects in addition to simulating background lighting.

5. Drag the direction handle in the proxy window that lies on the circumference of the light in the scene, the dot connected to the light source in the proxy window by a straight line; drag the dot to about 11 o'clock to direct the lighting. Also click+drag the center dot in the proxy window to reposition the light if necessary.

6. Drag the side dots on the circumference of the light away from its center to widen the Spotlight beam. The proxy window shows a hot spot and the image looks overexposed, but you're not done yet.

7. Drag the **Intensity** slider left to dim the spotlight. Then drag the **Ambience** slider to the right until the image in the proxy window looks well lit and well exposed.

8. Click the **Texture Channel** down arrow and then choose **Red Copy** as the channel you want to use to emboss the photo. Then drag the **Height** slider left to about 30. If you want to make the image look like an engraving instead of an embossed image, uncheck the **White Is High** box. Click **OK** to apply the Lighting Effects.

UNDERSTANDING YOUR LIGHTING EFFECTS OPTIONS *(Continued)*

- There are additional lights that you can add to your scene by clicking the **lightbulb** icon. You must select the light you've added by clicking on it in the preview window to then modify its attributes (Direction type, plastic Gloss, and so on). It's very easy to make a mistake and modify a light you don't want to modify in a scene of three or more lights. To delete a light, click it and then click the trash icon.

- The **Texture Channel** controls are for making embossed images. It's a good idea to have an alpha channel set up in your document before launching this filter, but you'll notice that if you click the down arrow, the color channels and layers that contain transparency are always available from the Texture Channel drop-down list. Once you've defined a texture channel, you have two controls. **White Is High** means lighter areas in the alpha channel correspond to bumping outward; if your potential embossed image looks to be puckering inward instead of bumping outward, uncheck White Is High. The **Height** slider controls the amount of the embossing. Start out with small values, such as 25% or less, because the effect can be more intense than when you see it in the preview window.

As you can see, with the possible exception of the price tag around the kid's neck (we weren't permitted to remove it at the statuary store), a simple photo of a detailed object now serves as a handsome piece of High Art. Don't use Lighting Effects on your entire photo collection, but let it serve as a safety net when you're in a rush for time and need interesting imagery.

Get More Filters for Free

Photoshop CS4 accepts a new architecture called Pixel Bender technology, which is hardware independent and can process in 8-, 16-, and 32-bit depth modes, so regardless

Proxy window
Light source control
Direction handle
Add a light
Spotlight shape control handle
Predefined and saved user lighting arrangements
Types of lights
Amount of light
Color
Spread for Spotlight
Light characteristics
Color
Delete selected light
Controls for embossing with a channel

of whether you want to filter a camera Raw image or a regular JPG, the plug-in modules for Pixel Bender are always available on the Filter menu. Developed by Adobe Labs, the Pixel Bender filter runs very fast on large images because it can process using both your Graphics Processing Unit (GPU, your video memory) *and* your computer's processors.

Pixel Bender didn't ship with Photoshop CS4, but the core—the host unit that will run many different plug-ins—is available for download after you register at Adobe Labs at **www.adobe.com/cfusion/membership/index.cfm?loc=en_us&nl=1&nf=1**.

Choose your operating system platform and then run the install program. Download **http://labs.adobe.com/downloads/pixelbender.html**. This is the core, but not the filters themselves that are being developed by independent programmers in a community effort. Not only are the individual plug-ins (called *.PBK and *.PBG files) free, but the list of effects is being continually updated.

Go to **www.adobe.com/cfusion/exchange/index.cfm?event=productHome&exc=26&loc=en_us**. Expand the files, and then manually copy the files to your new Adobe Photoshop CS4\Pixel Bender Files folder (where you installed Photoshop on your hard drive). Once you open Photoshop, you will have a new Filter entry, **Pixel Bender | Pixel Bender Gallery**, an interface much like the Filter Gallery, where you can choose installed plug-ins for the Pixel Bender "host" program from a drop-down list.

Figure 10-20: Pixel Bender is a host filter for independently developed plug-ins.

Figure 10-20 shows a fascinating effect applied to a colorful scene, very Escher-like in its vortex repeating quality. There are almost 20 filters for Pixel Bender to date and most of them are completely unlike the filter set that shipped with CS4. Your best guide to using these filters is Experimentation…and bring along Inspiration as a chaperone!

Chapter 11
Using Type and Type Effects

Text is an important accompaniment to images, and Photoshop handles text with the same grace and finesse as it handles your bitmap photographs. In this chapter you will discover how to create and edit type on images using typical formatting techniques, hyphenation, and justification. You will see how to perform the commonly needed tasks of checking spelling and finding and replacing text. Then, with the knowledge of text basics addressed, you will see how to play with your type: warping it, and transforming it by rotating, skewing, and resizing it. You will find out how to use layer styles that let you create special effects like drop shadows, beveling and embossing, inside and outside glows, and gradient fills. Finally, you will learn how to mask your type, thereby enabling you to copy images as fill for type, and how to make a *selection* of type, which you can then manipulate just like any other selection.

TIP

A new layer is not created when you create text in multichannel, bitmap, or indexed color modes, since they do not support layers. For these modes, type will not be vector based, but will be rasterized text on the background layer.

Create and Edit Text

When you use the Text tool to type text, it creates its own text layer, which can be edited until you *rasterize* it. Initially, text is vector based; however, when you rasterize it, it becomes a bitmap object. At this point, it can no longer be accessed as editable text (you can't easily correct spelling mistakes, for example). Some of the special tools and effects, such as the Paint tools and filter effects, can be used to enhance text once it is rasterized. See Chapter 2 for additional information on the differences between bitmaps and vector-based graphics.

When you select the Type tool, the Options bar becomes a Formatting toolbar. Figure 11-1 shows the tools available for creating and editing text.

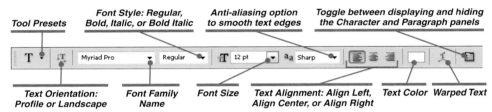

Tool Presets • **Font Style: Regular, Bold, Italic, or Bold Italic** • **Anti-aliasing option to smooth text edges** • **Toggle between displaying and hiding the Character and Paragraph panels**

Text Orientation: Profile or Landscape • **Font Family Name** • **Font Size** • **Text Alignment: Align Left, Align Center, or Align Right** • **Text Color** • **Warped Text**

Figure 11-1: **The Options bar contains formatting tools when you select the Type tool.**

COMMITTING TYPE

After your text has been entered and you are satisfied with the results, you *commit* the text to accept the changes. You can still edit the text after it has been committed. Just click the text layer and a text tool. Do one of these to accept, or commit, the changes:

• Click **Commit** in the Options bar.

   Click to cancel |—•⊘ ✔•—| **Click to commit**

• On the numeric keyboard, press **ENTER**.

• On the main keyboard, press **CTRL/CMD+ENTER**.

• Select another tool or select a menu option.

Create Text

You can enter text in two ways: as point type or as paragraph type. You indicate which type you are creating by the way you begin to insert the text: if you are creating point type, you click on the image and type; if you are creating paragraph type, click and drag and then type within a bounding box. Use point type when you have only a few words to enter. Use paragraph type when you are working with more than a few words. In both cases, a new type layer will be created.

ENTER POINT TYPE

As you are entering text, it doesn't wrap to the next line; rather, it continues on the same line. To enter point text:

1. Open an image and set attributes for the text (see the section "Format Type with the Character Panel" later in the chapter).

2. Select either the **Horizontal Type** tool or the **Vertical Type** tool.

3. Click in the image area, and the pointer changes into an I-beam pointer. Click where you want the text to begin. For horizontal type, the small intersecting line marks where the bottom of the type will appear. For vertical type, the intersecting line identifies the center of the type. Figure 11-2 shows both horizontal and vertical type on an image.

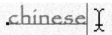

4. Select any formatting you want from the type options in the Options bar, the Character panel, or the Paragraph panel (see "Edit Type" later in this chapter).

5. Type your characters. Press **ENTER** to begin a new line.

6. Click **Commit** on the Options bar (see "Committing Type" earlier in the chapter).

ENTER PARAGRAPH TYPE

You type a paragraph of text into a *bounding box* that contains the text and creates a separate text object on its own layer. Then you set attributes for the paragraph (see "Format Paragraphs with the Paragraph Panel"). To enter paragraph text:

1. Select either the **Horizontal Type** tool or the **Vertical Type** tool.

2. Drag the pointer diagonally so that a bounding box is created.

Figure 11-2: *Point type entered using the Horizontal Type and Vertical Type tools creates a useful label for photos.*

NOTE

You can change from point type to paragraph type or vice versa. Select the type layer (not the text itself), and click **Layer | Type | Convert To Point Text** or **Convert To Paragraph Text**.

TIP

You can resize the bounding box using the handles on its perimeter; doing this changes the container for the text but doesn't affect the size of the text itself.

NOTE

If you press **ALT/OPT** as you drag to form a bounding box for paragraph text, the Paragraph Text Size dialog box appears. Type values in points in the **Height** and **Width** text boxes for the bounding box, and click **OK**.

Paragraph Text Size

Width: 271.08 pt   OK

Height: 136 pt   Cancel

3. Select any formatting you want from the type options in the Options bar, the Character panel, or the Paragraph panel (see "Format Type with the Character Panel" later in this chapter).

4. Type your characters. To break to a new line, press **ENTER**. The text will automatically wrap to the next line when it reaches the end of the bounding box.

5. Click **Commit** on the Options bar (see "Committing Type" earlier in the chapter).

Edit Type

You can edit your text by changing the font, text color, font size and style, leading, and kerning. You can tell when you are in Edit mode by looking for the Commit and Cancel Transform buttons in the Option bar. If these buttons are there, you are in Edit mode. This is most easily done using the Character or Paragraph panels.

FORMAT TYPE WITH THE CHARACTER PANEL

You can use the Character panel to edit the most common text attributes:

1. If it is not already showing, display the Character panel, shown in Figure 11-3, by clicking **Window | Character**.

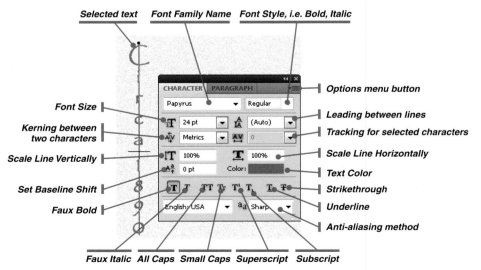

Figure 11-3: *The Character panel contains tools for editing text.*

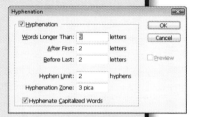

QUICKSTEPS

HYPHENATING AND JUSTIFYING TYPE

HYPHENATE WORDS

On the Paragraph panel, click the **Hyphenate** check box to have Photoshop automatically hyphenate words.

SET HYPHENATION RULES

1. Click the Paragraph panel **Options** button in the upper-right corner, and click **Hyphenation**. The Hyphenation dialog box appears.

2. Accept the defaults or change the following options:

   • **Words Longer Than __ Letters** Hyphenates only words longer than the given number of letters; the default is five letters.

   • **After First __ Letters** Requires a given number of letters to be typed before hyphenating.

   • **Before Last __ Letters** Requires hyphenation to occur at least that many letters from the end.

   • **Hyphenate Limit __ Hyphens** Limits the number of hyphens in adjoining lines; 0 provides no limit.

   • **Hyphenation Zone** Defines the distance (the default is 3 picas) from the end of the line within the bounding box that hyphenation will occur.

   • **Hyphenate Capitalized Words** Allows or restricts the hyphenation of capitalized words.

3. Click **OK**.

Continued . . .

2. Click the text layer in the Layers panel, and then select the text in the text box in the document by highlighting it with the appropriate text tool.

3. Select from among these options:

   • **Font** Changes the Font family name used.

   • **Font Style** Changes the look of the font. The options vary depending on the font used, but common styles are Bold, Italic, and Bold Italic.

   • **Font Size** Changes the point size of the characters.

   • **Leading** Changes the space between lines of text. Auto is the default. You usually want to select a leading larger than the size of the text so that the text is not too crowded. For example, if the point size is 20 points, you might use a leading of 24 or larger. However, using a reduced point size can be used to overlap lines of text for special effects.

     These lines use "auto" leading.

     These lines use reduced leading to squeeze lines together.

   • **Kerning** Changes the space between two characters. Place the pointer between the two characters you want to manipulate. You can move characters closer together or set them farther apart.

     Kerning

   • **Tracking** Changes the spacing for a selected line of characters. Using a higher number increases spacing; a negative number decreases spacing.

     Tracking reduces (-100) or increases (200) space between characters(0)

   • **Scale Vertically** Adjusts the height of selected text. This example reduces the second A to 50 percent.

     A ˄

   • **Scale Horizontally** Adjusts the width of selected text. Again, in this example, the width of the second A is reduced to 50 percent.

     A A

   • **Baseline Shift** Moves the selected characters above or below the baseline, such as in subscripts and superscripts.

   • **Text Color** Sets the color of text.

   • Several character attributes can be chosen for selected characters: **Faux Bold** (when your font has no bold family member), **Faux Italic** (when your font has no italic family member), **All Caps**, **Small Caps**, **Superscript**, **Subscript**, **Underlining**, and **Strikethrough**.

   • **Language** Establishes the language being typed.

   • **Anti-Aliasing** Adjusts the smoothness of the letters, from None to Smooth.

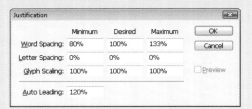

QUICKSTEPS

HYPHENATING AND JUSTIFYING TYPE (Continued)

SPECIFY NO BREAKS

To prevent a group of letters from being broken during word wrap:

1. Select the letters that are not to be broken.

2. Click the Character panel **Options** button in the upper-right corner, and click **No Break**.

SET JUSTIFY RULES

You can set the spacing between words, letters, and glyphs (any characters or symbols in a font, including nontext characters, such as Wingdings font characters):

1. Click the Paragraph panel **Options** button in the upper-right corner, and click **Justification**. The Justification dialog box appears.

2. Set the values to define the spacing between words, letters, and glyphs. Table 11-1 describes the limits for the spacing options.

3. Click **OK**.

FORMAT PARAGRAPHS WITH THE PARAGRAPH PANEL

When you type a paragraph into a bounding box, you have a Paragraph panel available for formatting line and paragraph spacing. Figure 11-4 shows the tools available with the Paragraph panel.

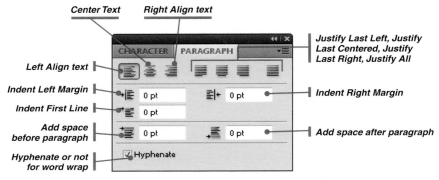

Figure 11-4: **Use the Paragraph panel to define paragraph attributes, such as alignment, spacing, and indentation.**

1. If the Paragraph panel is not displayed, click **Window | Paragraph**.

2. Set your paragraph parameters before typing text by clicking the attribute or filling in a text box (see Step 5).

3. Create paragraph text by selecting the **Horizontal Type** tool or the **Vertical Type** tool and then dragging a bounding box.

4. Begin to type the paragraph.

5. To change paragraph settings, select the paragraph and move your pointer over the Paragraph panel option icon, such as the **Indent Left Margin** icon. When your pointer becomes a pointing hand with a two-headed arrow, drag the scrubby slider to change the value.

ELEMENT	MINIMUM	MAXIMUM	NO EFFECT
Word Spacing	0%	1000%	100%
Letter Spacing	−100%	500%	0%
Glyph Spacing	50%	200%	100%

Table 11-1: **Defines Justification Rules**

Use Other Text Tools

Photoshop provides several other tools for working with your text. Among these are the Spelling Checker to proof your text, Find and Replace for making global changes, transforming text such as with Warp, Distort, or Skew functions, and working with text on a path.

Use the Spelling Checker

To check whether the words in your paragraph are spelled correctly, use the Spelling Checker feature. Photoshop uses an internal dictionary that comes with the product. You can add your own words to it. Your selected words are compared to the dictionary, and if the word is not there, Photoshop thinks your word has been misspelled. It displays your word, the word it thinks you may want, and a list of other words in case the first one doesn't correct. To use the Spelling Checker:

1. Select the text to be examined.

2. Click **Edit | Check Spelling**, or right-click the select text and choose **Check Spelling** from the context menu.

3. If a word cannot be found in the Photoshop dictionary, the Check Spelling dialog box appears, as shown in Figure 11-5, with the potential misspelling highlighted in your text, and identified in the dialog box as being "Not In Dictionary." Choose from among these options:

   - **Ignore**   Skips the word identified as a potential mistake
   - **Ignore All**   Skips all occurrences of this word
   - **Change**   Replaces the word displayed in the Not In Dictionary text box with the one displayed in the Change To text box
   - **Change All**   Replaces all occurrences of the identified word with the one displayed in the Change To text box
   - **Add**   Adds to Photoshop's dictionary the word displayed in the Not In Dictionary text box

4. Click **Done** to close the dialog box. If the Spelling Checker finds no more misspelled words, it displays a message that the spelling check is complete.

Word identified as being potentially misspelled   **Recommended word to replace the misspelled one**

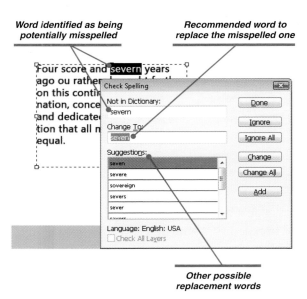

Other possible replacement words

*Figure 11-5: **The Spelling Checker feature identifies all words that are not in the Photoshop dictionary as potential misspellings.***

QUICKSTEPS

TRANSFORMING TYPE

You can transform type by manipulating the bounding box surrounding it. Text transformations available on the text bounding box do not include Perspective, Distort, and Warp. If you need these transformations, you use the Create Warped Text function on the Options bar, covered later in this chapter.

SELECT A BOUNDING BOX

To display the bounding box with handles for rotating and resizing, select your text layer and press **CTRL/CMD** (to toggle the bounding box on and off), press **CTRL/CMD+T**, or click **Edit | Free Transform**.

RESIZE A BOUNDING BOX

1. Place your pointer over the bounding-box handles until you see a double-headed arrow.

2. Drag the handles until the bounding box is the size you want. To change the size proportionally, press **SHIFT** while you drag.

> Four score and seven years ago our fathers brought forth on this continent, a new nation, conceived in liberty, and dedicated to the proposition that all men are cre-ated equal.

ROTATE A BOUNDING BOX

1. Place the pointer outside the bounding box until the pointer morphs into a curved double-headed arrow.

2. Drag the pointer in the direction the box is to be rotated. Press **SHIFT** while you drag to change the rotation in 15-degree increments. Press **CTRL/CMD** while you drag the center point to another place, even outside the bounding box. The new location of the center point becomes the center of rotation for the text. Then you can rotate the bounding box around a wider circle.

Continued . . .

Find and Replace Text

To find text and replace it with other text:

1. Right-click the text and select **Find And Replace Text**, or click **Edit | Find And Replace Text**. The Find And Replace Text dialog box appears.

2. Under Find What, type the text to be searched for and replaced.

3. Under Change To, type the new text.

4. Select any of the following options:

- **Search All Layers**   Searches for the text in all layers of an image
- **Forward**   Searches forward from one text object to another
- **Case Sensitive**   Restricts the search to the case of the text in the Find What text box
- **Whole Word Only**   Searches only for whole words that match the text in the Find What text box
- **Find Next**   Searches for the next occurrence of the word in the text
- **Change**   Changes the selected text to the text in the Change To text box
- **Change All**   Changes all occurrences of the text in the Find What text box to the text in the Change To text box
- **Change/Find**   Changes the selected text to the text in the Change To text box and then continues the search

5. Click **Done**.

Warp Text

You can create interesting effects on text by warping it for logos and other specialized work. You will need to experiment with the controls to find the perfect result for your warped text.

1. In the Layers panel, double-click the **T** icon on the layer containing the text to be warped. The text is highlighted.

TRANSFORMING TYPE *(Continued)*

USE THE OPTIONS BAR TO TRANSFORM TEXT

You can also use the Options bar, shown in Figure 11-6, to make changes to text. When the text is selected and you have used **CTRL/CMD+T** or the menu to display the transform bounding box:

- Click a point on the **Reference Point Position** icon to locate the reference point within the text box.

- Place the pointer over the X or Y until a hand appears—the scrubby slider. Drag it right or left to move the bounding box right or left (X sets the horizontal position of the reference point), or up or down (Y sets the vertical position of the reference point). You can also type the specific value into the text box.

- Click the triangle between the X and Y to toggle between using specific or relative positioning of the reference point. Then drag the appropriate scrubby sliders of the X, Y, or W to set those values.

- To set the horizontal and vertical scale of the bounding box and text, place the pointer over the W (**Set Horizontal Scale**) or H (**Set Vertical Scale**) until a hand appears. Drag the scrubby slider to increase or decrease the width or height of the bounding box. You can also type a value in the text box.

- Click the chain icon between the W and H to maintain the aspect ratio.

- Place the pointer over the **Rotate** icon and drag the scrubby slider to rotate the text.

- Place the pointer over the H (**Set Horizontal Skew**) or V (**Set Vertical Skew**) and drag the scrubby slider to skew the text horizontally or vertically.

Continued . . .

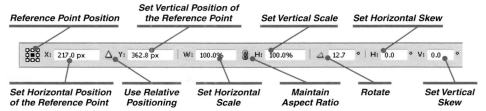

Reference Point Position | Set Vertical Position of the Reference Point | Set Vertical Scale | Set Horizontal Skew

Set Horizontal Position of the Reference Point | Use Relative Positioning | Set Horizontal Scale | Maintain Aspect Ratio | Rotate | Set Vertical Skew

*Figure 11-6: **Use the Options bar to skew text within the bounding box.***

2. Right-click the highlighted text and click **Warp Text** from the context menu. The Warp Text dialog box, shown in Figure 11-7, is displayed.

*Figure 11-7: **The Warp Text dialog box presents options for the style of warp you want.***

3. Click the **Style** down arrow, and select a warp style.

4. Click **Horizontal** or **Vertical** to orient the text horizontally or vertically.

11
12
13

UICKSTEPS

TRANSFORMING TYPE *(Continued)*

SKEW TEXT IN A BOUNDING BOX

1. Select the text layer that you want to skew.

2. Right-click the text and select **Skew** from the context menu, or click **Edit | Transform | Skew**. The pointer changes into an arrow that you can use to drag the handles, thus skewing the shape of the bounding box.

FLIP THE TEXT

To flip the text, click in the text to select it, press **CTRL/CMD**, and drag the bounding box across itself to the other side. For example, click the right handle and drag it to the left until the text flips. You can also right-click the text and click **Flip Horizontal** or **Flip Vertical** for printing T-shirt transfers and other reversed signage.

5. Drag the **Bend** slider to exaggerate or lessen the warp of the text. You can also type a percentage in the Bend text box to set the degree of warp.

6. Drag the **Horizontal Distortion** slider to increase or decrease the horizontal warp, or you can type a percentage in the text box.

7. Drag the **Vertical Distortion** slider to increase or decrease the vertical warp, or type a percentage in the text box.

8. Click **OK** when the warp effect is as you want.

Create Text on a Path

You can type text along a path, such as that shown in Figure 11-8. First you create a path and then you type text, pulling it along the path:

1. Select a tool, such as the **Pen** tool or the **Freeform Pen** tool, to create a path. (See Chapter 5 for additional information on creating paths.)

Figure 11-8: **Type text on a path for special effects.**

2. Click **Paths** on the Options bar, and draw the path. Text will appear in the direction that a path is drawn, so if you draw a line from left to right, that is how letters will be inserted. If a path is too short or the text comes to the end of the path before all the letters are on the path, the letters will follow the path and curve around the end of it.

3. Select the **Horizontal Type** tool for text parallel to the path, or select the **Vertical Type** tool for text perpendicular to the path.

4. Place the pointer above the path until it morphs into an I-beam. Click the path, and an insertion point appears.

5. Type your text.

Edit Text on a Path

To edit the text on a path by inserting and deleting letters and making formatting changes:

1. Select the text layer containing the text to be edited.

2. Click either the **Horizontal Type** tool or the **Vertical Type** tool.

3. Click the text string to place the insertion point, or highlight the text to select it.

4. Make your changes.

Flipping and Moving Text on a Path

To move text along a path or to flip it to the opposite side of a path, follow these steps:

1. Select the Selection Tool or the Path Selection Tool.

2. Hold the tool over the type until it changes to an I-beam with an arrow.

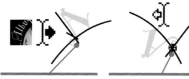

Normal type direction   *Flipped type direction*

   • To move the tool along the path, drag the the I-beam along the path.

   • To flip the text to the opposite side of the path, drag the I-beam across the path.

   • To move text on the other side of a path without also flipping it upside down, select the text. On the Character panel, set the **Baseline Shift** option to a negative number. To move whole characters across the path, enter a number equal to the point side of the type.

Figure 11-9: *You can type text around a closed path to create unusual effects.*

Create Text Within a Closed Path

To type text within a closed path, such as a circle or ellipse, create a path around a shape and type text, dragging the text where you want it:

1. Select a shape tool, and draw a shape, such as the oval shown in Figure 11-9.
2. Click **Path** on the Options bar to make the shape into a path.
3. Click the **Horizontal Type** tool or the **Vertical Type** tool, and place the insertion point on the path.
4. Type the text.
5. Adjust the positioning using the **Path Selection** tool or the **Direct Selection** tool to pull the text string one way or the other. You may also want to rotate the text, format it, or apply layer styles to it before you finish.

Use Special Effects with Text

You can apply special effects to your text using options from the Styles panel. You can also create masks to select or fill type with images.

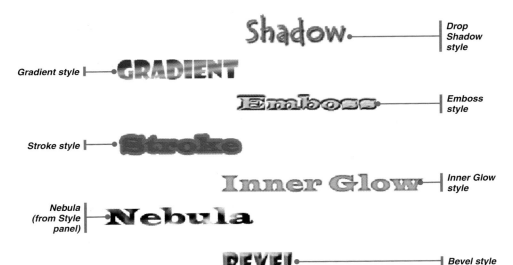

Figure 11-10: *Examples of effects you can create using layer styles*

Add Special Type Effects with Layer Styles

Photoshop has several predefined, or preset, styles that you can use to create drop shadows, embossing or beveling, inside and outside glows, gradient coloring, patterns, and more. Figure 11-10 shows examples of some effects described in this section that can be applied to type. Three commonly used styles are described next.

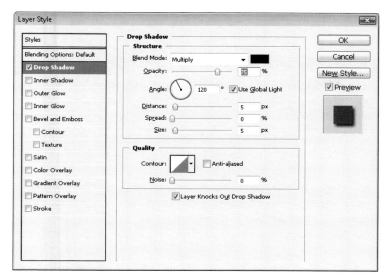

Figure 11-11: *The Layer Style dialog box can create and control special effects, such as the Drop Shadow style.*

TIP

To open the Layer Style dialog box, click the **Layer Style** button at the bottom of the Layers panel.

CREATE DROP SHADOWS

To create a slight shadow on selected type:

1. Select the text to which you want to apply the effect.

2. Click **Layer | Layer Style | Drop Shadow**. The Layer Style dialog box appears with the Drop Shadow options displayed, as shown in Figure 11-11. (You can also click the **Add A Layer Style** button on the Layers panel, and then click **Drop Shadow** to display the relevant options in the Layer Style dialog box.)

3. Experiment with the options and view the results in the preview:

- **Blend Mode** By default, this is set to **Multiply**, and the default color is black. (You can change the color by clicking the color preview and selecting a color from the Color Picker dialog box.)

- **Opacity** The Blend Mode determines how much of the image underlying the shadow is visible. At a value of 100, the shadow obscures anything underneath it.

- **Angle** Directs the source of the light.

- **Use Global Light** When checked, keeps all layers with effects in synch. If you have, for example, two different type layers with a Drop Shadow style, click **Use Global Light** to make Photoshop keep the Angle of the light on both layers the same, which is great for making a complex composition visually integrated.

- **Distance** Controls how far the shadow is offset from the type.

- **Spread** Relates to the percentage of thickness a shadow has, and it is related to the Size option.

- **Size** Controls how sharp or fuzzy the shadow is.

- **Contour** Opens a submenu of shadow curves or shapes.

- **Anti-Aliased** Blends the edges of the letters with the surrounding pixels of color to eliminate jagged edges.

- **Noise** Makes the shadow smoother, clumpier, or noisier. Drag the slider to add noise to the shadow.

- **Layer Knocks Out Drop Shadow** Determines whether the shadow will be visible on a semitransparent layer. When the check box is selected, the type layer knocks out the shadow, so if you turn the layer fill down, you can still see where the type cuts the shadow. If the check box is unselected and you turn the layer fill down, as the type disappears, the shadow still shows fully—a shadow with no type, and interesting effect to suggest text is carved out of objects on layers beneath it.

4. When you are satisfied, click **OK**.

QUICKSTEPS

FINDING AND USING LAYER STYLES

Preset layer styles can be found in a couple of places in Photoshop CS4. There is a difference between adding a layer style (singular) via the Add A Layer Style command on the Layers Panel and using the presets on the Styles (plural) panel. If you want a single effect for a layer—such as a Drop Shadow, you can choose it from the Add Layer Style drop-down list on the Layers panel. However, if you want to apply several effects (styles) at once, you use the Styles panel, with collections of style "recipes" that produce more elaborate looks through the use of multiple styles than a single style alone.

USE THE STYLES PANEL

1. Click **Window | Styles**. The Styles panel is displayed. This contains thumbnails showing what the style effects will look like.

2. Select the text layer to which the layer style will be applied.

3. Click the style, or drag the style to the selected text.

4. Press **SHIFT** while you drag to add the selected style to those already applied to the selected text. Without pressing **SHIFT**, the selected style replaces any styles currently applied.

USE THE LAYER STYLE DIALOG BOX

1. Select the text layer to which the style will be applied.

2. Click **Layer | Layer Style**, and click an option to display the dialog box for layer styles. (An example of the dialog box is shown under "Create Drop Shadows.") You can also click **Add A Layer Style** icon *fx.* from the bottom of the Layers panel and click the option you want from the context menu.

Continued . . .

BEVEL AND EMBOSS TYPE

To create either beveling or embossing on type:

1. Select the layer containing the text to which you want to apply the effect.

2. Click **Layer | Layer Style | Bevel And Emboss**. The Layer Style dialog box appears. (You can also click the **Add A Layer Style** icon *fx.* on the Layers panel and click **Bevel And Emboss** to display the Layer Style dialog box.)

3. The options for controlling the beveling and embossing are displayed in the dialog box, as shown in Figure 11-12. As you select options, you can view the results in the preview box.

- **Style**   Displays a menu of styles you can use: **Outer Bevel** forms the bevel beyond the edge of the original type; **Inner Bevel** forms the bevel from the edge of the text inward; **Emboss** makes the type look as if it were stamped, or standing apart from the background; **Pillow Emboss** is a more rounded look; **Stroke Emboss** adds an edge to the outline.

- **Technique**   Displays three options: **Smooth** blurs the edges; **Chisel Hard** makes it look crisp and defined; **Chisel Soft** is less sharp than Chisel Hard but more defined than Smooth.

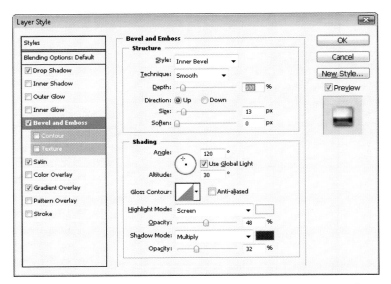

Figure 11-12: The Bevel and Emboss effects can give your text depth and a more dimensional look.

QUICKSTEPS

FINDING AND USING LAYER STYLES

(Continued)

3. Choose the settings for the option you selected. The choices will vary, depending on which style you picked. See "Add Special Type Effects with Layer Styles" for specifics on the common styles used.

4. Click **OK**.

TIP

To copy an effect from one layer to another, right-click the "fx" legend at the right of a layer, and click **Copy Layer Style**. Then **CTRL/CMD**+click other layers that you want to have the style, right-click, and then click **Paste Layer Style** off the context menu.

CAUTION

If your text does not conform to the path or if the path disappears, make sure you are on the right layer.

- **Depth**   Sets the depth of the bevel or embossing.
- **Direction**   Determines whether the surface of the type is up and rounded or down and indented.
- **Size**   Determines the size of the shading—that is, how deep into the text it is.
- **Soften**   Blurs the shaded part of the bevel or embossing.
- **Angle**   Establishes the degree of the light source and whether all the type has the same light source.
- **Altitude**   Determines how high the light source is.
- **Gloss Contour**   Displays a menu of options for the shape, or contour, of the bevel.
- **Anti-Aliased**   Smoothes the edges of the contour.
- **Highlight Mode**   Applied to the highlights of the bevel or embossing. By default, this is set to **Screen**, and the default color is white.
  - **Opacity**   Connected to Highlight Mode and varies it. Drag the sliders to set the values.
- **Shadow Mode**   Applied to the shadows of the bevel or embossing. By default, this is set to **Multiply**, and the default color is black.
  - **Opacity**   Can be varied for the Shadow Mode. Drag the slider to set the values.

4. When you are satisfied, click **OK**.

MAKE TYPE GLOW INSIDE AND OUT

The Inner Glow and Outer Glow effects make your type look as if there were a light source either inside or behind the type. You'll want to experiment with the options to get the effect you want:

1. Select the layer containing the text to which you want to apply the effect.

2. Click **Layer | Layer Style | Inner Glow**. The Layer Style dialog box appears. (You can also click the **Add A Layer Style** button ![fx] on the Layers panel, and then click **Inner Glow** to display its options on the Layer Style dialog box.)

3. The options for controlling the inside and outside glows are displayed on the dialog box, as shown in Figure 11-13. As you select options, you can view the results in the preview box. You can see that many of the options are the same as with the Drop Shadow or Bevel and Emboss effects. The following lists some of the options unique to Inner Glow.

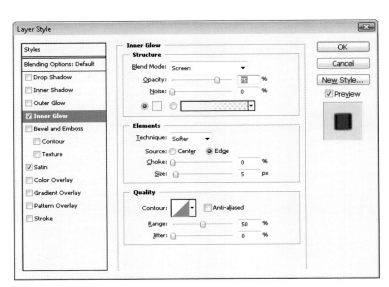

Figure 11-13: *The Inner Glow effect makes your type look as if there were an inside source of light.*

- **Noise**   Makes the glow harsher and is actually a good way to simulate fluorescent lighting with objects and text and can prevent banding when printing. Drag the **Noise** slider to add more noise to the glow. Specify a value between 0 (no noise) and 100 (maximum noise).

- **Fill**   Can be solid or you can select a graduated color scheme from the drop-down list. Click the small color swatch to determine the color for the glow and click the down arrow on the larger swatch for the gradient.

- **Technique**   Determines whether the effect is blurry or sharp.

- **Source**   Determines whether the light source is coming from the center of the type or from the inside edges.

- **Choke**   Increases or decreases the perimeter of the matte of the glow.

- **Size**   Defines the size of the glow.

- **Contour**   Pertains to the pattern of the fading of the glow.

- **Range**   Describes where the contour will be applied to the glow.

- **Jitter**   Increases or decreases the variations around the layer.

4. When you are satisfied, click **OK**.

Create Text Masks

You can use a text mask either to create a selection of type or to fill type with the background from one image or layer that you want to use on another image or layer. It is like making a cutout of one image to use in another.

1. In the Layers panel, select the layer that contains the image you want to use.

2. Select the **Horizontal Mask Type** tool or the **Vertical Mask Type** tool.

3. Set your formatting the way you want, as described previously in this chapter. Click the image to set the insertion point. The document should immediately turn to Quick Mask tint overlay color, and as you type, your text appears as clear areas in the Quick Mask (see Figure 11-14).

*Figure 11-14: **Quick Mask indicates selected areas, while the text you type reveals underlying layer content.***

4. Type the words you want to mask, and then click **Commit**. You will now see a selection marquee representing your text.

5. You can do several tasks, although you cannot edit the type as text at this point (no editing can be done after clicking Commit):

- Copy and paste the contents within the marquee selection to a new layer—put a selection tool inside the marquee, right-click, and then click **Layer Via Copy**. The background image is not affected.

- Move the selection marquee (with a selection tool inside the marquee); it can be dragged to another position, the underlying content can be copied, the selection can be filled, or it can be treated like any other Photoshop selection.

The text shown in Figure 11-15 is a copy of the photo area on the bottom layer and has been repositioned in the document on the top layer.

Figure 11-15: *The photo areas of the selected words "Puget Sound Sunset" were copied and then repositioned.*

How to...

- Choose a File Format
- Saving to Acrobat PDF Format
- Save to PSD
- Save as a PNG
- Use JPEG
- Use TIF
- Save a GIF
- Use EPS Under Certain Circumstances
- Prepare Your Images for Printing
- Print to an Inkjet Printer
- Choosing a Rendering Intent
- Preview Print Jobs with Soft Proofing and Gamut Warning
- Using CMYK Inks and RGB Color Profiles
- Care for Inkjet Prints
- Create a Contact Sheet
- Create a Personal Web Gallery
- Learn the Basics of Commercial Printing
- Print on Something Other than Paper
- Use a Service Bureau for High-End Output

Chapter 12

Printing and Exporting Images

The photos and artwork you create with Photoshop can have a life of their own *outside* of Photoshop; this chapter dives into personal and professional printing of your work, as well as exporting from Photoshop to file formats you can share online with others. Tips and techniques for prepping your work for a commercial printer are also covered.

Choose a File Format

Photoshop can save your work to dozens of different file formats, although you and your clients probably will only need PSD, PDF, PNG, JPG, TIF, GIF, and EPS. So which one should you use to save your hard work? If you will be working with this file again in Photoshop, you'll want to be sure to save it in Photoshop's native format PSD so that all of Photoshop's specialized layers and other effects are saved. But you will also probably want to save a copy of your file in some other file format, such as JPG or PNG for use on the Web or TIF, EPS, or PDF for printing.

QUICKSTEPS

SAVING TO ACROBAT PDF FORMAT

Adobe's Acrobat PDF file format is useful for e-mailing to clients, and the quality of text and graphics in a PDF is generally suitable for sending to a commercial printer. PDFs can retain font information as an embedded subset of the font you use; text is vector in structure, so it prints crisp at any resolution, but only the characters used are embedded, making it difficult for recipients to unlawfully extract a commercial typeface from the PDF document. A PDF saved from Photoshop can display the text layer intact when you open it in Photoshop, depending on the backward compatibility setting you choose when you save and the version of PDF to which you save. Here is how you can create a PDF file from Photoshop:

1. Click **File | Save As** and Photoshop displays a small reminder box that if you could care less about PDF options, a quick way to save a copy of your file is via the Actions panel, which has a high-quality, press-ready Action all set up for you in the Default Actions folder.

2. Choose the options that best apply to your intended audience from one of these categories in the Save Adobe PDF dialog box:

   - **General** This category offers a number of presets (click the **Adobe PDF Preset** down arrow) that are a good jumping-off point if you want to customize the settings. If you or your client has a specific version of Acrobat, click the **Compatibility** down arrow and choose the version of Acrobat Reader as the target. Also, there are a number of standards for PDF files for PDF Exchange (PDF/X) you might or might not need to set. When you select an Exchange

Continued . . .

Save to PSD

You should use Photoshop's native file format, PSD, whenever you think you'll want to perform future editing to a composition. PSD retains layer information, alpha channels, text, paths, and all special effects such as Layer Styles you might have placed in the document. When you save to PSD file format, a dialog box is displayed offering only one option: to enable backward compatibility, or not. Maximize Compatibility means that the file will degrade gracefully to successfully open in previous versions of Photoshop—although features specific to CS4 might be simplified or removed when, for example, a Photoshop 7 user opens the file. The data is there; it simply is hidden to prevent previous Photoshop versions from faulting on data they weren't designed to handle.

Save as a PNG

A Portable Network Graphic (PNG) file can be created by clicking either **File | Save As** or **File | Save For Web & Devices**. It's usually more error-proof to save in the Save For Web & Devices feature, particularly if your composition has transparency. A PNG file can only have one layer, with or without transparency, and no alpha channels. In addition to being great for the Web, it's also useful for archiving photos that have transparency; PNG's file format is lossless, and it's understood by many other graphics applications. See Chapter 13 for details on PNG's use on the Web.

QUICKSTEPS

SAVING TO ACROBAT PDF FORMAT
(Continued)

as a preset, the standards are identified in the Standard drop-down list, and a brief summary is displayed in the Description text box. The Exchange Standard eliminates discrepancies in the document that relate to font embedding and color trapping for commercial output. Therefore, if your press operator can't handle a PSD file, you should set an appropriate PDF/X version; a PDF is not editable by a commercial press operator without Photoshop, so removing halftone screen and transfer (brightness) functions before you send this file to a printer ensures fewer "show-stoppers."

● **Compression** These settings give you the opportunity to create a custom downsampling of your PDF file so, for example, a copy you need to e-mail is 72 pixels per inch (ppi) instead of the more press-ready image resolution of 266–300 ppi. However, choosing [Smallest File Size] from the Adobe PDF Preset drop-down list automatically calculates the best-quality, smallest file for e-mailing. Of some importance under Compression are the options to use JPEG, Zip, or No Compression. Zip compression creates larger saved files than JPEG compression, but Zip is lossless compression while JPEG is lossy. If you're a purist about your imaging work, you might want to choose lossless or no compression. (See Chapter 2 for a discussion of the compression techniques.)

Continued . . .

Use JPEG

This file format should only be used on a copy of your original Photoshop composition, because it uses lossy compression (data that is judged to be unimportant is discarded, to save on overall file size). Great for the Web and e-mail attachments, JPEG images can be created via **File | Save As** and **File | Save For Web & Devices**; Save For Web & Devices is a better route because you can preview how the lossy compressed file looks before you save it. Refer to Chapter 13 on how to prepare a JPEG for posting on a web page.

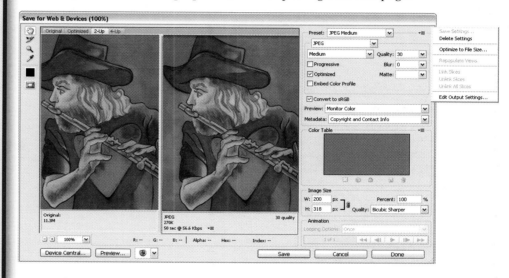

Use TIF

The Tagged Image File (Format) is one of the oldest high-fidelity formats for images, and its current "custodian" (the party who determines its standards and features in the future) is Adobe Systems. At present, the TIF file format has almost every capability that PSD does—special effects and text, along with paths in a saved TIF can be successfully reopened in Photoshop. However, many other applications cannot parse (understand, decode) the special data, although

SAVING TO ACROBAT PDF FORMAT

(Continued)

- **Output** This category gives you the chance to specify a Color Conversion for when you send a PDF to a commercial press and the RGB visual data needs to be read as CMYK data. If you're uncertain of what the destination's color space is, you can choose No Conversion; a good print house should be able to work with Adobe's native color space for a conversion because Adobe RGB color space is based on the CIELAB color model, which is device independent.

- **Security** This category enables you to set up security for your document if it's very sensitive in content and you're e-mailing it to an insecure ftp site. However, you shouldn't be doing this in the first place (password protection is relatively feeble against cracks using supercomputers), and it's very common to password-protect *yourself* or your client from the document!

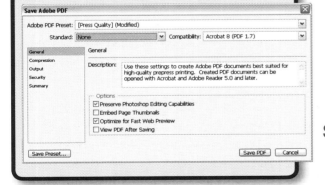

they can indeed open the TIF file format. The best you might get, for example, if you try to place a Photoshop TIF with layers in a Microsoft Word document, is that the layers will be flattened (this is called "gracefully degrading" data). But the worst is that an application might not recognize the special data, or even crash. If a client requests a TIF image, it's probably best to assume they don't own the latest version of Photoshop—so go ahead and flatten a copy and delete alpha channels unless the client specifically asked for alpha channels.

TIF file types can also be saved using compression; the Layer Compression area of the dialog box is quite explicit about saving fast or saving small. If you work cross platform, you might want to use the Byte Order of the intended recipient of your file.

Save a GIF

The Graphic Interchange Format (GIF) is a very old and not terribly color-capable file format for high-quality images. GIFs are Indexed Color mode, capable of only containing up to 256 unique colors, and as a result files are quite small.

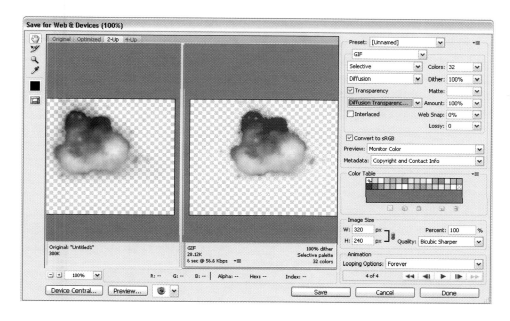

GIF images are still used on the Web for small icons and animations; the best way to save a copy of images and the only way to save an animated GIF is via **File | Save For Web & Devices**. See Chapter 13 for the steps on how to build a GIF animation.

Use EPS Under Certain Circumstances

Encapsulated PostScript (EPS) is falling out of favor commercially, giving way to PDF, but it's still a useful file format for sharing graphics, text, and images with coworkers who don't own Photoshop. Briefly, an EPS file contains printing instructions about the graphical content of the file; if the file contains both vector (such as text) and bitmap data, it will be hard to impossible for anyone to view the file in programs other than Photoshop, although vector-only contents can often be opened using Illustrator, CorelDRAW, and Xara Xtreme. An EPS file can contain printing plates for CMYK, Duotone, and two-color print jobs, and when you choose this file format for saving a copy of a file, you're given the option to include a small thumbnail that others can see for the purpose of accurately placing the data file in DTP programs such as InDesign. EPS files will be your least common choice of formats in everyday imaging and file-sharing work.

When you save to EPS, it's a fairly standard convention that the file should be in CMYK color mode, but it's not a mandate and you can indeed save an RGB image to EPS. If you have layers or alpha channels, you must save the file **As A Copy**; however, additional channels are accepted as EPS data—this is how spot color plates are saved for custom inks used in commercial signage. After you choose a filename and click **OK**, you will see the options for Preview and Encoding.

NOTE

Only PSD, JPEG, and TIFF file formats will retain user-entered metadata. See Chapter 3 on how to embed metadata using either Photoshop's **File | File Info** command and Adobe Bridge to add metadata to scores of images at one time.

The Preview is a coded-in thumbnail that is used for placement in DTP applications; a grayscale, 8-bit per pixel offers a better preview than 1 bit per pixel for placement in a document. Ask your coworker or press operator what sort of encoding they want; although ASCII is commonly accepted, if you work on the same operating system as the print shop does, they might ask for Binary encoding, which speeds up rendering time a little. Unless you're a press operator or really, really know what you're doing, *do not* check Include Transfer Function or Include Halftone Screen. An EPS file usually cannot be edited or otherwise tweaked by a press operator; if you use screening angles for the wrong imagesetting device, the operator can't change this, it adds up to needless expense and migraines. Expect an EPS file to be a lot larger than its original PSD file; PostScript information adds significantly to pixel data.

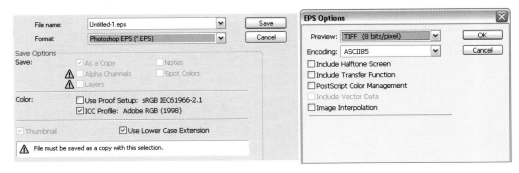

Prepare Your Images for Printing

Although pressing **CTRL/CMD+P** prints documents in Windows and the Mac in most applications, you get more out of prints generated from Photoshop with the investment of a few additional moments of time and a little understanding of what it takes to print terrific-looking images. Color management, resolution, and color spaces are all important to get every pixel looking its best, whether you pull prints from a home inkjet or intend to have your work commercially printed for magazines and posters. The following sections take you through the smartest and quickest workflow for ensuring that what you see onscreen is basically what you see in print.

USE COLOR MANAGEMENT

Every device that accepts color images will display, modify, and reproduce color differently. A color management system is your best insurance to get color consistency between your monitor and an output device; without consistency, you have no certainty of color accuracy from day to day. Additionally colors can shift from device to device: your images are all *about* color—in a nutshell, you *need* color management. The Adobe Color Management (ACM) system that is built into Photoshop and other Adobe products is based on the universally accepted International Color Consortium's ICC (color) profile.

What you see on your screen will never be *100 percent* the same as what you see in printed output because the colors on your monitor are produced by mixing light, whereas printed colors are produced by mixing pigments or dyes. Light uses an additive color model, while printed material uses the subtractive CMYK (or other) model. When you use the appropriate ICC profile for your output device, Photoshop can more accurately reconcile the differences between the colors you see on your screen and those that can be printed by your chosen device. If you don't bother to use Photoshop's color management tools, the color accuracy of your printed output becomes highly unpredictable, with some colors almost certainly being noticeably off-color.

If you have a properly calibrated monitor, you can effectively use the Adobe preset and third-party add-in color profiles available for various devices such as printers, print presses, monitors, and web browsers. Photoshop also has a very useful feature called Soft Proofing that helps you see what your image will look like when output.

CAUTION

Color management is useless without calibrating your monitor. Be sure to read Chapter 4 before printing.

Print to an Inkjet Printer

In Photoshop, you have access to both your system's printing options and Photoshop's own printing options. Fortunately, you can access your operating system's functions—to decide on which printer to use and to set up the size of the page you have physically loaded into the printer's tray—all from within

Photoshop's Print dialog box. The following sections take you through your options and guide you through potential stumbling blocks that might thwart your very best print from Photoshop.

SIZE AN IMAGE FOR PRINTING

Before printing, it's a good idea to ensure that the image is scaled to fit on the printable page. Photoshop has options in the Print dialog box for scaling your image to the page, but the amount of image data sent to a printer affects the time it takes to print an image. Photoshop does not touch the image itself when you set printing options; let's say you have a 26×18-inch image at 300 ppi. The image file size is 120MB and it's too large to fit on an 8½×11-inch sheet of paper. The quick and dirty remedy is to scale the image down using the features in Photoshop's Print dialog box, but you're still sending 120MB of file information to the printer, and the printer will take a seeming eternity to render the print as it examines and then discards the excess of file information.

Instead of wasting your time and electricity, to scale an image, follow these steps:

1. Click **Image | Duplicate**. Click **OK** to accept the default name of the file. You're doing this to not mess up your valuable original image.

2. Close the original image and then click **Image | Image Size** (**CTRL/CMD+ALT/OPT+I** is one of the handful of keyboard shortcuts you really do want to commit to memory).

3. In the Image Size dialog box, shown in Figure 12-1, click **Bicubic Sharper (Best For Reduction)** on the bottom drop-down list as the reduction method.

4. Click **Inches** in the Document Size increments drop-down list (unless you use European increments, then choose mm or cm); make sure that **Constrain Proportions** is checked.

5. Type **10.5** in the greater of the two dimensions boxes; 10.5 inches clears the standard paper size limit of 11 inches.

6. Image resolution corresponds to the maximum number of inkjet dots or laser printer toner dots. Typically, the true printing resolution of an inkjet printer today doesn't exceed the need for a corresponding 225 to 255 ppi, so in this example type **255** in the Resolution field. As you can see at the top of Figure 12-1, the file size is reduced dramatically and the file will take an order of magnitude shorter time to print.

7. Click **OK** to resize the image; it's basically ready to print.

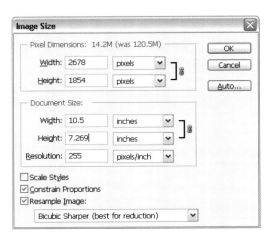

Figure 12-1: Photoshop's Image Size command can scale a copy of your image to make it print-ready.

ENTER THE PRINT DIALOG BOX

Before you actually pull a print of your own, simply peruse Photoshop's Print dialog box first; open any image you have on hard disk and then press **CTRL/ CMD+P**. Figure 12-2 shows your options in the first of two fields within this dialog box: click the **down arrow** in the upper-right corner of the Print dialog box, and click **Output**. Here are the features that are relevant to inkjet printing in this section; more details concerning high-quality commercial printing are covered later in this chapter:

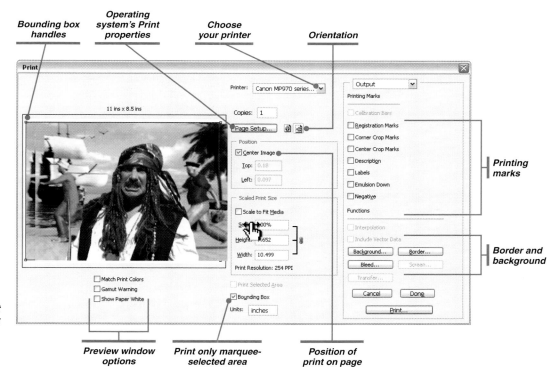

Figure 12-2: Photoshop's Print (Output) dialog box

- **Printer, Copies, and Page Orientation** The two icons tell Photoshop which page orientation (profile or landscape) to use. You can also override this setting by using your system's printing options box; click **Page Setup | Finishing tab**. Naturally, defining your printer and the number of copies are musts. It's usually wise to print only one copy of an image to see how it comes out before printing a dozen greeting cards, for example.

- **Position**   You'd need a compelling reason not to center your image on the page, such as wanting to write a note on the page after it's been printed. But if you do want to vary the position, remove the **Center Image** check mark and type the positions for the top left of the image.

- **Scaled Print Size**   If you click the **Scale To Fit Media** check box, Photoshop auto-scales the image to fit on the printable page. You might not want this; for example, you might want a 5×7-inch print. If you uncheck this check box, you're free to manually scale the image for printing. To do this, you drag the scrubby slider (place your cursor over the text label **Scale**, **Height**, or **Width**), or enter values manually. You can also manually scale the image by dragging the bounding box handles in the preview window. Although it is the default to show the bounding box, if it is not shown initially, click the **Bounding Box** check box.

- **Print Selected Area**   You must create a marquee selection in your image (using the Rectangle tool or other selection tool) prior to entering the Print dialog box. With this option checked, only the selected area of an image is sent to your printer.

- **Registration Marks**   Use this feature if and when you print color separations. It's a useless feature for printing composite images; registration marks are used by printers to ensure that the individual C, M, Y, and K plates are aligned at press time. Registration Marks are unavailable when you're outputting to a defined color inkjet; inkjets print finished composite photos and not black and white separations.

- **Corner and Center Crop Marks**   These are useful options for trimming your printed images to fit in a picture frame. See the Bleed option later in this list.

- **Description and Labels**   If you're printing a picture for framing, there's no reason to have text outside of the image. But if you're scrapbooking, you might want to include descriptions. Descriptions are automatically added from metadata information you must first add to an image through **File | File Info**.

- **Emulsion Down and Negative**   These options are for printing color separations, discussed later in this chapter. Don't check them for inkjet printing.

- **Background**   Use this option to choose a background color to be printed on the page outside the image area. Click **Background**, and then select a color from the Color Picker. This option does not affect your document, but only the print background of your document.

- **Border**   Prints a black border around an image; you cannot choose any other color. Type a number (it is limited to a size equal to or smaller than .15 of an inch or equivalent for other units) and choose a unit value to specify the width of the border.

If you want a *fancy* border, use Photoshop's Shapes tool or a third-party plug-in filter to create one prior to printing.

- **Bleed**   Prints thin crop marks inside rather than outside the image. Use this option to trim the image within the graphic. For example, you'd use this option on an image that does not print exactly to a picture frame size.

- **Print preview options**   Found beneath the image preview, these options are enabled when you choose Photoshop Manages Colors under Color Handling in the Color Management pane. **Match Print Colors** displays a very good onscreen simulation of how the colors in your image will actually look when printed. **Gamut Warning** displays an overlay in the image preview window of "problem areas"—areas that fall outside of the printer's color range capability, and will most likely print terribly. Fluorescent colors, bubble gum colors, and any area that is oversaturated will print dull. Cancel out of your print job if you see a visible Gamut Warning in the preview window; later in this chapter you'll learn how to correct gamut discrepancies between screen and printed images. **Show Paper White** is a preview compensation in the event that you're not printing to high-quality white-balanced paper but instead to newsprint or other tinted paper. Your preview will most likely look brownish, and that's what you'll get in your print; generally you should stick to glossy high-quality photographic paper for imagery you'll be proud of in print.

You're more than halfway to achieving the print of your dreams now. Click the **down arrow** in the upper-right corner (where you chose Output) and now click **Color Management**. In the Color Management fields, shown in Figure 12-3, set these options:

- **Document or Proof**   Click either one of these buttons; the Document setting will send color settings to your inkjet printer using the color profile of the image; this is set in **Edit | Assign Profile** in Photoshop before you use **File | Print**. If at this point you don't fully understand color profiles, it won't kill your intended print—it will just wound it a little! See Chapter 4 for tips and documentation on color profiles and how they relate to color management. If you click **Proof**, Photoshop assumes you want to print a "hard proof"—a print that simulates what a commercial print job will turn out like, using the CMYK parameters you've previously defined in **Edit | Color Settings** (see Chapter 4). If this is a print for your portfolio or to give to your mom, choose Document; the colors will be more vivid than a commercial press simulation of your work.

TIP

Once you have options set up for printing, it's nice to save the settings for future work. To keep your options and close the Print dialog box without actually printing a piece, click **Done**. To print one copy of an image, press **ALT/OPT** and then click **Print One**.

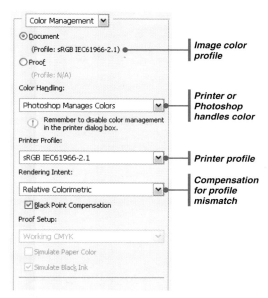

Figure 12-3: The Color Management settings in the Print dialog box

QUICKFACTS

CHOOSING A RENDERING INTENT

A *rendering intent* refers to a set of rules that a color management system uses to manage color as you move from color space to color space and device to device. It's typical for non-PostScript printers (inkjets don't use PostScript) to "presume" Perceptual rendering intent, but printer specs change almost daily; you're usually safe letting Photoshop decide how colors are handled. Different rendering intents favor different aspects of color such as saturation or the relationship between colors. Your choices in the Rendering Intent drop-down list are

- **Perceptual** Favors changing colors in ways that most closely match the way the human eye sees color; so this is good when you are printing photographs.

- **Saturation** Good for charts, cartoons, and so forth in which bold color is used to tell the story and where accuracy or subtle nuanced color is not needed.

- **Relative Colorimetric** Usually the best choice if you are printing documents on a press in the United States and Europe because it shifts all out-of-gamut colors into gamut. In Japan, commercial printers are set up differently and Perceptual should be used for commercial print work instead.

- **Absolute Colorimetric** Clips out-of-gamut colors and emphasizes maintaining color accuracy. Some devices or media such as paper and video produce better results when this rendering intent is used.

Photoshop is pretty good at picking the right rendering intent for the output device, so when in doubt it is safe to choose to go with the default rendering intent Photoshop's various dialog boxes provide.

- **Color Handling** The decision of whether to let Photoshop or your inkjet printer handle colors is only really determined by printing a copy each way. It totally depends on the make and model of your inkjet printer. Through experience, the authors have witnessed—using three different makes and models of printers—that most of the time (but not always), Photoshop sends better color data handling info to the printer than the printer's interpretation. The exception is if your inkjet can actually read color management data; a Canon Pixma inkjet can read color profiles, works well with the sRGB color space, and typically renders a more faithful representation of digital work than Photoshop does.

- **Printer Profile** Either read the manual that came with your inkjet or go online to the manufacturer's web site and see what color profile the printer is set up to use. Generally, an image's color profile should match the color profile of the printer. For example, you might be disappointed if your document is assigned the Adobe RGB color space while your printer prints to sRGB. Colors can be either too brilliant or too dull in the case of a profile mismatch.

- **Rendering Intent** Rendering Intent is your parachute and your lifesaver—it is used to reconcile the difference between your document's color profile and your printer's, on-the-fly, so you don't have to cancel a print and return to pondering Photoshop's Edit menu. This option deserves a more lengthy explanation. See the "Choosing a Rendering Intent" QuickSteps for details.

CONSIDER OTHER PRINT SITUATIONS

If for some reason your print is too large to fit on the page and you click Print, you'll get an attention box from Photoshop telling you this; your options are to Proceed or Cancel:

- If you click **Cancel**, the whole print setup is cancelled and you're returned to Photoshop's workspace.

- If you click **Proceed**, you're taken to your system's printing options box where you can choose your printer. Some (but not all) printer drivers offer scaling options for printing so you might not have to cancel your intended print.

Similarly, if Photoshop detects that the resolution capability of your printer is greater than the resolution of the digital image you intend to print, you'll receive an attention box. However, if you want a down-and-dirty print, you might be pleased if you continue and print. Inkjet printers don't use

PostScript halftone dots to render images—they spray ink on a semiporous page and physically the inks will blend, making somewhat less of a coarse image. For now, click **Cancel**, and it's time to explore other, commercial printing possibilities.

Preview Print Jobs with Soft Proofing and Gamut Warning

Clipping is one of the issues that arise when printing from a large additive color space, such as your monitor's RGB space, to the comparatively small subtractive color space of inkjets and other CMYK printing methods. If you saw a tint overlay in image areas earlier when exploring the Print preview, these areas are out of the printer's color gamut and will be clipped. *Clipping* is the unwanted discarding of original document colors when you print; colors that cannot be described using subtractive pigments are called out-of-gamut colors (a *gamut* is a color range, also known as a *color space*).

PREVIEW ON YOUR SCREEN BEFORE PRINTING

There is a way to see an approximation of how your image's colors will print via the View menu, and there is also a way to reduce how far out of gamut image areas might be for printing. Use the following steps with any of your images to bring areas back into a printer's color gamut:

1. Click **View | Proof Setup | Custom**.

2. In the Customize Proof Condition dialog box (see Figure 12-4), click **sRGB IEC61966-2.1** in the Device To Simulate drop-down list. The chances are very good that your inkjet printer is hard-wired to the sRGB color space.

3. In the Rendering Intent drop-down list, you have the four options discussed earlier in the "Choosing a Rendering Intent" QuickSteps. If your piece is an illustration, you might want to choose **Saturation**, which gives up color accuracy in favor of brilliant, juicy colors. However, if you print more photographs than illustrations, choose **Relative Colorimetric**, which shifts out-of-gamut colors to the closest reproducible color in the destination color space, using the source document's highlight regions as a base point.

Figure 12-4: **The Customize Proof Condition dialog box**

4. Check **Black Point Compensation**. This option ensures that the shadow detail in the image is preserved by simulating in Photoshop's workspace the full dynamic range of the printer. Also choose this option if you plan to use black point compensation when printing.

5. Click **OK** and your screen image looks as close as possible to a physical print, but note that showing dots of ink on a piece of paper—on your monitor—is like judging the color of a sweater you buy from a printed catalog.

DETECT OUT-OF-GAMUT COLORS

Gamut Warning is an onscreen color overlay on your photo that indicates areas that are out of gamut and will not print properly. However, most of the problem with out-of-gamut colors is that they have too much saturation. Without touching hue or brightness, thus ensuring a lot of color consistency, you can bring colors in your image back into printer gamut using the Sponge tool *on a copy of your photo*. Here are the steps to take to correct an image's out-of-gamut colors for more accurate printing:

1. Press **F8** to display the Info panel. If the top-right field is not set up to show CMYK values, click the **eyedropper**-arrow next to this field and then click **CMYK** as the color model.

2. Click the **Sponge** tool on the Tools panel, and then choose **Desaturate** on the Options bar. Set the **Flow** (the amount, or intensity) to less than 50% and choose a brush tip on the Options bar that is in scale with the elements in your photograph.

3. Hover (don't click) over some areas in the image. As shown in Figure 12-5, there are exclamation marks to the right of the CMYK values on the Info panel in a lot of areas over which the cursor lies. These areas are out of gamut for your custom soft proof and need to be corrected.

4. Click **View | Gamut Warning**. A tint overlay appears over image areas that are out of gamut as defined by your preview settings. Depending on the color content of the image, you might need to change the Gamut Warning color to better see the warning. For example, if your image has a lot of reds, you press **CTRL/CMD+K** and then, on the Transparency & Gamut page, specify a contrasting Gamut Warning color such as green or blue.

5. With the **Sponge** tool, stroke over areas that are highlighted with the Gamut Warning tinted overlay. As you can see in Figure 12-6, the tint is disappearing from the document; what's actually happening is that these areas are decreasing in saturation and thus move into a printer's color range.

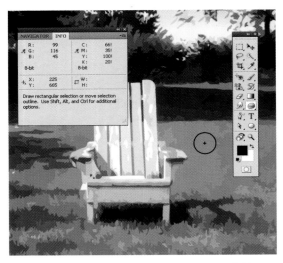

*Figure 12-5: **An exclamation mark next to a CMYK value means the area won't print accurately.***

*Figure 12-6: **Reduce saturation to move colors into printable range.***

Care for Inkjet Prints

If you really want your pictures to last, archival inks are usually mated to specific archival paper when you buy them; the experts know the chemical interaction of ink on paper, so trust the experts, because ink and paper go hand in hand usually. Archival ink goes for about $60 for the C, M, Y, and black set, and you can get archival paper, acid-free, for around $1 per 8½×11-inch page. Archival inks are pigment based, while standard cartridges are filled with less-permanent dyes.

Once you've made your print, bear in mind these physical realities about your digital prints:

- Treat printed sheets as fine art and handle them to avoid scuffing. If you stack prints to store unframed ones, interleave them with soft, smooth, acid-free paper or acid-free glassine slip sheets.

- If you're thinking of laminating prints, pretest a laminate before applying it. Liquid laminates such as Clearshield, FrogJuice, and Golden MSA Varnish are compatible with many archival papers.

- If you want *mounted* prints, follow museum mounting techniques, including Japanese hinges and Mylar corners. Detailed information about fine art care and treatment standards is available at **www.artfacts.org**.

- Although glass frames are much better (and classier) than acrylics (inkjet ink seeps into the acrylic over time), don't let the print *touch* the glass. Instead, buy or make a matte, or use a frame that stands off from the face of the print.

- Display your work in room lighting, avoiding direct sunlight. Inkjet colors shift and fade at uneven ratios, like store signs whose cyan ink has disappeared.

- Store blank paper at 72°F, and after a year, buy fresh paper. Unused paper should be stored in its original packaging in the poly bag.

Create a Contact Sheet

A *contact sheet*, a page filled with a collection of image thumbnails, is even more useful in the digital world of photography than it was in the physical, film-based world of photography. Unlike film, you can't hold a DVD or a disk drive up to the window or put it on a light table to see what images are stored there!

NOTE

To the disappointment of previous users of Photoshop, many of the neat Scripts are being phased out by Adobe Systems, such as Picture Package printing. However, the script itself is still supported by CS4; if you don't care to work in Bridge, you can download and install scripts available from Adobe.com.

If you're upgrading from a previous version of Photoshop, the Contact Sheet Script is no longer on the File menu—contact sheets are now created in Adobe Bridge.

To create a contact sheet of some or all files in a hard disk folder:

1. Launch Bridge.

2. Press **CTRL/CMD+K** (**Edit | Preferences** in all Adobe programs), then click **Startup Scripts** on the list and put a check in the **Adobe Bridge CS4** box. By default, Adobe has not enabled scripts, scripts drive contact sheets and other former Photoshop Script choices, and scripts can slow down Bridge performance. You may need to close and restart Bridge after clicking **OK**.

3. If Output isn't on the Application bar, click the **workspaces** down arrow and choose **Output**. The Output panel is displayed. Use the scroll bar as needed to display all the options described in the following steps.

4. Navigate the **Folders** panel for the collection of images you want produced as a PDF contact sheet. Once the folder is opened, you can select only the images you want from the Content panel by **CTRL/CMD**+clicking their thumbnails; they'll display in the Preview panel, and once they're there, you can drag on thumbnails to arrange them.

5. In the **Output** panel (see Figure 12-7), click the **PDF** icon, and then choose your printer's page size and orientation from the **Document** area.

6. Choose in the **Layout** area a layout that suits your needs. For example, if your contact sheet has eight images, in landscape orientation, choosing two rows of four columns will display nice large thumbnails; thumbnails don't necessarily have to be thumbnail-sized!

7. Click **Refresh Preview** to see how your PDF file is coming along in the **Output Preview** panel. Do this often throughout the following steps.

8. In the **Overlays** area, choose a font, a color for the font, and whether you want the file extension printed below each thumbnail or not. If you uncheck both Filename and Extension, nothing will print.

9. You can make a slideshow out of a PDF document, whose recipient can enjoy auto-turning pages with Transition effects and durations for the show. Set up your Hollywood epic using the **Playback** options.

10. Protect your work from an unintended recipient copying your photos from the PDF by typing a polite but firm ownership statement in the appropriate **Watermark** field.

11. The Save button might be hidden on the Output panel; use the scroll bar as needed until you can see the bottom of the panel. Check **View PDF After Save**, click **Save**, and you now have a PDF contact sheet, as shown in Figure 12-7.

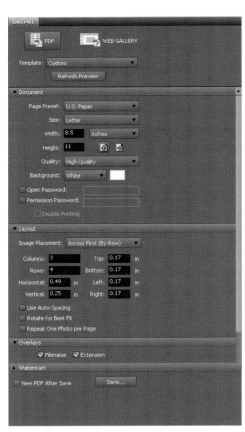

*Figure 12-7: **Create a contact sheet, or several, directly within Adobe Bridge.***

Create a Personal Web Gallery

Creating a gallery for a web site is only marginally more difficult than printing a PDF contact sheet. Be aware that if you're dreaming of an extraordinarily interactive, jazzy, slick, and unique web gallery, you'd contract a designer to do this sort of thing. It's not super robust, but Web Gallery creation is performed in Bridge, and the code Bridge generates is very clean XHTML and conforms to web standards. You can perform some customizing to the eight templates Bridge offers, and users can anticipate that additional templates will be offered in the future on Adobe's Exchange web site.

To create a Web Gallery, you can either upload the code and images to an ftp site supplied by your ISP, or you can save the code and images to your computer hard disk. If you upload to an ftp site, you will need to know its address and an ID name and password with which you can log on. Here are the steps to create and upload or save a Web Gallery:

1. In Bridge, click **Web Gallery** in the Output pane.

2. Select the images you want to feature on your Web Gallery from the Content pane, and then arrange them to your liking in the Output Preview pane (see Figure 12-8).

Figure 12-8: **Bridge's Web Gallery creation features consist largely of making choices and dragging files you want in your online gallery to the appropriate onscreen locations.**

3. In the Output pane, choose a template from the **Template** drop-down list and then click **Refresh Preview** to see it in the Preview pane. Some templates have a choice of style: click the **Style** down arrow to pick other style options for your page.

4. Scroll down and set colors for the page's **Background**, the **Title** on the page, the **Menu** visitors use to navigate through your images, and how the border of the **Thumbnail** reacts when the visitor clicks and hovers over the thumbnail.

5. In the **Appearance** area, you might or might not want Bridge to auto-generate the filename's title below the main display of each image; sometimes this is a visual distraction, while other times a filename might be personal. You can set the Thumbnail Size in this area (Medium is usually good, considering a lot of visitors have relatively large monitors today), and the size of the main image on the page, called the Preview Size. You can also make the preview images cycle in your uploaded collection at any speed (Slide Duration), and you have a passel of neat Transition Effects at your disposal from the drop-down list.

6. In the **Create Gallery** area, name your gallery by typing in the **Gallery Name** field. If you don't, visitors will read "Adobe Web Gallery" when they land on your gallery— flattering for Adobe Systems but probably not what you envision!

7. Click the **Save To Disk** button if you're unsure of your ISP's ftp login information, then click **Browse** to locate a good folder location on your hard drive. Click **Save** to save the Web Gallery on your hard disk. At a later time, you can send the files to your ISP for them to put in place. Alternatively, click **Upload**, fill in the ftp address and your login information, and then click **Upload**. Be patient at this point and don't click anything in Bridge; Bridge needs to connect to your host's server and upload your files.

8. When Bridge notifies you that it's finished, you can close Bridge, open your favorite web browser, and surf to your new Web Gallery online, and live.

Learn the Basics of Commercial Printing

The "Prepare Your Images for Printing" section earlier in this chapter contains valid information not only for personal inkjet printing, but also for commercial printing, the sort that involves line screens, CMYK and custom colors, and color separations. Although Photoshop can generate color "seps," you need to understand that unless you work at a print house, you don't create your own color separations; you give a press operator a disk with either a PSD file or a PDF. Why?

- High-resolution commercial printing is usually produced from color separations that are written to a material such as film; paper like you'd buy at an office supply store can't hold the sheer volume of printing dots required for a high-quality reproduction nor does paper have the tensile strength of film for accurate reproduction of pixels to dots. Commercial printers historically have used a PostScript device called an *imagesetter* for making color seps for printing plates. An imagesetter is a piece of hardware that is sufficiently expensive that you do not *go* to an office supply store and put one on your credit card!

- When press plates are made from color separations, these plates are mounted on presses whose precise calibration is a mystery to all but the operator. You don't know the ink pressure, nor how much undercolor removal (UCR) needs to be adjusted so puddling doesn't occur during printing. A press operator knows the physical characteristics of a specific print press and how it needs to be recalibrated as wear and tear take their toll. They can compensate for printing characteristics by adjusting the seps. You, sadly, cannot.

Take heart: You're a creative spirit, a photographer or a retoucher, and physical output is just a different type of art from what you perform. This is the stuff business relationships are made of; read on to see what you can do to help this business partner by setting up a few things with your Photoshop work so the printer can reproduce your efforts and skill, using *their own* efforts and skill.

UNDERSTAND (AND OBEY) THE TIMES TWO RULE

Separation plates necessarily have to be made of dots—*halftones* whose size corresponds to *continuous tone* colors you see onscreen and in physically printed material. Resolution plays a big part in *not seeing* the *dots*; the higher the resolution in the image file you send to a commercial printer, the smaller the printed dots, until at a certain point the resolution is high enough that the average audience cannot see the dots without using a photographer's loupe.

What makes PostScript the printing method from digital media the *de facto* standard is how the dots are arranged line per line. Non-PostScript printers occasionally don't even bother to align halftone dots with the precision necessary from which to make high-resolution separation plates. These lines of dots are arranged on the C, M, Y, and K plates at different angles to prevent a patterning effect. There is additionally something called *line frequency* (how many dots per line), and happily for you, this mind-boggling math is at an end if you only understand the "Times Two Rule:"

> *For the best reproduction, the digital file must be of twice the pixel per inch (ppi) resolution as the line per inch (lpi) value of the printing screens.*

To make this less abstract, we typically use 300 ppi, *at printing size* (measured in inches or cm, or mm) for digital files to be reproduced in "coffee table book" quality, 2540 dpi and occasionally higher. The reason for this value (300 ppi) is that it's a little more than twice the line/inch value of high-quality printing: 133 lpi. In theory, your images can be 266 ppi for a 133 lpi screen, but "300" is so easy to remember that even Adobe Systems recommends this value.

PREPARE YOUR FILES FOR THE INTENDED OUTPUT

The most common means of transporting a digital file to a commercial printer, a photofinisher, or other party who will render your digital work to a physical surface is a CD or DVD. To write files to a CD, you can use your operating system's accessory or a third-party program such as Nero.

File sizes are a relative issue. For 5×7s, a 9MB image—5×7 at 300 ppi—is fine. Use Photoshop's Image Size command, covered earlier, before saving a copy or an image to TIFF format. Similarly, an 8×10 at 300 ppi is a 20.6MB file. Photofinishers occasionally prefer to have your camera's memory card over a CD, but these are unedited images—call ahead and ask them if they'll take a thumb drive.

With most online services, you're provided the option of uploading files or snail-mailing them on CD or DVD, which is welcome if you have a dial-up connection. Online photofinishers almost always have an "upload wizard" to simplify file transfer. In terms of acceptable file formats, TIF is ubiquitous, but the TIF file must be uncompressed with layers flattened, and no saved selections to alpha channels. Some photofinishers will accept JPEG images, but these lossy file formats aren't really acceptable for serious imaging work. Many online places ask for image resolutions of 250–300 ppi, and although they'll accept smaller files, they make the disclaimer that larger prints—8×10s and up—will look grainy; you'll be able to see the ink, pigment, or dye dots.

CAUTION

If you are considering an online service or a local photofinisher for high-quality prints, ask about Photoshop first. You might be asked not to write PSD image files to the CD; photofinishers use TIF images primarily (and JPEGs), and usually can't work with layered images. A good rule of thumb is if your operating system shows an icon of an image in Thumbnails folder view, don't copy it. Your last name or telephone number also makes a good volume label for the CD you burn.

TIP

The high-end professional places require that you download a color profile to use on images for print to ensure the best quality.

Try increasing the saturation of an image to be printed on a novelty item to an extent that verges on the unrealistic to compensate for CMYK pigment's inherent narrow color space; naturally, do this to a *copy* of your work. Expect your image to last longer—you should be able to expect a machine-washed image, on a mug for instance, to last over 6 years without apparent fading or chipping of the image. A photofinisher will provide the dimensions for your photo or artwork, and they will probably ask for a 300-dpi image in TIFF file format.

If you have access to an inkjet, you can print your own T-shirts quicker and for about the same price as you could order online. A ten-pack of T-shirt transfer paper runs $1 per page, and you can usually buy it at the supermarket or office supply stores.

Print on Something Other than Paper

Mugs, canvas bags, and T-shirts are the most common items you can have your images affixed to, but you can find via an online search specialty paraphernalia printers, offering to print on items ranging from baseball caps to wall clocks to men's boxer shorts. In terms of availability, you can have these gift items ordered through just about any local photofinisher; the service takes about a week because the photofinisher usually has to send out for these items.

Expect to pay about $10 for a coffee mug, $20 for a baseball cap, and $25 for a messenger-style bag with your photo on it. As far as quality is concerned, you must expect the colors to be a little dull due to the media onto which your image is rendered.

Use a Service Bureau for High-End Output

There are two types of service bureaus:

- The standard service bureau
- The full-service bureau

Standard service bureaus offer short-run offset printing and basically serve business needs—you want a *full-service* bureau for artistic needs. Service bureaus can turn your images into overhead transparencies and, more importantly, 35mm slides. Although slide projectors have mostly given way to LCD projectors (owned by large organizations and typically $1200 and up), there's something convenient and personal about 35mm slides (*chromes*); they're extremely portable and suit the need to present images from your trip to Europe to clubs and small community groups.

If you live in or near a city of 100,000 or more, chances are you and the disc you burn are only a short drive from a service bureau. You need to call ahead and ask for pricing, turnaround time, and file format and image size. Many service bureaus can turn around a 35mm slide in 24 hours. Suppose you want 35mm slide work—after asking these questions, you follow these steps:

1. The bureau wants at least a 6MB image. Not a problem; today's digital cameras produce 12MB images and higher, and you know how to resize your image using steps discussed earlier in this chapter.

2. The bureau typically asks for *35mm portrait aspect ratio*; again, no problem if you haven't cropped your 35mm image. Click **Image | Image Size**. In the Image Size dialog box, uncheck **Resample Image**, and then type **1** in the smaller of the Height or Width boxes. If the other field turns to **1.33**, you're all set to write the file to disc. Alternatively, click the **Crop** tool, type **1.33** in the Width field and **1** in the Height field on the Options bar. If the image looks bad with the proposed cropping, click the **Cancel** icon.

If the two techniques above fail, use these advanced steps to manually change the aspect ratio to that of 35mm:

1. Click **Image | Image Size**, and then uncheck **Resample Image**.

2. Type **3.75** in the lesser amount proportion box, then click **OK**. You're going to create a 4×5.32-inch image, which is a multiple of 1/1.33; the 3.75 is to allow a little background on the narrower side of the photo, because background color or texture on only two sides of a photo looks unprofessional.

3. Double-click the layer title on the Layers panel to turn the photo into a layered image if it's not so already.

4. Click **Image | Canvas Size**. Type **4** and **5.32** inches in the fields, depending on whether the image is tall (portrait) or wide (landscape). Click **OK**.

5. On the Layers panel, click the **Create A New Layer** icon and then drag this layer title to below the photo layer.

6. Fill the bottom layer with a solid color or a pattern.

7. Flatten a copy of the image, save to TIFF or other file format the service bureau requests, and then burn a disk for the service bureau.

CAUTION

A service bureau isn't responsible for matting your images before writing them to 35mm slides, and often they'll just go with white (clear) to proportion your work. Then your projected slide will blast your audience in a dimmed room with white on its sides, and no one will thank you.

Chapter 13

Preparing Your Images for the Web

This chapter shows you how to use Photoshop's tools for preparing images for display on the World Wide Web. You will learn how to optimize images and create animations, image maps, and rollover effects using Photoshop CS4.

Optimize Images for the Web

Images for use on the Web need to be "lean and mean"—the file size needs to be as small as possible with a minimum of loss in image quality. Smaller file sizes result in images that are transmitted and displayed faster, thereby reducing the time it takes a web page to load. Three factors determine the file size of an image (for a set width and height): the file format (usually GIF, JPEG, or PNG), the number of colors (determined, in part, by the file format chosen), and the dimensions of the image—its height and width as measured in pixels per inch. Of the file types, GIF and JPEG formats are the most common. PNG is not as widely supported, although it is gaining popularity in recent years

TIP

The Save For Web & Devices dialog box automatically converts the image resolution to 72 pixels per inch (ppi), long considered the highest resolution needed for web work. If you wish to use a different image resolution, you must use Save As instead of Save For Web & Devices.

NOTE

When you save an image for the Web, you can consider resizing the image to web-friendly dimensions. Most users today run 1024×768-pixel screen displays. When posting to online galleries, you can prep your work to accommodate the host's gallery space, minus any headers a web page might have. Essentially, if you're posting to a gallery, you could and should go 900 pixels wide and as high as the page will accommodate: 600 is usually fine.

due to the fact that PNG uses lossless file compression. Characteristics of these common file types include:

- **GIF (Graphic Interchange Format)**   Images in this format use Indexed Color mode, containing a maximum of 256 colors. Images with large areas of solid color and sharp detail work best as GIFs, such as with icons and animations. GIF also supports transparency, allowing the area under the transparent portions of the GIF to be visible.

- **JPEG (Joint Photographic Experts Group)**   This format compresses an image, using lossy compression, to reduce the file size. When images are compressed in this format, data is lost—specifically, similar colors are removed from the image during compression. The amount of data lost depends on the amount of compression applied. JPEG supports 24-bit color, which yields approximately 16 million colors. This works well for web images.

- **PNG (Portable Network Graphic)**   This format comes in two varieties: PNG-8, which is similar to GIF; and PNG-24, which is similar to JPEG but uses lossless compression (no colors are removed). PNG files are often used to contain transparent image areas. Using Photoshop, the files are reduced to a single layer, and retain no alpha channel or image resolution information, unlike TIFF and other less-optimized image file formats.

- **WBMP** (Wireless Application Protocol Bitmap Format)   This format is ideal for optimizing images to be used for mobile instruments. It is 1-bit-per-pixel color mode, and thus color images are reduced to either black or white pixels.

You set the file type, number of colors, and resolution when you save images.

Optimize Using the Save For Web & Devices Dialog Box

Photoshop uses the Save For Web & Devices dialog box to optimize files for the Web. You can display four file versions of an image, optimizing each and then saving all four or one, if you choose. You can apply certain other adjustments in this dialog box, such as to change image size or to apply transparency. As you set the optimization options, the estimated file size and download time are shown below the preview window, as shown in Figure 13-1. Here are the steps and possibilities:

1. With an image open in Photoshop, click **File | Save For Web & Devices**. The Save For Web & Devices dialog box appears, as shown in Figure 13-1.

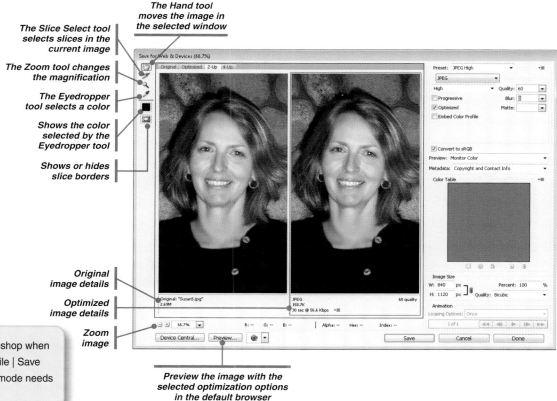

The Hand tool moves the image in the selected window

The Slice Select tool selects slices in the current image

The Zoom tool changes the magnification

The Eyedropper tool selects a color

Shows the color selected by the Eyedropper tool

Shows or hides slice borders

Original image details

Optimized image details

Zoom image

Preview the image with the selected optimization options in the default browser

CAUTION

Don't tinker around with color modes in Photoshop when you're preparing a photo for the Web. Using File | Save For Web & Devices can handle all your color mode needs automatically *on a copy* of your original.

Figure 13-1: This Save For Web & Devices dialog box shows the 2-Up tab selected.

2. Click the **2-Up** tab so that you can see the original and modified images side by side as you set the options.

3. Depending on your image type, read one of the following sections to learn how to optimize your image. The optimization options vary by file type.

OPTIMIZE A GIF OR PNG-8 IMAGE

GIF and PNG-8 images are similar and use an indexed color panel. Previewing the settings you choose is the key to a small, good-looking GIF or PNG export. The optimization options are shown in Figure 13-2.

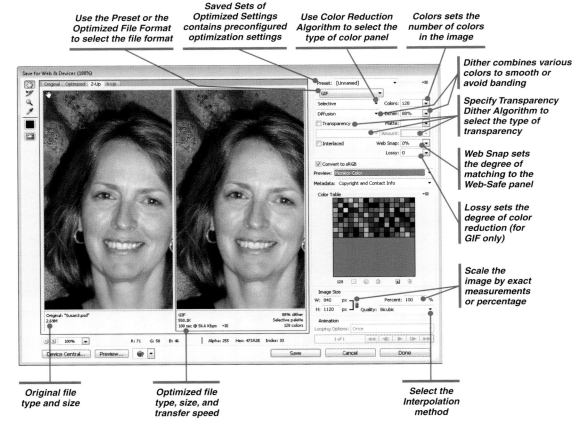

Use the Preset or the Optimized File Format to select the file format

Saved Sets of Optimized Settings contains preconfigured optimization settings

Use Color Reduction Algorithm to select the type of color panel

Colors sets the number of colors in the image

Dither combines various colors to smooth or avoid banding

Specify Transparency Dither Algorithm to select the type of transparency

Web Snap sets the degree of matching to the Web-Safe panel

Lossy sets the degree of color reduction (for GIF only)

Scale the image by exact measurements or percentage

Original file type and size

Optimized file type, size, and transfer speed

Select the Interpolation method

Figure 13-2: Optimization options for GIF and PNG-8 images

To optimize a GIF or PNG-8 image in Photoshop:

1. Click the **Optimized File Format** down arrow and choose **GIF** or **PNG-8**.

–Or–

Click the **Preset** down arrow, and click one of the **GIF** options or **PNG-8**. The options particular to this file format are displayed. (If the GIF is intended as an animated GIF, the animation preview controls will also be available.) Notice that if you choose a GIF-24 to GIF-128 option, the Color Table preview displays the closest match of original image colors to new color approximations for the limited palette of unique colors.

NOTE

An *algorithm* is a procedure or formula for solving a problem. Photoshop uses algorithms for color reduction and dithering, among other things.

2. Select the desired options, as shown in Figure 13-2:

- Click the **Color Reduction Algorithm** down arrow, and click the desired color-reduction algorithm (see Table 13-1).

NAME	WHAT IT DOES
Perceptual	Creates a panel that gives precedence to colors for which the human eye has greater sensitivity.
Selective	Favors broad areas of color and the preservation of web-safe colors.
Adaptive	Samples and uses the colors in the image rather than creating a full-spectrum panel.
Restrictive (Web)	Limits the panel to the 216 web-safe colors.
Custom	Enables you to create a custom panel by selecting the colors for the panel from the Color Table dialog box.
Black & White	Uses only black and white, which produces an effect similar to the halftones that are used in newspapers.
Grayscale	Uses only shades of gray, including black and white.
Mac OS	Uses the default Macintosh 8-bit system panel.
Windows	Uses the default Windows 8-bit system panel.

Table 13-1: Color Reduction Algorithms

NOTE

Dithering is a technique that Photoshop uses to suggest a color when a color is unavailable in the selected color table. For example, if there is no room in a color table for purple, Photoshop carefully arranges alternating pixels of available red and blue to simulate purple (when viewed from a distance, the red and blue visually merge to suggest purple). Dithering is also used to prevent banding and to ensure smooth color blending in images.

- Click the **Dither Algorithm** down arrow, and click the desired option (see Table 13-2). If you specify a Dither Algorithm, click the **Dither** down arrow, and drag the slider to specify the percentage of dithering. If you have a large variety of colors in the original image, specifying a larger amount of dithering may help reduce the file size. Note that using **Diffusion Dithering** slightly increases file size, but improves a GIF's appearance: you work between the number of colors and the Dither Amount scrubby slider to arrive at the best size/best image or animation.

- If you want an area of your GIF or PNG-8 image to be transparent, click the **Transparency** check box. Then click the **Transparency Dither Algorithm** down arrow and choose one. (See Table 13-2.) For example, if you intend to put an animation on a web page that features a particular color or pattern and want the GIF's background to drop out, click the **Transparency** check box. Note that unlike Photoshop compositions, whose layers can feature gradual transitions from totally opaque to transparent, GIF files are limited to one specific drop-out color. It is not possible using the GIF file format to, for example, make both green *and* purple areas drop out to transparent.

- If you want your GIF or PNG-8 image to be interlaced, click the **Interlaced** check box. This causes the image to load in a web page in several passes rather than in a single pass, which enables viewers with a slow connection to see part of the image immediately.

NAME	WHAT IT DOES
Diffusion	Applies a random pattern across adjacent pixels. You control the amount of dither using the Dither slider. More dither increases the number of colors and the file size.
Pattern	Applies a pattern similar to a halftone. The effect is usually obvious and unwanted; the pattern can take on more visual importance than the content of the image.
Noise	Applies a random pattern similar to Diffusion but with less scattering of random pixels in areas where simulating an unavailable color requires dithering.

Table 13-2: Dithering Algorithms

- Click the **Colors** down arrow, and select the number of colors you want in your GIF or PNG-8 image. You can also click the **Colors** spinners to specify the number of colors in the compressed image. Fewer colors means a smaller file size, so try to use as few colors as possible while maintaining some semblance of your original design.

- Click the **Matte** down arrow, and select the desired matte color from the drop-down list (see Table 13-3). This sets the color against which transparent pixels will be dithered, creating a smooth blend of transparent pixels with the matte colors. If you've selected a matte option, drag the **Amount** slider to specify the value.

- Set the amount of web snap by clicking the **Web Snap** drop-down list and dragging the slider. This shifts the colors in the image to the closest web-safe color—the higher the value, the more colors will be shifted.

- For GIF images, click the **Lossy** drop-down slider and drag the slider to specify the lossy value. Specifying a high lossy value removes more colors from the compressed image, resulting in a smaller file size with poorer image quality.

NOTE

Matte, the opposite of transparency, fills transparent pixels with a chosen color to display a solid background rather than a transparent one.

NAME	WHAT IT DOES
None	Makes pixels with more than 50 percent transparency fully transparent and pixels that are 50 percent or less fully opaque.
Eyedropper Color	Uses the color selected with the Eyedropper tool.
Foreground Color	Uses the foreground color in the Tools panel swatch.
Background Color	Uses the background color in the Tools panel swatch.
Black or White	Uses black or white, respectively, for the matte color.
Other	Allows you to select a color using the Color Picker dialog box.

Table 13-3: Matte Descriptions

- **Convert To sRGB**, selected by default, converts the image's colors to sRGB if they are not already, so that the colors on the various web browsers will look as much as possible like the optimized file being saved.

- To see how light or dark an image will appear on a computer system, click the **Preview** down arrow and choose an option. This allows you to take a look at various systems; it does not change the image. Monitor Color, the default setting, displays the image as it is. Macintosh (No Color Management) shows a gamma of 1.8—slightly lighter than Windows (No Color Management) of 2.2 gamma. Use Document Profile displays the image at whatever profile is available for color-managed images.

- Click the **Metadata** down arrow to specify what information will be carried in the image. The information can be entered or looked at by clicking **File | File Info**. If you didn't previously save metadata using File Info or by using Adobe Bridge, there will be no metadata to write; you cannot enter metadata directly into Save For Web & Devices.

- Under **Image Size**, you can scale the saved JPEG by using the scrubby slider to enter a width and height, or a percentage change. (Hold the cursor over the label and drag to change the values in the text box.)

3. Click **Preview** beneath the previewed image to see what your optimized image will look like in your default browser window.

4. When you're satisfied with your selections, click **Save**. The Save Optimized As dialog box appears.

5. In the **Save In** drop-down list, select the location for your image, and type the filename in the **File Name** text box. Verify the file type and then click **Save**.

TIP

Color profiles are instruction sets that are tagged to an image file that instruct printers and applications (a web browser, Photoshop, other graphics and DTP applications) how the image should be displayed. Characteristics such as brightness and saturation take on a consistency when viewed on different devices when these devices can read color profiles…and the user takes the time to tag an image with a specific color profile.

OPTIMIZE A JPEG IMAGE

JPEG files are recommended for photographs and continuous-tone images because they support more colors than the GIF format. Some of the options differ from those for GIF and PNG-8 files, as shown in Figure 13-3.

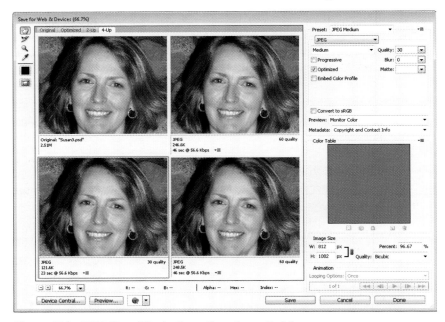

Figure 13-3: JPEG files differ in the options for optimizing.

To optimize a JPEG image in Photoshop:

1. With your image open in Photoshop, click **File** and then click **Save For Web & Devices**.

2. Click the **Preset** or **Optimized File Format** down arrow, and click a **JPEG** option.

3. Choose the options you want:

  ● Click the **Compression Quality** down arrow, and select an option from the drop-down list. Higher compression settings produce fewer colors and smaller images.

TIP

You can optimize a PNG-24 image by clicking **PNG-24** in either the Preset or Optimized File Format drop-down list. The PNG-24 format is similar to JPEG format, but PNG-24, unlike JPEG, uses a *lossless* compression algorithm. This means that PNG-24 images tend to be larger, but PNG-24 can preserve 256 levels of transparency.

TIP

To choose the target file size of the saved JPEG image, click the **Options** down arrow in the upper-right corner of the dialog box and click **Optimize To File Size**. In the dialog box, fill in the desired file size and select the initial settings under **Start With** and **Use**. Click **OK**.

TIP

The Compression Quality drop-down list in the Save For Web & Devices dialog box for a JPEG file offers preset compression settings. You can also set the level of compression using the Quality slider. This gives you greater control over the compression level and resulting file size.

- If you want the image to download in successive passes rather than in one pass, click the **Progressive** check box. A progressive JPEG is similar to an interlaced PNG; it's akin to streaming data, and broadband audiences don't need (and probably won't see) this enhancement.

- If you want to preserve the ICC profile (the color space) for the image, click the **ICC Profile** check box. (If it is unavailable to you, your image does not have an ICC profile.)

- If you want the image optimized, click the **Optimized** check box. This feature, which is not supported by older browsers, creates a slightly smaller file with no additional lossy compression data loss.

- If you want to use a compression setting not specified in the Compression Quality drop-down list, click the **Quality** down arrow and drag the slider to set the compression amount.

- Click the **Blur** down arrow and drag the slider to set the amount of blur. This applies a Gaussian-type blur (an adjustable hazy effect caused by adding detail to the pixels) to the image and decreases the file size. Recommended values are 0.1 to 0.5.

- Click the **Matte** down arrow to select the matte color. The matte color is the fill color for pixels that were transparent in the original image.

- For the JPEG file to conform to current web standards for color profiling (currently the standard is sRGB, but this is changing as web browsers are able to detect metadata color profile information), check the **Convert To sRGB** check box. If you test check Convert To sRGB, you may see a big color difference between the original preview window and the preview of the saved JPEG.

- Other options are described in the previous section, "Optimize a GIF or PNG-8 Image."

4. When you're satisfied with your selections, click **Save**. The Save Optimized As dialog box appears. Click the **Save In** down arrow, and navigate to the folder in which you want to save the image. Type the filename in the **File Name** text box, and click **Save**.

SAVE OPTIMIZED IMAGES

The process for saving optimized images is similar to that for saving any other image:

1. Click the **Save** button in the Save For Web & Devices dialog box. The Save Optimized As dialog box appears.

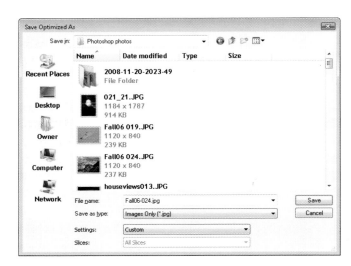

TIP

When you're using the Save For Web & Devices dialog box to optimize images for the Web and you create settings you'd like to use on other images, you can "remember" them. After creating the settings, click **Done** located on the bottom of the dialog box to remember and leave the dialog box. To remember, but stay in the dialog box, **ALT/OPT**+click **Remember**. To cancel the changes you've made and leave the dialog box, click **Cancel**; to cancel the changes but remain in the dialog box, **ALT/OPT**+click **Reset**.

TIP

To open the Output Settings dialog box from the Save Optimized or Save Optimized As dialog box, click the **Settings** down arrow, and click **Other**.

2. Click the **Save In** down arrow, and navigate to the folder in which you want to save the file.

3. Type the filename in the **File Name** text box.

4. Verify that the **Save As Type** is the format you want and for which you have optimized the file.

5. Click the **Settings** down arrow, and click the desired option from the drop-down list. See "Set Output Options" next for details.

6. If there are slices in your image, click the **Slices** down arrow, and click one of the following options:

   ● **All Slices**   Saves all the slices in the image

   ● **Selected Slices**   Saves only the selected slices

   ● **All User Slices**   Saves only the user slices in the image

7. Click **Save**, supply a name for the output settings, and click **Save** again.

Set Output Options

Use the Output Settings dialog box to set the output options for Photoshop. In Photoshop, open the Output Settings dialog box from the Save For Web

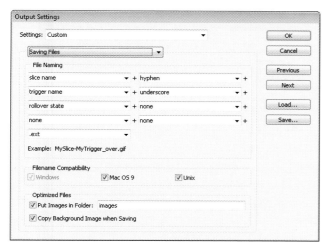

Figure 13-4: *The Output Setting dialog box sets options for Photoshop output files, such as background images, slices, saving files, or HTML.*

& Devices dialog box. Only the Save For Web & Devices dialog box allows you to save custom settings. When you save custom settings, they appear on the Preset drop-down list.

1. With an image open in Photoshop, click **File | Save For Web & Devices**.

2. Click the **Optimize** down arrow to the right of Preset, and then click **Edit Output Settings**. The Output Settings dialog box appears, as seen in Figure 13-4.

   You can select the different groups of output options from the drop-down list below the Settings field in the Output Settings dialog box. For example, you can click the down arrow and click HTML to set HTML output options. The HTML options are listed in Table 13-4.

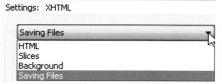

HTML OPTIONS	DESCRIPTION
Output XHTML	Ensures the generated code conforms to the Extensible HTML standard. If selected, some other options (such as Tag Case) are unavailable due to XHTML requirements. XHTML has more stringent syntax than HTML.
Tags Case	Sets the case of the HTML tags. The options are Lowercase, Uppercase, and Mixed Case (leading caps).
Attribute Case	Sets the case of the HTML tag attributes. The options are Lowercase, Mixed Case, Mixed With Initial Lower, and Uppercase.
Indent	Sets the type and amount of indent for indented lines. The options are Tabs, None, 1 Space, 2 Spaces, 4 Spaces, 5 Spaces, and 8 Spaces.
Line Endings	Sets the line endings for different operating systems. The options are Automatic, Mac (Macintosh), Win (Windows), and Unix.
Encoding	Sets the character encoding for the generated code. The options are Automatic (iso-8859-1), Western (iso-8859-1), Mac OS Roman (x-mac-roman), and Unicode (utf-8). The iso-8859-1 character set is the standard set of characters used in Western European languages. Unicode (utf-8) is a better choice if you need to support other languages.
Include Comments	Includes HTML comments within the HTML <!-- --> delimiters. Comments help you understand what is happening on the page.
Always Add ALT Attributes	Includes the ALT attribute for those HTML tags where it is applicable, such as the image (IMG) tag. Web accessibility standards require the ALT attribute for all nontext elements. The ALT value will be empty, so you will need to enter the tag information separately.

Table 13-4: *Descriptions of HTML Settings*

HTML OPTIONS	DESCRIPTION
Always Quote Attributes	Places quotes around the values of HTML tag attributes. HTML does not require quotes, but XHTML and XML (Extensible Markup Language) do.
Close All Tags	Inserts the closing HTML tags for all tags that require them. HTML is generally forgiving of unclosed tags, but XHTML and XML are not.
Include Zero Margins On Body Tag	Adds the Margin attribute set to 0 to the BODY tag. This starts the page content in the upper-left corner of the browser with no margin. This is not supported by all browsers.

Table 13-4: Descriptions of HTML Settings (continued)

3. Click **Next**. The Slices section appears. (You can also click the down arrow below the Settings field, and click **Slices** from the drop-down list.)

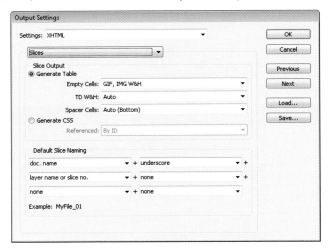

Click one of the following options for slices in your document and then set the default slice naming:

- **Generate Table**   Creates an HTML table for displaying the slices.

    - **Empty Cells**   Sets the rules for how empty table cells are generated: GIF, IMG W&H (GIF spacer image using the IMG tag with width and height specified); GIF, TD W&H (GIF spacer image using the table data tag [TD] with width and height specified); and NoWrap, TD W&H (text is not wrapped, using the TD tag with width and height specified).

    - **TD W&H**   Sets when width and height values will be generated. The options are Auto, Always, and Never.

- **Spacer Cells**   Controls whether or not a row of spacer cells will be generated. Some browsers allow space between cells, which destroys the effect of slices. A row of spacer cells at the top or bottom of the table can help ensure that the table will have the overall width specified. The options are Auto, Auto (Bottom), Always, Always (Bottom), and Never.

- **Generate CSS**   Generates a Cascading Style Sheet (CSS) rather than a table to display the slices. When you click the Generate CSS option, the Referenced option becomes available.

  - **Referenced**   Sets how the CSS elements will be referenced in the code: By ID (a unique ID value set in the code), Inline (style elements set in the DIV tag), or By Name (classes referenced by a unique ID).

- **Default Slice Naming**   Provides options, through a series of drop-down lists, for automatically generating a filename for each slice.

4. Click the **Next** button. The Background section appears. (You can also click the down arrow below the Settings field, and then click **Background** from the drop-down list.) This option places a background image on the web page. The View Document As option determines whether the background is an image or a solid color:

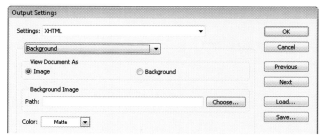

- **Image**   Enables you to type the path to the image in the **Path** text box, or you can click the **Choose** button and browse to an image file.

- **Background**   Gives you only the Color option.

  For a solid color, click the **Color** down arrow, and click an option from the drop-down list. Your choices are None, Matte (the current matte color), Black Or White, or Eyedropper Color (to select one of the current panel colors); or you can click **Other** to choose a color with the Color Picker.

5. Click the **Next** button. The Saving Files section appears. (You can also click the down arrow below the Settings field, and click **Saving Files** from the drop-down list.)

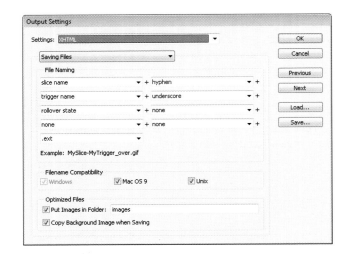

In the File Naming section, use the series of drop-down menus to specify how the various files generated are named when you save the document. Accept the defaults, or choose different options from the drop-down lists.

6. After clicking the desired File Naming options, specify settings for the following options:

- **Filename Compatibility** Enables you to specify the operating systems with which the files will be compatible. Your native operating system is chosen by default. You can choose to generate files compatible with Windows, Mac OS 9, and Unix.

- **Put Images In Folder** Enables you to store the images in a separate folder from the HTML documents. We recommend accepting the default **Images** folder option. (*Images* is the default folder name for almost all host server software.)

- **Copy Background Image When Saving** Creates a copy of the specified background image when the document is saved.

7. Click **Save**. The Save Output Settings dialog box appears.

8. Type a name for the output settings file, and then click **Save**.

Use Animated GIFs

Animations are a group of images that are displayed sequentially, creating a transition from second to second. Although automatically self-running animations are a standard on web pages, animated web content can also be triggered by a user action—for instance, when a viewer hovers a pointer over an image and something happens to it, such as it morphs into another image or is highlighted. Animations are an important part of web sites today. Photoshop has two levels of animation, depending on the version of product you have. Photoshop Standard's animation features are described in this book; Photoshop Extended contains both GIF animation and fairly comprehensive digital video creation and editing features.

Create a GIF Animation

GIF animations are great for banners and other elements on web pages; however, it's a good idea to begin with a concept. A good place to begin is with an idea of a story, a miniplot. What you can visually say within the limitations of a short, small, animated GIF often boils down to two elements:

QUICKSTEPS

MAKING PART OF AN IMAGE TRANSPARENT

With GIF, PNG-8, and PNG-24 images, you can select a color to be transparent in the final image. This is commonly done when you're displaying a web page image over a web page with a colored background. Choose the same color for the transparency in the image as the background color of the web page, and the image appears to be part of the background. However, notice that unlike Photoshop compositions, whose layers can feature gradual transitions from totally opaque to transparent, GIF files are limited to one specific drop-out color. It is not possible using the GIF file format to, for example, make both green *and* purple areas drop out to transparent.

Continued ...

QUICKSTEPS

MAKING PART OF AN IMAGE TRANSPARENT *(Continued)*

SELECT A COLOR TO BE TRANSPARENT

1. If your image is not in Indexed Color mode, click **Image | Mode | Indexed Color**. The Indexed Color dialog box appears.

2. Click the **Palette** down arrow, and click **Custom**. Or, if your image is already in Indexed Color mode, click **Image | Mode | Color Table**. In either case, the Color Table dialog box appears.

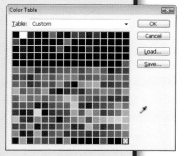

3. Click the **Eyedropper** tool and then click the color in the image that you want to be transparent. The corresponding color swatch in the Color Table becomes transparent.

4. Click **OK** to close the Color Table dialog box. If necessary, click **OK** again to close the Indexed Color dialog box. The image will appear unchanged in Photoshop; however, the transparency will be apparent when you add the image to a web page.

- **A character** You the artist decides on the subject you want to animate. A human figure is very ambitious; an object such as a star or a still photo that changes color over time is much easier to create from photos of your own, or Photoshop Shapes.

- **An animation treatment** You have a wide range of animation techniques at your disposal, but the four most common (and easiest to build) are listed here, followed by an advanced technique:

  - **Transitions** A fade from one scene to another, a wipe, a Venetian blinds effect, and all the other transitions you see on television shows.

  - **Builds** Your animation starts with an empty screen and then gradually fills up. Use of a text build can make an effective and eye-catching advertising message.

  - **Morphs** You can change one shape to a different shape through Photoshop's tweening features, demonstrated later in this chapter.

  - **Filters** You can make a stunning animation by using filters, either applying in a build or a transition. Later in this chapter you'll learn the steps used to make an animation using some interesting Photoshop filters.

  - **A cycle** This is a very ambitious GIF endeavor and you should be a skilled illustrator or be familiar with a 3D modeling program to attempt it. You can make a character walk, eat, or perform any repetitive action through the use of an animation cycle. Traditional animators have used cycles for more than 50 years because it requires less manual labor. If they need a character to walk across a screen, they build a single walk cycle and then repeat it, eliminating the drudgery and time of drawing 100 cells.

UNDERSTANDING THE ANIMATION PANEL

You work extensively between the Layers panel and the Animation panel to build the stock for your animation that you then export via **File | Save For Web & Devices**. Figure 13-5 shows the Animation panel along with callouts to its controls. Choose **Window | Animation** to display the panel. The following is a list of which controls do what:

- **Animation frame** This area provides a thumbnail of a specific GIF animation frame. When the frame is highlighted, this means that it's the current editing fame, but you don't perform edits on the frame, but instead on a layer in a Photoshop document using tools, filters, and also the Layers panel. You can drag a frame to reposition it on the Animation panel and you can choose multiple frames for editing: press **SHIFT** while you click to select sequential frames, or press **CTRL/CMD** while you click to select nonsequential frames.

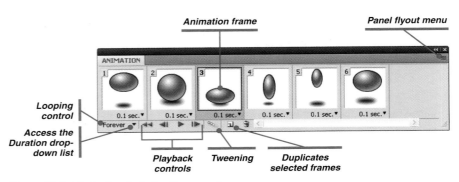

Animation frame

Panel flyout menu

Looping control

Access the Duration drop-down list

Playback controls

Tweening

Duplicates selected frames

Figure 13-5: *Photoshop's Animation panel*

- **Duration down arrow**   You click this arrow to define the time for the chosen (highlighted) frame(s). If you have multiple frames selected, setting one duration sets all the selected frame durations.

- **Looping control**   A GIF animation can play only once when it loads in the audience's browser, or it can repeat twice, a hundred times, or forever. **Forever** is usually a good choice, so the audience can decide on how long to view the animation, and this is why your animations should begin and end on the same frame.

- **Playback controls**   These VCR-like buttons let you play, stop, and go to the first or the last frames in your animation timeline.

- **Tweening**   Use this feature to have Photoshop create frames in between selected frames. Opacity, movement, and other attributes of frames are averaged to produce a smooth animation.

- **Duplicates Selected Frames**   This button duplicates one or more of the frames you've chosen and put copies after the current frame.

- **Panel flyout menu**   Here you find some features you can also access directly on the panel, such as Delete Frame (clicking the Trash icon when a frame is selected does the same thing), and also commands you don't find elsewhere, such as Reverse Frames.

Build an Animation

The concept in the following example is to create an antique version of the color photo onscreen, progressing from the full-color original to a sepia tone, woodcut version. To do this, you'll create a Smart Object from the image layer, apply a filter as a Smart Filter, and then duplicate the layer to use in different frames.

TIMING OF GIF ANIMATIONS (Continued)

The following is a list of durations in human terms and what you'd use the duration for:

- **No Delay**   This duration tells the web browser not to wait at all after loading the first frame to move to the next frame, and so on. It's best used for full-motion animation you'd create by importing still frames from movies.

- **.1 sec.**   A tenth of a second between frames is useful for a "build" type animation, where elements successively populate the screen, such as the characters in a line or text.

- **.2 sec.**   This duration creates an *almost* unperceivable pause in the animation. There is a visual difference the audience will appreciate between a .1 and .2 second duration.

- **.5 sec.**   A brisk pause, useful for letting a character in an animation do a "take," as in the reaction of a character hearing, "Honey, I burned the house down."

- **1 sec.**   A brief pause, useful for letting the audience read one or two words before moving on to the following frame.

- **2 or more sec.**   A true break in the action. Use longer durations to let the audience appreciate a message, a logo, a slogan, or a piece of artwork. Slideshows timed to 8 seconds per frame provide the audience with a good time to assess a piece of artwork or a photo without becoming bored.

USE FILTERS TO SET UP AN ANIMATION

The advantage to using Smart Filters is that you can mask areas to reveal the progression from color to a filtered sepia tone image:

1. Open the image you want to use in an animation, and click **Window | Animation** to display the Animation panel. If you don't see the Animation (Frames) view of the Animation panel (it might happen if you have Photoshop Extended), click the **Convert To Frame Animation** icon on the lower right of the panel.

2. Right-click the background layer title on the Layers panel and then click **Convert To Smart Object** from the context menu. The background layer is renamed "Layer 0" (see Figure 13-6).

*Figure 13-6: **Create a Smart Object from the background layer.***

3. On the Animation panel, choose 2 seconds for the duration of the first frame by clicking the down arrow on the lower right of the frame (the individual image frame) and selecting **2.0**. In film, this is called an *establishing shot*.

Figure 13-7: Apply one or more filters as Smart Filters via the Filter Gallery.

4. On the Tools panel, set the current foreground color to deep chocolate and the background color to pale sand. You'll use the Stamp filter shortly—this filter uses foreground and background color swatches to process the image.

5. Click **Filter | Filter Gallery**.

6. Click **Stamp** in the Sketch collection. Choose about **25** for the Light/Dark Balance and then drag the **Smoothness** slider to about **5**.

7. Click the **New Effect Layer** icon at bottom right, and then choose **Halftone Pattern** from the Sketch folder (see Figure 13-7).

8. Set the **Size** to **2**, the **Contrast** to about **45**, and the **Pattern Type** to **Line**. This is not exactly the desired effect since the Halftone Pattern is applied at the top filter and Stamp should be the last filter for a more antique look.

9. Drag the **Halftone Pattern** title to the bottom of the list, as shown in Figure 13-7. Click **OK** to apply the filters as Smart Filters.

ANIMATE USING THE FILTER LAYER MASK

You now have the resource for creating the GIF animation. In the following steps you create a transition over time by duplicating the layer and then progressively reveal the filter effect by painting on the Smart Filter mask:

1. Click the **Smart Filters** thumbnail on the Layers panel, the all-white thumbnail, to tell Photoshop you want to edit the mask and not the image linked to it.

2. With black as the current foreground color, press **ALT/OPT+BACKSPACE** to fill the Smart Filter layer mask with black, removing the filter effect from frame 1 and this layer in the document.

3. Click the **Duplicate Frame** button on the Animation panel. Set the duration of the new frame to **0.2** second.

4. Drag the layer on the Layers panel into the **Create A New Layer** icon. Because by default, the original Smart Object layer is titled **Layer 0**, the new layer should be auto-named **Layer 0 copy** (just for reference here, and the following one will be named Layer 0 copy 2, etc.).

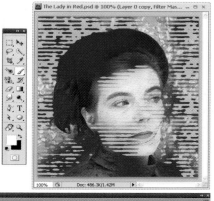

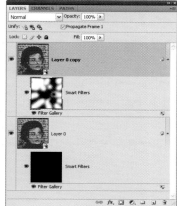

*Figure 13-8: **Hide more and more of the original image by exposing the Smart Filter's effect.***

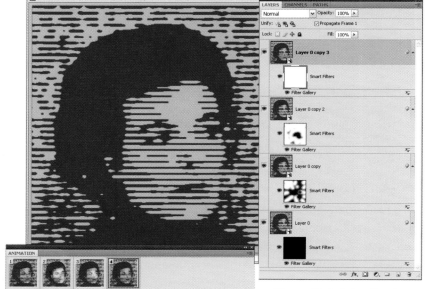

*Figure 13-9: **Animation is automation when you use Smart Filters.***

5. Click the **Layer 0 copy** Smart Filters thumbnail on the Layers panel to select it; because this layer is on top in the Layers stack, its contents are now frame 2 on the Animation panel.

6. Press **X** to make the current foreground color white. Then click the **Brush** tool on the Tools panel, and set the size to about 1/10 the height or width of the document. You are ready to paint on the Smart Filter mask, revealing some of the effect.

7. Paint an asterisk sort of shape on the frame 2 image, hiding original areas; don't paint too much—leave black areas that you'll fill in for frame 3, the third of four frames for this animation. See Figure 13-8.

8. Repeat Steps 3 through 7, filling in **Layer 0 copy 2** almost completely.

9. Click the **Duplicate Frame** button on the Animation panel. Set the duration to **0.2** second. Then click the second duplicate layer title so it's the active editing layer. Use the white foreground and the Brush tool to paint as you did in Step 6 to reveal more of the filter effect, working from the outside inward.

10. Repeat Steps 3 through 6, and then fill **Layer 0 copy 3** completely with white. Set the duration to **2** seconds. The Layers panel should look like Figure 13-9 now.

TIMING AND EXPORTING YOUR ANIMATION

Two things remain—simple things—to prep your document for animation export. First, because each duplicate layer you created is visible, the top layer is visible for all four frames. This is hardly an animation just yet!

1. Click frame 3's thumbnail on the Animation panel, and then on the Layers panel, click **Layer 0 copy 3**'s eye icon to hide this layer when frame 3 plays.

2. Click frame 2's thumbnail on the Animation panel, and then on the Layers panel, click **Layer 0 copy 3** and **2**'s eye icon to hide these layers when frame 3 plays.

3. Click frame 1's thumbnail on the Animation panel, and then on the Layers panel, click **Layer 0 copy 3, 2** and **Layer 0 copy**'s eye icon to hide these layers when frame 3 plays.

4. Click the **Play** button on the Animation panel to preview the animation now. Click **Stop** when the amusement wears off and you want to get to the final preparation step.

It would be good if this animation returned to the first frame, in a backward transition. Here's how to copy frames on the Animation panel:

1. SHIFT+click the second and third frames on the Animation panel, and then duplicate them by dragging their thumbnails into the **Duplicate Selected Frames** icon.

2. Drag the new duplicate frames to the end of the animation.

3. With the frames still selected, click the panel menu icon and click **Reverse Frames**.

EXPORT THE DOCUMENT AS AN ANIMATED GIF

It's likely that your document is too large in height and width to make an effective animated GIF for the Web; typically, GIFs are no larger than 200 pixels on a side. The good news is that the dimensions and other techniques for reducing the saved file size of the GIF animation can be handled all within Save For Web & Devices, as follows:

Click the Color Table down arrow when exporting to GIF. By default, the color table is displayed in order of hue (from red, to orange, and so on). However, if you need to reduce the table of **colors further** to make images smaller, you can click **Sort By Popularity**. Then click the bottom color(s), the least popular (the least frequent in the GIF image), and click the **Trash** icon. This usually makes the saved file size a few bytes smaller at very little chance of visibly altering the exported GIF's colors.

1. Click **File | Save For Web & Devices**.

2. Click the **Optimized File Format** down arrow (second from top), and click **GIF** from the list. Click the **Preset** down arrow and click **GIF 128 Dithered**. This preset offers a good balance between reducing the number of possible colors (thus decreasing file size) and retaining fair visual fidelity.

3. In the **Image Size Height** or **Width** field, type **200** (or less), put your cursor in a different field, and Photoshop automatically scales the dimension of the field you didn't type in.

4. Check the estimated file size of the optimized file preview—see Figure 13-10. Generally, if the projected image size is more than 100K, the animation will play sluggishly in browsers that use dial-up connections. If you're over 100K, go to Step 6.

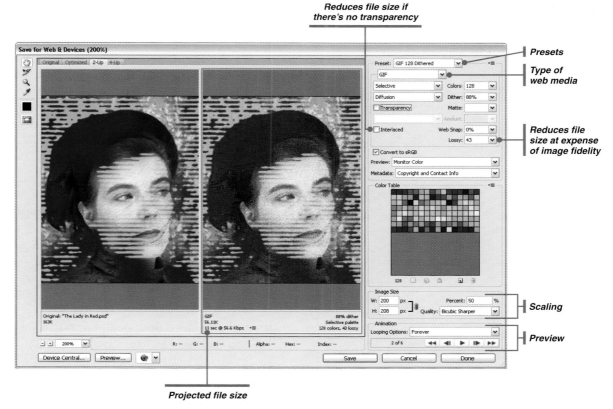

Reduces file size if there's no transparency

Presets

Type of web media

Reduces file size at expense of image fidelity

Scaling

Preview

Projected file size

Figure 13-10: Saving a GIF animation can only be performed via Save For Web & Devices.

5. Uncheck the **Transparency** check box if your animation has no transparent regions—this example did not use transparency on layers. By unchecking the box, you'll notice that you shave a few K off the estimated saved file size.

6. Click the **Lossy** down arrow and drag the slider a little to the right. Check the preview image and then check the estimated saved file size. Work between what you think will look good and the saved file size by dragging the **Lossy** slider back and forth. As the name suggests, Lossy performs some color averaging, reducing the quality of the saved GIF animation. The fewer unique colors used in the saved GIF, the smaller the saved file size.

7. Click **Save**, find a good location on hard disk for the GIF file, click **Save** in the Save Optimized As dialog box, and you're done.

When you return to Photoshop, you might want to choose to save the document again. If you close the file, Photoshop will tell you the file has changed. This is called a "false flag" in programming terms; the file hasn't changed, but it's been handled by Save For Web & Devices, a separate module in Photoshop, and Photoshop is flagging you on a possible change because the document has "left" its workspace for a moment.

USE TWEENING

The creation of animations can be simplified by the use of *tweening*. Tweening creates intermediate frames in an animation. For example, if you insert one tweening frame between two target frames, this frame consists of the two frames neighboring it, a mix of 50 percent opacity of the two, to average position, colors, or other changes. You create the start and end frames, and tweening creates the specified number of frames in *between* those frames; hence, the term tweening. Tweening can be applied to single or contiguous frames:

- If applied to a single frame, you select whether to tween between it and the previous or following frame.
- If you select two contiguous frames, the tweened frames are placed between the selected frames.
- If you select more then two contiguous frames, the intermediate frames are modified.
- If you select the first and last frames, they are treated as contiguous. This is useful for smoothing animations that loop more than once.

NOTE

In the future, you can view your animation by dragging the file into a web browser window.

To use tweening:

1. In the Animation panel, select the frames to tween.

2. Click the **Tween** button. The Tween dialog box appears.

3. Click the **Tween With** down arrow, and click the desired option. If you selected a single frame, the options **Next Frame** and **Previous Frame** are available. If you selected more than one frame, only the **Selected** option is available.

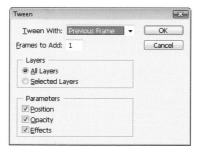

4. Type the number of frames to create between the selected frames in the **Frames To Add** text box. This option is not available if you selected more than two frames. In that case, only the selected frames are tweened.

5. Click the desired **Layers** option: **All Layers** modifies all the layers in the selected frames; **Selected Layers** modifies only the layers selected in the Layers panel. Static layers do not need to be modified by tweening, but you may have objects on multiple layers that do.

6. Accept the **Parameters**, which are all selected by default. You can also clear a parameter check box to deselect the parameter and not apply it to the tweening. You have the following tweening parameters with which to work:

   - **Position** Varies the position of the objects evenly between the starting and ending frames.

   - **Opacity** Varies the opacity of the objects evenly between the starting and ending frames. This is useful for making smooth fades.

   - **Effects** Varies the layer-effect parameters evenly between the starting and ending frames. For example, a drop shadow effect could be used to give the impression of a light source moving across the animation, thereby changing the angle of the shadow.

7. Click **OK** to apply your settings.

OPTIMIZING ANIMATIONS

You can optimize animations as GIF images only, since this is the only image format that supports them. If you optimize an animation as a JPEG or PNG, only the current frame of the animation will be displayed. In addition to the optimization options available for all GIF images, with animations, you can limit optimization to only the areas that change between frames, which greatly reduces the size of the final file:

1. Click the Animation panel flyout menu on the upper right of the panel, and then click **Optimize Animation**. The Optimize Animation dialog box appears.

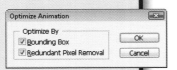

2. Choose from the following options:

   ● **Bounding Box**   Crops each frame to the area that has changed from the preceding frame. This option is recommended because it makes for a smaller file, but it isn't supported by all GIF editors. If your animations will be edited in other programs, you should determine if this feature is supported; otherwise, deselect it.

   ● **Redundant Pixel Removal**   Makes all pixels that are unchanged from the previous frame transparent. This option is also recommended to reduce the final file size. This feature requires that the Transparency checkbox in the Save for Web & Devices dialog box be selected.

You can switch from the Slice tool to the Slice Select tool by pressing **CTRL/CMD**.

Slice an Image

With Photoshop, you can *slice* an image, to "cut" a *copy* of the image into sections. The copy is made up of the slices, which can be named and saved. You then can apply different effects to each slice or designate each slice as a hyperlink and place them on a web page. The web site reassembles them so that, to the viewer, the slices appear as a single image, even though each slice may have different properties and actions, such as varying hyperlinks.

There are two tools specifically for working with slices that are found in the Crop menu:

● **Slice tool**   Cuts slices in an image. The slices are numbered sequentially left to right.

● **Slice Select tool**   Selects a slice so it can be modified, resized, or moved.

You have three types of slices to choose from:

● **Auto slices** are created automatically. These are the areas in an image that are not defined by one of the other slice types. For instance, when you delete a slice, an auto slice replaces it. Or, when you define slices on only part of an image, auto slices define the rest of it. This is so the image is balanced or does not contain gaps that would distort the image. Auto slices can be converted to user slices.

● **User slices** are created by using the Slice tool.

● **Layer-based slices** are selected layers in the Layers panel. You select a layer and then click **Layer | New Layer-Based Slice**. This command is unavailable for the background layer; you'll need to create a duplicate to use this command. You can "promote" a layer slice to a user slice.

VIEW SLICES

Slices are viewed both in Photoshop and the Save For Web & Devices dialog box. You can distinguish between different types of slices by looking at the lines that define them and the color of their symbols. Figure 13-11 shows an example.

● User and layer-based slices have solid lines and blue symbols by default.

● Auto slices have dotted lines and gray symbols by default.

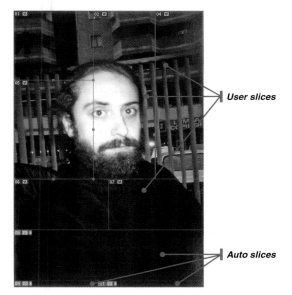

User slices

Auto slices

Figure 13-11: An image can be sliced into parts and then reassembled on a web site.

NOTE

Slices are always rectangular when you use Photoshop. You cannot have an oval or irregularly shaped slice.

TIP

Press **SHIFT** while you drag to constrain the slice to a square, and press **ALT/OPT** while you drag to draw from the center.

Slices are numbered starting with the slice nearest the upper-left corner of the image and moving to the lower-right corner—a numeric symbol is in the upper-left corner of each slice. As you add or remove slices, the numbering for individual slices will change to reflect the changes. Each slice also has a *badge*, or icon, that displays the properties of the slice.

CREATE USER SLICES WITH THE SLICE TOOL

To create a user slice:

1. Click the **Slice** tool in the Tools panel (with the Crop tool).

2. Click the **Style** down arrow, and click the desired option. This option determines how the slices you create are drawn. Choose from the following options:

- **Normal**   Uses dragging to set the slice area. A good way to do it is to drag diagonally across the area of the image you wish to make into a slice.

- **Fixed Aspect Ratio**   Uses a fixed width-to-height ratio, which you set by typing values in the Width and Height text boxes. Or, set the size of the slice by dragging, and the slice is proportionate to the values you type in the Width and Height text boxes.

- **Fixed Size**   Creates a slice of a specific size in pixels that you type in the Width and Height text boxes.

3. With Normal and Fixed Aspect Ratio slices, drag to select the area of the slice.

4. With a Fixed Size slice, click to create the slice, and then drag the selection outline to the desired area.

CREATE LAYER-BASED SLICES

A layer-based slice consists of the entire selected layer. These slices are useful for rollovers. If you apply an effect, such as a drop shadow, to the layer to create a rollover state, the slice automatically adjusts to include the pixels created by the effect. To create a layer-based slice in Photoshop, click the layer in the Layers panel. Then click **Layer | New Layer Based Slice**. Be aware that these slices can be unwieldy if they are too big.

CREATE SLICES USING GUIDES

You can also create user slices using guides:

1. Place the guides on your image.

2. Click the **Slice** tool and click **Slices From Guides** in the Options bar. Existing slices on the image are deleted.

EDIT AND DELETE SLICES

You can edit and delete slices and divide them. You can also reorganize them in the stack.

1. Right-click the slice to be changed or deleted.

2. From the context menu, select one of these options:

- Click **Delete Slice** to delete the selected slice. Another way to delete slices is to select slices to be deleted, click **Slice Select**, and press BACKSPACE.

- Click **Edit Slice Options** to open a dialog box for altering the slice characteristics, including the Slice Type (choose between No Image, Image, or Table), Name, URL, and Dimensions of the slice.

- Click **Divide Slice** to open a dialog box to specify the number of slices horizontally or vertically the selected slice is to be divided.

- Click a positional command to change the position of the slice in the stack: you can bring it to the front of the stack or to the back, or send it one slice forward or backward.

- Click **Promote To User Slice** to change a layer slice to a user slice.

- Click **Combine Slices** to merge selected slices.

UICKSTEPS

SAVING SLICED IMAGES

The procedure for saving slices in Photoshop is virtually the same as with saving any other image:

1. Click **File** and then click **Save For Web & Devices**.

2. Apply the desired settings as outlined earlier in this chapter.

3. Click **Save**. The Save Optimized As dialog box appears.

4. Click the **Slices** down arrow, and select an option from the drop-down list: **All Slices**, **All User Slices**, or **Selected Slices**.

5. Click **Save**.

Index

References to figures are in italics.

A

Add Anchor Point tool, 127
Adjustment Brush tool, in the Camera Raw
    Editor, 62
Adjustment layer, 130
Adobe Bridge. *See* Bridge
Adobe Color Engine (ACE), 75
Adobe Color Management (ACM), 263
Adobe Gamma, Control panel, 68–71
airbrush feature, 177
animated GIFs, 292–293
    exporting as an animated GIF, 298–300
    optimizing animations, 302
    timing and exporting, 297–298
    timing of GIF animations, 294–295
    tweening, 300–301
    using filters to set up an animation, 295–296
    using the filter layer mask, 296–297
Animation panel, 293–294
anti-aliasing, 111, 112
    removing fringe pixels, 115, 186
Application bar, opening files from, 4
Art History Brush, 192, *193*
auto slices, 302

B

Background Eraser tool, 119–121, 181, 183–184
background layer, 130
    unlocking, 133
batch renaming files, 51–52
bitmap images, 23–25
    See also images
Bitmap mode, 25, 30
Black and White dialog box, 93, 213
black and white photographs
    editing in RGB mode, 208
    See also Grayscale mode

Blur filters, 224–226
Blur tool, 186
bounding boxes, 241
    manipulating, 246
    skewing text in, 248
Bridge, 39–40
    building workspaces, 45–46
    Collections and Smart Collections, 41–43
    Content panel, 43–44
    downloading raw image files to, 35–37
    Favorites list, 41
    Filmstrip layout, 45
    Filter panel, 43
    Folders panel, 40
    image views, 44–45
    Keywords, 45
    launching executable files, 40
    Light Table layout, 45
    opening files, 5
    opening images in Photoshop from the Bridge,
        53–54
    viewing and writing metadata, 46–50
    workspace, 40
Brush tool, 176–177
    changing brush tip groups, 177–178
    creating a custom brush library, 180
    creating custom brushes, 178–179
    deleting brushes, 181
    displaying a custom brush library, 181
    editing a mask with, 143
    Flow option, 178
    Mode option, 178
    Opacity option, 178
    options, 18–19
Burn tool, 190–191, 207

C

caching, 79
calibration, 68
    calibrating your monitor, 68–71
    hardware, 72

Camera Raw Editor
    adjustment sliders, 58–59
    Camera Calibration tab, 66
    Detail tab, 64
    HSL/Grayscale tab, 64–65
    interface, 54–56
    Lens Corrections tab, 65–66
    navigation arrows, 58
    opening, 54
    Preferences, 63
    Presets tab, 66
    saving or resetting processing work, 56
    Settings menu, 57
    Split Toning tab, 65
    Tone Curve tab, 63–64
    tools, 59–63
    workflow options, 57–58
    zooming, 57
camera raw images, 53–54
    defining properties of a processed raw file, 57
    See also Camera Raw Editor
cartoons, converting photos into, 222–223
Character panel, 242–243
clipping, 269
clipping masks, 130, 145–146
closing Photoshop, 3
CMYK Color mode, 30
CMYK inks, 271
collapsing panels, 9
Collections, 41–43
color, 14
    Kulor panel, 15
    Match Color adjustment, 94
    out-of-gamut colors, 270
    replacing lighter colors with darker ones,
        161–162
    setting foreground and background colors, 20
Color Balance, 89
color gamut, 73
Color Halftone filter, 222–223
color management, 263

Free Transform, 112–113
Freeform Pen tool, 126–127
full-service bureaus, 277–278

G

gamma
    adjusting, 69
    See also Adobe Gamma
gamut, 269
Gamut Warning, 270
Gaussian Blur, 224
general preferences, 7
ghosted images, 150–151
GIF format, 260–261, 280
    optimizing images, 281–285
    See also animated GIFs
gradient masks, 144–145
Gradient tool, 186
    applying a gradient fill, 186–187
    editing a gradient, 188–189
    evening out overall photo tones, 212–213
    Gradient Editor dialog box, *188*
    Gradient presets, 187
Graduated Filter tool, in the Camera Raw Editor, 62–63
Grayscale mode, 30, 31–32, 92–93
grids, turning off, 11
Grow command, 118–119
Guides, Grids & Slices, preferences, 8

H

Hand tool
    in the Camera Raw Editor, 60
    panning an image, 13
    zooming, 12
hardware calibration, 72
Healing Brushes, 203–204

Help
    tutorials, 2
    using, 14
Highlights. *See* Shadows/Highlights
histograms, 77
    bad histograms, 80
    balanced vs. unbalanced, 79–80
    and cache, 79
    Histogram panel, 77–78
History panel, 20–22
    snapshots, 22
HTML settings, 289–290
Hue/Saturation, 90–92

I

image canvases, creating from a preset, 6
image orientation, 38
image views, 44–45
images
    arranging in workspace, 12–13
    bitmap images, 23–25
    changing resolution, 28
    compression, 26–27
    dimensions vs. resolution, 27
    ghosted, 150–151
    panning, 13
    resampling, 28–29
    resizing, 28
    rotating, 13
    slicing, 302–304
    stacking, 52–53
    vector images, 25–26
importing digital photos, 34–35
Indexed Color mode, 30, 32
inkjet printing, 263–269
    care for inkjet prints, 271
    CMYK inks and RGB color profiles, 271
interface, preferences, 7

International Color Consortium (ICC), 71
interpolation methods, 8–9
IPTC metadata, 46–47

J

JPEG format, 26, 259, 280
    optimizing images, 286–287

K

keyboard shortcuts
    assigning, 9–10
    Preferences dialog box, 7
    zooming, 12
Keywords, 45, 48–49
Kulor panel, 15

L

LAB Color mode, 31
labels, 50–51
    See also tags
Lasso tools, 106–108
layer blend modes, 150
    Behind painting mode, 173
    Clear painting mode, 171–172
    Color Burn mode, 161–162
    Color Dodge mode, 162–164
    Color mode, 168–169
    Darken mode, 154–156
    Difference mode, 166–167
    Dissolve mode, 151–152, *153*
    ghosted images, 150–151
    Hard Light mode, 163
    Hue mode, 167–168
    Light mode, 164–165
    Lighten mode, 152–154
    Lighter and Darker Color modes, 159–161

restoring photographs (cont.)
  removing dust and scratches, 202–204
  removing red eye, 214
  removing the color, 213
  revealing hidden detail, 211–212
RGB Color mode, 30, 32
RGB color profiles, 271
Rotate View tool, 13
Rounded Rectangle tool, 194
  See also Shape tools

S

S Curve, 83–84
  See also Curves
Saturation. *See* Hue/Saturation; Variations adjustment
Save For Web & Devices dialog box, 280–288
saving files, 37–38
scanning images, 32–33
  line art, 34
  preparing vintage pictures for scanning, 198–199
  straightening a scanned photo, 198–200
screen modes, 17
scrubby sliders, 16
selections
  adding to, 113
  adding to a mask, 143
  anti-aliasing, 111, 112
  contiguous and noncontiguous, 104
  converting a selection to a border, 113
  copying to a new document, 117
  copying to a new layer, 116–117
  creating a layer mask from, 143
  creating from a mask, 143
  cropping to fit a selection, 114
  deselecting, 114
  duplicating the contents of, 117
  excluding areas from, 111
  expanding or contracting selections, 114, 118–119
  feathering, 111, 112
  fixed-aspect ratio, 104

fixed-size, 103, 104
loading, 116
making multiple selections, 113
making with the Lasso tools, 106–108
making with the Magic Wand tool, 103–104, 105
making with the Marquee tool, 102, 103
making with the Quick Selection tool, 105
moving a selection border, 111
moving the contents of, 117
painting with Quick Mask mode, 206
refining edges, 106–107
reselecting, 114
saving, 115
subtracting from, 113
touching up, 123
transforming a selection, 112–113
using paths for, 124–128
using the Color Range command, 109–110
  See also Quick Masks
service bureaus, 277–278
shadows, 224–226
Shadows/Highlights, 87–88
Shape tools, 194–195
shapes, editing, 195
Sharpen tool, 186
  Smart Sharpen command, 202
shortcut menus, 14
shortcuts. *See* keyboard shortcuts
Similar command, 119
Single Column Marquee tool, 103
Single Row Marquee tool, 103
Slice Select tool, 302
Slice tool, 302
slices, 302
  creating layer-based slices, 303
  creating user slices with the Slice tool, 303
  creating using guides, 304
  deleting, 304
  editing, 304
  saving sliced images, 304
  viewing, 302–303

sliders, 13
  scrubby sliders, 16
Smart Collections, 41–43
Smart Filters, 219–221
Smart Objects, 57–58
Smart Sharpen command, 202
Smart Sharpen filter, 230–231
Smudge tool, 186, 204–205
Soft Proofing, 263
Spelling Checker, 245
Spin effect, 229
Sponge tool, 190–192, 207
Spot Healing Brush, 203–204
Spot Removal tool, in the Camera Raw Editor, 61–62
stacking documents, 14–15, 52–53
starting Photoshop, 2
Status bar, 4
  zooming, 12
steeltones, 91–92
Straighten tool, in the Camera Raw Editor, 61
Styles panel, 252
Swatches panel, 14

T

tags, 51
  See also labels
text
  adding special effects with layer styles,
    250–254
  beveling, 252–253
  committing, 240
  creating, 240–242
  creating on a path, 248–249
  creating within a closed path, 250
  drop shadows, 251
  editing on a path, 249
  embossing, 252–253
  finding and replacing, 246
  flipping, 248
  flipping and moving on a path, 249

formatting with the Character panel,
242–243
formatting with the Paragraph panel, 244
hyphenating words, 243–244
Inner Glow and Outer Glow effects, 253–254
justifying, 244
paragraph type, 241–242
point type, 241
Spelling Checker, 245
text masks, 255–256
transforming type, 246–248
warping, 246–248
See also bounding boxes
TIF format, 259–260
Times Two Rule, 274–275
tone correction
with Curves, 81–82
evening out overall photo tones, 212–213
with Levels, 82–88
tools
cycling through using the SHIFT key, 19
options, 18–19
switching in a menu, 19
Tools panel, 17–18
displaying in two columns, 18
Transform Selection command, 112–113

transparency
making part of an image transparent, 292–293
working with, 130
Transparency & Gamut, preferences, 8
tutorials, 2
tweening, 300–301
type, preferences, 8
Type tool, 240

U

undocking documents, 14–15
undoing actions, 20, 22
See also History panel
Units & Rulers, preferences, 8
Unsharp Mask filter, 231–232
unstacking documents, 14–15
upsampling, 8
user slices, 302, 303

V

Variations adjustment, 96–97
vector images, 25–26
See also images

W

Warming Filters, 95
WBMP format, 280
Web Galleries, creating, 273–274
White Balance tool, in the Camera Raw Editor, 60
Working CMYK View mode, 30
working color space, 74
workspace, 3–4
arranging images in, 12–13
Bridge, 40, 45–46
customizing, 9

X

XMP metadata, 47–48

Z

Zoom tool, 11
in the Camera Raw Editor, 60
zooming an object at the camera, 227–228
zooming in and out, 11–12
in the Camera Raw Editor, 57